LEAVING LEGACIES of LAWLESSNESS

New Insights into Benghazi
and Government Corruption

Annette Mick

authorHOUSE®

AuthorHouse™
1663 Liberty Drive
Bloomington, IN 47403
www.authorhouse.com
Phone: 1 (800) 839-8640

Published by AuthorHouse 01/18/2017

ISBN: 978-1-5246-5470-2 (sc)
ISBN: 978-1-5246-5469-6 (e)

NEW INSIGHT INTO
BENGHAZI AND GOVERNMENT
CORRUPTION

E dward Snowden had taken asylum in Russia because of the information
he had leaked to the public which proved that the NSA was spying on
Americans. The U.S. government wanted every country that Snowden was
in at the time, that they knew of, to extradite him to the United States. Not
a single country would do so. He did not leak any secrets or put anyone's
lives in danger but of course those in the government claimed that he did.
But the government would not produce any evidence that would prove
that claim. Edward Snowden did commit a crime. But so did the US
Government. Snowden felt he had a responsibility to warn the U.S. citizens
as to what the government was doing.

Documents that were released by Edward Snowden included details
on the SSO unit. Internet service providers which include AOL, Apple,
Google, Facebook, Microsoft, PalTalk, YouTube, and Yahoo allowed
the NSA to collect communications data for analysis under the PRISM
program. Also part of SSO are the programs which tap fibre-optic cables
around the world. And through this industry cooperation some of the
access to these fibre-optic cables is achieved. And without the knowledge of
the companies included, there are other operations taking place.

Also revealed was NSA compromising smartphones and calling
patterns. The CO-TRAVELER system enables the NSA to gather
location data to gain knowledge of relationships between individuals.
Mobile apps are also targeted by NSA programs which collect cookies and
data. Text messages are also collected.

Documents also released by Edward Snowden show a program called Boundless Informant. This program maps and graphs data from every Digital Network Intelligence (DNI) record in the SIGINT (signal intelligence) system and gives a full view of collection capabilities of GAO. The XKeyscore database allows the NSA to analyze data from the combination of data from PRISM, SCS sites (also called F6 sites) and FORNSAT sites.

An NSA program, Project BULLRUN, attempts to defeat the encryption used to secure network communication technologies.

The documents also uncover operations that are mainly undertaken by the NSA's Five Eyes partners in the UK, Canada, Australia, and New Zealand. There are close staffing and funding relationships between these agencies. The NSA also has jointly staffed projects, which shares NSA tools and raw data about US citizens with signals intelligence agencies in Germany, Israel, and Sweden.

So Edward Snowden revealed the extent of the spying capabilities used by the government against American citizens. So his crime essentially was not criminal. But when President Obama goes around Congress and dictates law and allows this spying on American citizens he is committing a crime. He is acting as a dictator. Why does Congress allow this? And how does the U.S. allow a person to run for the Office of the President of the United States when leaked emails proved she was using a non-secure email system that contained classified and top secret information which was hacked by foreign governments. And she was using the State Department as Secretary to gain favor of companies and governments who donated to the foundation and then in return she gave these countries access. And how can she be allowed to have had used this office's employees to work on deals that enriched her foundation on the government's time? But most of all she broke the law. And unlike Edward Snowden, she put names of CIA officers in her emails and put their lives in imminent danger.

Has our government in part or as a whole, forgotten what America, our Constitution, our flag stands for? From the president to the Justice Department to the FBI, there is so much corruption in our government.

When we had our first black president elected, he then supported the MLB movement. This did not help the black community. It caused racial tension and violence. He did not emanate Martin Luther King Jr.'s values. His loyalty is to the Muslims not the black community.

This book is dedicated to those who fought and for those who lost their lives in Benghazi; Dave "D.B." Benton, Mark "Oz" Geist, Kris "Tanto" Paronto, Jack Silva, John "Tig" Tiegen, David Ubben, Glen "Bub" Doherty, Tyrone "Rone" Woods, Sean Smith, Ambassador Chris Stevens. And to those who cannot be named but you know who you are.

CHAPTER 1

When the American flag floats in the soft breeze the first reaction is pride and gratitude. Pride for the flag. Pride for what the flag stands for. Pride in being an American. And then - sadness sets in. Our flag still stands for the same values. But, America, looking back over the past at 6 to 8 years does not look the same. Imagine Francis Scott Key as he stood up high, overlooking the battle, the rockets red glare the bombs bursting in air, he saw through the night that our flag was still there. The pride he must have felt in the dawn's early light that the Star Spangled Banner still waved o'er the land of the free, and the home of the brave. He would still be proud today. But he would not be pleased with the state that America is in now. He saw firsthand the sacrifices that were made so that we could have the United States of America. He saw firsthand the sweat, blood, and death it took to have our great United States. Let us not lose what was so important to our forefathers, to those who fought and who died to create America. To those soldiers in Arlington Cemetery with the swath of white headstones adorning their resting place, and to those who are still fighting to keep America safe.

From the book "Our Flag" published in 1989 by the House of Representatives;

"The colors of the pales (the vertical stripes) are those used in the flag of the United States of America; White signifies purity and innocence, Red, hardiness & valor, and Blue, the color of the Chief (the broad band above the stripes) signifies vigilance, perseverance & justice."

Justice. It is not a word that is attributed to Hillary Clinton whether in reference to, or in being delivered, by her.

"That n*****."

"Watch out. This is just the beginning of the tornado."

1

Those were Tracey Martin's answers to the questions asked by Tom Bauerle.

The first answer was what Hillary had called a black gentleman who had brought her something in which she was not pleased. Tracey Martin along with French president, Jacque Chirac's wife, were in the room with Hillary at that time.

The second answer is what Tracey Martin said to expect if Hillary is elected president.

Tracey Martin was the traveling chef for the Clinton's during their first four years in the White House. The Chef who had hired Tracey for the White House, Walter Scheib, was killed on June 13, 2015. The questions were asked by Tom Bauerle radio talk show host on WBEN radio. After having Tracey Martin on his radio show Baurle's family member received a call at 2 a.m. from a phone number that was in the DNC emails that were released. How could this number have accidentally been called by a person named April Mellody whose number was included in the DNC emails? Was this an accident? Not likely. Was this a threat? Most likely. Tom Bauerle had Tracey Martin on his radio show on July 27, 2016 "to discuss in detail how he had discovered firsthand, as a former Clinton employee, that there were two different Hillary's".

Since July 27th Tracey Martin's life has been turned upside down. He has had 10 different threats against his life and has had his phone hacked.

On Friday July 29th, two days before the call from a DNC member, Tracey Martin was on Baurle's show.

"But this is as chilling as it is real."

"Isn't it interesting that during the Democratic Convention, someone very close to me received a 2 a.m. phone call and a conversation on their voicemail?

"Two days before the call was made Tracey Martin appeared on my show. The one time travel chef for the Clinton White House spoke the real truth about the racist Hillary Clinton. Tracy's phone was hacked within days of being on my show. And his life has been turned upside down.

"Where is the media outrage about her hypocrisy or Tracy's phone being hacked? Oh, the guy who hired Tracey to work for the Clintons? He's dead. One of those hiking accidents where you drown. A lot of people seem to end up dead when it comes to these Richard 3rd like characters.

"This call to my loved one was made very early on Friday July 29th. And wouldn't you just know that phone number is on the Wikileaks DNC emails?"

Baurle had mentioned on his radio show the probability of the election being rigged by satellites. He had talked about "the recent and very close together deaths of John Ash (bosom Clinton pal) and former president UN General Assembly, the brilliant world-renowned Molly MaCauley (who knew how satellites can be used to rig elections) who tragically reached out to Ash according to... sources, and 27 year old Seth Rich who did voter Outreach work for the muckraking DNC and until July 10, 2016, had his whole life before him". These people died within days of each other.

Also Shawn Lucas died. He was lead attorney and process server who had served papers to the DNC Services Corp., and to Chair person Debbie Wasserman Schultz at DNC headquarters in New York in the fraud class action suit against the Democratic party on behalf of Bernie Sander's supporters.

Former President of the United Nations General Assembly, John Ashe, died on June 22nd, 2016. It was first reported as a heart attack before being changed to death by dropping a barbell on his throat at his home, which was the cause of death the police had given. He was to appear before Congress two days before he died. Or more likely murdered. He was to be questioned about the Clintons and the Chinese billionaire Ng Lap Seng. Ashe was about to begin trial for a bribery charge involving Chinese businessman Ng Lap Seng, who had been implicated but not charged in the 1996 "China-gate" scandal for funneling illegal donations to Bill Clinton's re-election fund through Arkansas restaurant owner, Charlie Trie. Ashe was supposed to testify about Hillary's links to Ng Lap Seng.

Shawn Lucas died on July 3, 2016. He was found on his bathroom floor. The reason of his death is unknown.

Molly Macaulay, 59, was fatally stabbed in the neck on July 8, 2016, while she was walking her dogs. Homicide is very rare in the affluent neighborhood where Molly Macauley lived. Macaulay specialized in satellites and the space program. She was a valued member of the Space Policy Community for decades and renowned for her expertise on the economics of satellites especially in the Earth Observation Arena. She had testified before Congress many times and was the author of more than 80 Journal articles, books, and book chapters. She had worked with the United Nations which is most likely how she knew John Ashe who she reached out to concerning satellites capability of rigging the election. McCauley was a past member of the Space Studies Board (SSB), and of the Aeronautics and Space Engineering Board (ASEB) of the National Academies of Science, Engineering, and Medicine, and served on many of its study committees.

Two days later on July 10, 2016, Seth Rich died. Rich was beaten, shot, and killed but was not robbed. He still had his wallet, watch, and phone when police discovered his body. He was shot three times, once in the back.

Seth Rich had previously worked on the failed US Senate campaign of Nebraska businessman, Scott Kleeb, who's Clean Energy business had come under investigation after losing $300,000 in 2010, and another $300,000 in 2011, despite having been subsidized by the Clinton Global Initiative. Someone may have pressured Rich to leak what was going on. Julian Assange subtly suggested that Rich was the source of the Wikileaks exposed DNC emails. News agencies were following a lead that Rich was going to the FBI to speak to special agents about an "ongoing court case" possibly involving the Clinton family.

Brad Bauman, the man hired by the Rich family to end the "conspiracy theories" that surrounded the unsolved murder, is a public relations manager with the Pastorum Group and specializes in "crisis communications" for none other than the Democrat Party.

The Pastorum Group was founded by Joseph Cohen. Cohen is described as a campaign veteran who has previously worked at SEIU, the Democratic National Committee, and Obama for America.

Bauman is said to have been a former executive director of the Congressional Progressive Caucus. He released the following statement to the International Business Times on behalf of the Rich family;

"The family welcomes any and all information that could lead to the identification of the individuals responsible, and certainly welcomes contributions that could lead to new avenues of investigation. That said, some are attempting to politicize this horrible tragedy and in their attempt to do so are actually causing more harm than good and impeding on the ability for law enforcement to properly do their job. For the sake of finding

Seth's killer, and for the sake of giving the family the space they need at this terrible time, they are asking for the public to refrain from pushing unproven and harmful theories about Seth's murder."

The case of Seth Rich's murder was on Crime Watch Daily. On the program it was adamantly stated that Rich's parents did not feel that it was a targeted hit. The program though seemed as if it's purpose was to denounce any involvement of the DNC in Seth Rich's murder. A little too strongly.

Victor Thorne died on August 1st 2016, his 54th birthday, supposedly by suicide using a shotgun.

Thorn had written four books on the Clintons and had a forthcoming book that was supposedly a treasure trove of Hillary opposition research. Thorn had made several appearances on the Russell Scott Show, and told Scott, "Russell, if I'm ever found dead it was murder. I would never kill myself."

Joe Montano died of an apparent heart attack in his Falls Church Virginia home in late July 2016, after the WikiLeaks DNC email leaks. Montano,47, was an aide to the democratic vice-presidential nominee, Tim Kaine. Montano had been employed by him for several years. He was working for the DNC when he died. Some have connected Joe Montano's death to that of Seth Rich's death. They both were working for the DNC.

Tyler Drumheller died on August 2, in 2015, said due to pancreatic cancer. Tyler Drumheller was a former officer with the CIA and the division chief for the directorate of operations (DO) for clandestine operations in Europe. He exposed the U.S. use of discredited sources used to make the case for the war in Iraq.

In March 2011, Sidney Blumenthal sent an email which included 'apparently highly sensitive information' to then US Secretary of State with details received from Drumheller, who had spoken with a CIA colleague mentioning the name of an intelligence source. He was also due to be questioned by the House Oversight Committee on Benghazi. Emails show that Tyler Drumheller had produced intelligence on Libya and other foreign countries during the war against Gaddafi. This intelligence was passed by Sidney Blumenthal to Hillary. Drumheller also worked with, David L. Grange, head of Osprey Global Solutions. Grange is a retired major general with a Special Forces background who was sending people to terrorist places to collect intel which was then sent to Hillary. It is not known who paid Osprey Global Solutions. Possibly, Aegis, which at the time chair of the Intelligence Committee, Mike Roger's wife was running at that time. The two were focused on Libyan border security issues, of course involving a large amount of money. Emails also show that Drumheller was working for CBS at the same time. And this was the time period that 60 minutes came across the Benghazi scandal. It was concerning Dylan Davies, a British citizen, hired by the Blue Mountain Group to train the Libyan guards. Davies had an eyewitness account of what happened in Benghazi. Drummheller had tried to persuade Lara Logan not to do the report on Dylan Davies. The supposed "problem" that CBS had with Davies was that, although all of his facts coincided with U.S. Government reports and Congressional testimony, an article in a newspaper had said that Davies had told his boss that he had not gone to the compound. His boss had ordered him to stay in his villa. So 60 minutes apologized and said they had made a mistake by reporting the story. The story itself was not a mistake. The mistake was that Davies' facts was a damning condemnation of the Obama administration's and Hillary's conduct.

Also the death of Army Major General, John G. Rossi, two days before assuming his new command seems somewhat suspicious. His new command was to be the Commander of the Army Space and Missile Defense Command /Army Forces Strategic Command. The cause of death was yet to be determined and was under investigation.

"At this point we don't have any indication of foul play," a spokesman for Army Criminal Investigation Command, Chris Gray, said. Major General John G Rossi was found dead in his on-post home at Redstone Arsenal on Sunday July 31, 2016.

What adds to the suspicion of Major General John G Rossi's death is that he is the same John G Rossi who was Col. John Rossi, deputy commander of fires and effects, who addressed members of the media during a morning news conference Nov. 5, 2009, following the largest mass shooting at a military installation.

At that time Major General John G. Rossi was the Fort Hood deputy commander for fires in 2009, as a colonel and served as the post spokesman after Army psychiatrist Maj. Nidal Malik Hasan killed 13 people and wounded more than 30 others in a shooting rampage.

"Thirteen gave their lives in service to their nation. These heroes are so much more," Rossi had stated.

Rossi would have received his third star before assuming his new command as U.S. Army Space and Missile Defense Command and Army Forces Strategic Command.

Even though an autopsy was performed no results had been reported.

Did he know something about Nidal Malik that could not be allowed to become known publicly with the presidential election coming up in approximately 4 months after his death?

The former U.S. Army psychiatrist Nidal Malik was sentenced to die for the 2009 Ft. Hood shooting that killed 13 and wounded 32. He had released a letter saying he wanted to become a citizen of the militant group Islamic State. What a surprise.

Nidal Malik Hasan addressed a handwritten letter to Islamic State leader, Abu Bakr Baghdadi, requesting membership with ISIS.

"It would be an honor for any believer to be an obedient citizen soldier," Hasan wrote in his letter.

The amount of money spent on Hasan that cost taxpayers the following:

The Bell County Sheriff's Office was paid approximately $650,000 to hold Hasan.

*$200,000 spent on daily helicopter rides to commute Hasan from the jail to Fort Hood.

*Tens of thousands of dollars were spent to provide Hassan a private Fort Hood office for Hasan. He represented himself at the trial.

*$5 million was spent on travel for government lawyers, money given to expert witnesses, the buying of vehicles and cell phones, major security renovations at the base.

*$300,000 in military pay between his arrest and his dishonorable discharge in September 2013. Why would he be paid after killing 13 Americans? It is outrageous.

"I mean, it's just a bunch of overkill," attorney John Galligan told KXAS-TV. "Unnecessary funds that were spent," said Hasan's civil attorney, John Galligan, for all of the expense.

The U.S. government has refused to label Hasan's attack an act of terrorism.

Rep Pete Hoekstra, member of the House Permanent Select Committee on Intelligence, referred to the "troubling refusal by Obama officials to acknowledge that the shooting likely was an act of homegrown terrorism."

"The government has tried to deny that this was an act of terrorism. I think that, I hope that if people hear the words from Hasan's own mouth that they will understand that this was an act of terrorism," Manning said, who was one of those who were shot by Hasan.

The Army does not consider the shooting to be an act of terrorism on the military by an enemy combatant. So far they have denied the victims requests for combat-related pay and medals that come with additional benefits.

Then why was Hasan allowed all the special treatment after killing 13 Americans, 12 soldiers and an expectant mother who begged for her life?

And then in November 2016, it was reported that Major General John G. Rossi's death was ruled a suicide.

Another DNC worker was killed in an explosion. No other information has been released.

John Jones was killed on August 15, 2016. Jones was Julian Assange's lawyer. Approximately a month after, Julian Assange the founder of WikiLeaks, released a batch of incriminating Hillary Clinton emails. Assange's lawyer was run over by a commuter train in Britain. Jones was a top human rights lawyer. His specialty was extradition, war crimes, and counterterrorism. Shortly before his death, Democratic Strategist on CNN, host Bob Beckel, called for Julian Assange's assassination on TV. His exact words were, "Just kill the son of a b****." And Hillary had said of Assange, "Can't we just drone this guy?"

John Jones was working to prevent the extradition of Julian Assange. Jones worked on the same legal team as George Clooney's wife, Amal. The Clooney's are big supporters of Hillary.

Authorities were quick to rule Jone's death as a suicide but WikiLeaks stated it was foul play. He left a wife and two children.

Michael Ratner died on May 11th, 2016. He was an attorney for Wikileaks and Julian Assange. He had sued the George HW Bush Administration to try to stop the Gulf War, and the Clinton Administration to try to stop strategic bombing during the Kosovo War. He had spoken out on behalf of Jeremy Hammond and Chelsea Manning, alleged Wikileaks sources. Chelsea Manning was facing court-martial for disclosing files to WikiLeaks which included evidence of war crimes in Iraq.

Michael Ratner on Hammond, "Jeremy Hammond pleaded guilty to one count of conspiracy, of hacking into a protected computer. That count finishes the case in terms of any other charges. It carries up to a maximum of 10 years in prison. He doesn't have to get that, and in fact the demand is that he get time served. This is part of the sledgehammer of what the government is doing to people who expose corporate secrets, government secrets, and really the secrets of an empire. And the people who should have been on that trial are the very people who Jeremy admitted to hacking into, which is the Stratfor people who have engaged in corporate spying, along with government cooperation, the public safety people in Arizona, the FBI, etc."

Gavin MacFadyen, founder of the Center for Investigative Journalism, and director of WikiLeaks, has also died. The cause of death has not been made public. Although he was 76, his death is somewhat suspicious. In the original post from his wife, Susan, she had written that her husband had died from "a short illness," but then that line was removed.

And after Julian Assange had released thousands of emails showing Hillary's corruption, his internet was turned off after Hillary's Goldman Sachs speeches were made public. The Obama administration had pressured the Ecuadorian government to stop the leaking of Hillary's emails. Wikileaks tweeted that heavily armed police appeared outside the Ecuadorian Embassy in London where Julian Assange has political asylum. This happened after John Kerry pressured Ecuador to shut Wikileaks down for good. Reports had shown a removal van outside of the Ecuador embassy in London which questioned the eviction of Assange. But Ecuador has denied the eviction of Assange from the embassy so far.

In 2011, Ögmundur Jonasson, a former Icelandic minister, said US authorities told him that there was an 'imminent attack' on Iceland's government databases. They said that hackers were trying to destroy software systems in the country and that the FBI would send agents to investigate.

Jonasson said, "I was suspicious. Well aware that a helping hand might easily become a manipulating hand!"

Jonasson, now serves as a member of the Icelandic Parliament. He said that when a 'planeload' of FBI agents arrived he realized the real reason for their visit.

He said that the FBI wanted Iceland's 'cooperation set up to frame Julian Assange and WikiLeaks'.

Jonasson said the FBI was seeking Iceland's "cooperation in what I understood as an operation set up to frame Julian Assange and WikiLeaks".

"Since they had not been authorized by the Icelandic authorities to carry out police work in Iceland, and since a crack-down on WikiLeaks was not on my agenda, I ordered that all cooperation with them be promptly terminated.

"I also made it clear at the time that if I had to take sides with either WikiLeaks or the FBI or CIA, I would have no difficulty in choosing: I would be on the side of WikiLeaks.

"I also made it clear they should cease all activities in Iceland immediately," Jonasson said.

Think about when this took place. In 2011. That was when the Arab Spring began. The Arab Spring was the uprisings in Tunisia, Egypt, Libya, and Syria.

The death of Janet Reno is even suspect. It was reported that she died due to problems from Parkinson's disease. But Janet Reno has been the one believed to have given the full out assault order on the Branch Davidian compound in Waco, Texas. But leaked emails show that the all out assault order came from the White House and very likely from Hillary herself.

CHAPTER 2

THE LADY

I wonder what she thought As she stood there, strong and tall. She couldn't turn away, She was forced to watch it all. Did she long to offer comfort As her country bled? With her arm forever frozen High above her head. She could not shield her eyes She could not hide her face She just stared across the water Keeping Freedom's place. The smell of smoke and terror Somehow reduced her size So small within the harbor But still we recognized... How dignified and beautiful On a day so many died I wonder what she thought, And I know she must have cried.

After the murder of Molly Macauley, the satellite expert who knew how the elections could be rigged by satellite, it would not be shocking if the voting computers were calibrated to change votes to Hillary.

Hackers have already hacked the voter registration systems of more than 20 states in recent months, a Homeland Security Department official said.

There are concerns that foreign hackers might cause a lack of integrity of the U.S. elections. But the concern should be of those in the U.S. rigging the election. Online polls taken have shown that once the submit button is tapped the answers that were chosen comes back different.

And suspicion continues to grow over George Soros providing voting machines for 16 states. On its website, Smartmatic, a UK-based company posted its flow chart which shows it had provided voting machines for 16 States which included Arizona and Florida, important battleground states. Mark Malloch Brown, Smartmatic's chairman is a former UN official. He also sits on the board of George Soros' Open Society Foundations. Brown also has connections to the Clintons through his work at two consulting firms who have Clinton ties. And the billionaire, Soros, is a large backer of Hillary. And Smartmatic has a bad record in free and fair elections. After the story broke, Smartmatic took down the flow chart from its website.

As an example of todays technology, Apple's new patent for an infrared signal would instantly disable the cameras on all equipped iPhones in the vicinity. This would prevent anyone from photographing or video recording in the direction of the infrared signal. But this should be illegal. This could be used to disable phones completely. Or it could be used to trigger phones to transmit their GPS coordinates. It could also be used to turn on microphones and cameras. Eric Snowden's revelations have shown what the NSA can do when they target an individual's phone. This system will allow anyone to instantly disable the cameras on every iPhone in the vicinity of the infrared signal. This would place customer's devices into someone else's control by remote.

And of course there is a Hillary connection to some of the satellite companies. Loral, a satellite company, is a large donor to the foundation and goes way back with the Clintons to their White House days.

CEO of Dish satellites, Charlie Ergen, donated $750,000 to Hillary's campaign.

Gilat satellites partnered with Hillary's campaign to allow them uninterrupted news-gathering capabilities during the election campaign. Hillary's team had low profile SOTM satellite on the Move antennas on their tour bus. This allowed reporters to present on the Move reporting and give live updates from the campaigning.

Below is a description of Gilat satellite company's capabilities as listed on their weibsite.

The Automated Election System;

One of the five highlights of the automated election system is;

* Control and Reports. Full control over all of the system throughout the entire election process and real-time status of every site.

The automated election systems project goals are to;
* Mitigate the factors that can potentially compromise election integrity.
* Reduce the time for calculating and announcing electoral results from days to hours.
* If required to recount votes perform this instantaneously, preventing any undesired repercussions.

Now we know that certain states elections in the primaries were rigged.

Voting machines can be calibrated to automatically select a particular candidate. Molly Macauley was most likely killed because she knew how the elections could be rigged by satellite.

And of course, George Soros' Open Society Foundation, sought to expand electronic and online voting systems nationwide. This was learned from a leaked foundation's document. Electronic voting has been a big concern in this year's election due to the claim that digital voting systems can be changed. In a leaked file, the online voting plan presents the Open Society U.S. Programs board meeting in New York, during September 29-30, 2014;

The board meeting dedicates a significant amount of time to the methods the foundation's US programs could use to further the use of President Obama's executive action authority to bypass Congress during Obama's final two years in office. Together with partner grantees the Open Society created a general list of potential president executive actions on numerous issues. And of course the Soros group made the expansion of online voting an important issue.

Also Soros has been a long time supporter of Hillary and may have ties to the North Carolina protests and the CIA has tied him to a bombing in then Czechoslovakia in 1987.

President Obama's presidential commission on Election Administration released its recommendations on, January 2014, for reform in the U.S. election process including; transitioning to voting via tablet computers and other technologies. The commission highlighted new technologies in which the voter can pre-fill sample ballots at home to be scanned later at the polling place. The commission also dismissed concerns about hacking.

The commission stated the fact that a tablet or off-the-shelf computer can be hacked or breakdown does not mean such technology is inherently less secure than existing belt marking methods if proper precautions are taken.

So those concerns were dismissed. The concerns were dismissed but that did not eliminate the possibility of such technology being less secure.

Intelligence officials revealed hackers, twice, attempted to hack State voter registration databases. The theft of up to 200,000 voter records in Illinois was one of the attempts by hackers to gain access to State voter registration databases, according to the officials. The FBI issued a nationwide flash alert in which to warn states to take immediate measures to protect the security of their online voting systems.

"It would be very difficult for any sort of cyber intrusion to alter the ballot count simply because it is so decentralized and so vast. It would be very difficult to alter the count," stated Director of Homeland Security, Jeh Johnson.

But with satellite capabilities, the threat was high. It is very probable the reason for the demands of the recount of votes and why Hillary is in on it now. She was certain she was going to win.

CHAPTER 3

O FLAG OF OUR UNION

O flag of our Union,
To you we'll be true,
To your red and white stripes,
And your stars on the blue;
The emblem of freedom,
The symbol of right,
We children salute you,
O flag fair and bright!

So why did FBI director James Comey recommend that no charges be brought against Hillary Clinton?

And why had President Obama nominated James Comey for the board at HSBC in June 2012? Comey was appointed March 4th, 2013, to the board at HSBC and then resigned on September 4th, 2013. And then Obama appointed James Comey as FBI Director in 2013. Was Marine Field McConnell's claim of theft of weapons systems being stolen by James Comey when at HSBC have anything to do with this?

James Comey was a partner at McGuire Woods Law Firm. He had successfully defended a company against claims that the company's machinery had caused asbestos-related injuries. From there he went into public prosecution. In 2003, he was appointed by George W Bush as Deputy Attorney General. Two years later he joined Lockheed Martin as senior vice president. He then joined the world of hedge funds at Bridgewater Associates. After that, he joined the board of HSBC Holdings. HSBC has been charged many times and paid billions of dollars to settle money laundering charges and mortgage abuses. They were involved in a large scale evasion scandal where HSBC allowed thousands of Americans and others which include arms dealers, and wealthy power players worldwide to avoid paying taxes by hiding their money in a Swiss bank. Mark Johnson, an HSBC executive, was arrested for conspiring to take advantage of insider information, along with other charges.

There are many connections between FBI director James Comey and Hillary Clinton. Comey had accepted for HSBC millions of dollars for a Clinton Foundation defense contractor. Included is Comey's former membership on a Clinton Foundation corporate partners board and his financial relationship with his brother Peter, who works at the law firm that does the Clinton Foundation's taxes. James Comey received appximately six million dollars from Lockheed Martin when he was chief officer there during his last year of employment. Lockheed Martin became a Clinton Foundation donor that very year. It became a Clinton Global Initiative member in 2010. Lockheed Martin is also a member of the American Chamber of Commerce in Egypt which paid Bill Clinton $250,000 to deliver a speech in 2010. In 2010, Lockheed Martin won 117 approvals for private contracts from Hillary's State Department.

In 2013, James Comey was a board member and a director of Financial System Vulnerabilities Committee Member of the London Bank HSBC Holdings. He had been nominated for this position by President Obama. Unsurprisingly HSBC Holdings and some of its branches were to partner with the Clinton Foundation. HSBC partnered with a Deuschte Bank through the Clinton Foundation to retrofit 1,500 to 2,500 housing units primarily in the low to moderate income sector in New York City. Retrofitting refers to a green initiative to conserve energy in commercial housing units. The Clinton Foundation records show that the foundation projected $1 billion in financing for this green initiative to conserve people's energy in low income housing units.

James Comey's brother, Peter, serves as senior director of real estate operations for the, Americas for DLA Piper. DLA Piper is the firm that performed an independent audit of the Clinton Foundation in November when Hillary's campaign was working to bury the email scandal. The employees of DLA Piper are a large donor to Hillary's campaign. And they are, as a whole, a large donor to the Clinton Foundation. DLA Piper placed number five on Hillary's top contributors list. They rank a little higher than Goldman Sachs.

At the beginning of the Obama Administration in January 2009, Peter Comey became a real estate and construction consultant for Procon Consulting. Procon provided strategic project management for the grouping of over 11,000 FBI personnel into one high security facility.

The FBI and Director James Comey were criticized for their request at Apple to install a back door for U.S. surveillance agencies to use. Former NSA and CIA director Michael Hayden stated "...frankly I think on balance, that actually harms American safety and security..."

Barack Obama, Hillary Clinton, FBI Director James Comey, and Loretta Lynch all have ties to the criminal organization that is HSBC.

HSBC Holdings is a British-based multinational banking and financial services company headquartered in London, United Kingdom. It is the world's fourth largest bank by total assets of U.S. $2.67 trillion. It was established in its present form in London in 1991 by the Hong Kong and Shanghai banking corporation limited to act as a new group holding company. The origins of the bank lie mainly in Hong Kong and to a lesser extent in Shanghai where branches were first opened in 1865. The HSBC's name is derived from the initials of the Hong Kong and Shanghai Banking Corporation. The company continues to see both the United Kingdom and Hong Kong as its "home markets".

In June 2012, James Comey, was nominated by President Obama for a post on HSBC board of directors. He was appointed on March 4, 2013, to the board of HSBC. Comey served on the HSBC Financial system vulnerabilities committee. He resigned after his confirmation to serve as the FBI director. Leaked files reveal the identities of at least 7 donors to the Clinton Foundation who were also HSBC clients. Those donors had contributed $81 million to the Clinton Foundation.

When Loretta Lynch was U.S. Attorney for the Eastern District of Manhattan, New York, she brokered a deal with Eric Holder that allowed HSBC to pay fines instead of facing criminal charges. With no criminal charges against HSBC, this Deferred Prosecution Agreement was highly criticized. Loretta Lynch and Eric Holder were accused of acting as if HSBC was 'too big to prosecute'. This connection between the four is most likely part of the reason that Hillary received a recommendation of no charges from FBI director James Comey. Comey's job, as HSBC board member for Financial Systems Vulnerabilities Committee, was formed immediately after HSBC settled with the federal government for laundering hundreds of millions of dollars for the criminal and deadly Mexican drug cartels.

In Hillary's economic policy address, she said she would "offer plans to rain in excess of risks on Wall Street and ensure that stock markets work for everyday investors not just high frequency traders and those with the best or fastest connections".

Hillary had targeted HSBC for "allowing drug cartels to launder money".

"There can be no justification or tolerance for this kind of criminal behavior," stated Hillary.

But Bill Clinton delivered a fix figure speech to HSBC Securities.

Douglas Holtz Eakin, president of the American Action Forum stated, "She's profited both directly and indirectly at the Clinton Foundation from the activities of all these firms and if she didn't like what they were doing, I don't understand why she would take their money."

And five other banks that were involved in scandals are big contributors to Hillary's campaign. Barclays, Citigroup, JPMorgan, Royal Bank of Scotland, and UBS, paid a combined amount of $5 billion in fines for rigging rates in May of 2015.

Hillary said, "We will prosecute individuals" referring to financial executives who gained personally from fraud.

"I will appoint and empower Regulators who understand that Too Big to Fail is still too big of a problem," Hillary stated.

But her words are in contradiction to her actions.

*****

It is illegal for foreigners to donate to U.S. political campaigns, but this law was challenged by two foreign Nationals in 2012. This law was declared constitutional by the United States Supreme Court with the vote being 9-0.

But there are always ways around this law. Hillary has found these by taking donations from foreign countries and governments to the Clinton

Foundation and its entities and for money paid for speaking fees. And the timing of these donations parallel with important decisions made by Hillary as senator from New York and as Secretary of the State Department. And most of these foreign donors benefited richly. Some of these decisions made by Hillary include; access to vital US nuclear technology, approval of controversial energy products, matters related to Middle East policy, the overseas allocations of billions in taxpayer funds, the Russian government's acquisition of American uranium assets which continue to give Hillary large sums of money.

The Clinton Foundation must be legally certified as a non-profit entity. But a 2008 leaked memo from attorney, Kumiki Gibson, to Bruce Lindsay, chairman of the Clinton Foundation, shows Gibson had been hired to do an independent assessment of the Foundation's practices.

Gibson's assessment included, "Important responsibilities regarding corporate filings are delegated to the [Foundation] CFO, who appears to delegate them to an outside organization, with very little oversight by the legal department. As a result, the Foundation is not in compliance with the filings rules, including in New York, which requires the Foundation to be certified to do business in the State."

"No matter what the leadership decides about the larger, over-arching question, it must act immediately to bring the Foundation into compliance with the law and standards that govern not-for-profits, and must create strong legal and HR offices so to prevent any lapses in the future."

"The Foundation does not have a record retention policy, and the procedures currently utilized in Harlem (which is the headquarters) may violate the law."

An unnamed executive of the foundation was 'being paid by the government and the foundation' which 'allowed the foundation to host what may have been a political event, apparently without official pre-approval from the foundation's legal department and without regard, before the fact, to the impact of that decision on the foundation's tax exempt status.' This was not reconciled in 2008 to the present.

The work of the Clinton Foundation seems to look good at face value but when looking deeper there are questions that cannot be answered. The disclosure of the amounts of money given to their Foundation are given in ranges, not exact amounts. And some donations are not even disclosed. So their net worth is not possible to be known.

Peter Schweitzer, in Clinton Cash, found a very clear "pattern of financial transactions involving the Clinton's that occurred contemporaneous with favorable U.S. policy decisions benefiting those providing the funds".

Washington Times reported in January 2009, that a secret party had paid an excessive amount for stock donated to the Clinton Foundation; "Former President Bill Clinton's Foundation, despite identifyng more than 200,000 of its donors in recent weeks, will not say who paid its windfall prices for stock in a struggling internet firm with links to the Chinese government... Mrs. Clinton's office and the foundation has declined to answer questions about a lucrative 2006 stock transaction details of which were reported by the Washington Times in March 2008.

"The Acoona Corp. donated between $250,000 and $500,000 to the Clinton Foundation after Mr. Clinton spoke at the company's launch in New York in 2004 according to donor information released by the foundation in December. The foundation sold its Acoona stock for $700,000 two years later according to the charity's tax return for 2006.

"Despite what the tax return suggests Acoona struggled mightily to turn a profit. In 2007, Acoona filed a prospectus with the Securities and Exchange Commission reporting more than $60 million in losses during three years. In the same prospectus it listed the China Daily Information Corp., a subsidiary of China Daily, the official English-language newspaper of the Chinese government as an official partner and 6.9 percent owner of the company... While the Clinton Foundation voluntarily disclosed the original donation of the stock it still is unwilling to say who was willing to pay so much for its holdings in the struggling company."

In May 1999, a bankruptcy attorney from Chicago, William A. Brandt, Jr., donated $1 million dollars to the Clinton Foundation. At that same time, the Clinton Justice Department was investigating Grant's testimony to Congress to determine whether he lied under oath concerning a Clinton fundraiser and the lobbying of federal officials. Three months later, in August, the Department of Justice dropped the investigation and decided that "prosecution is not warranted".

A report, From Russia with Money, by the Government Accountability Institute, shows how Hillary's State Department and the Clinton Foundation worked together.

The company, Joule, had received $35 million from a Putin-connected Russian government fund.

John Podesta, Hillary's campaign manager, served as a board member of Joule which included senior Russian officials.

Joule Global Stitching and Joule Global Holdings was a client of the Panamanian law firm, Mossack Fonseca. Mossack Fonseca is at the center of the the the Panama Papers investigation. The investigation was of global offshore money-laundering. At the same time, Hillary, then-Secretary of State was at the head of the transfer of U.S. advanced technology as part of her "reset" strategy with Russia. Some of that technology had military usage capabilities. According to both the FBI and the U.S. Army, this greatly enhanced Russia's military's technological capacities.

Viktor Vekselberg laundered money through Metcombank, a Russian regional bank, owned 99.978 percent by Vekselberg, with the money transferred by Deutsche Bank and Trust Company Americas in New York City, with the money ending up in a private bank account, in the Bank of America, that is operated by the Clinton Foundation.

Viktor Vekselberg, a Russian investor with ties to the Russian government, and Vekselberg's Renova Group, a Russian conglomerate with interests in energy, oil, and telecommunication was one of the Russian entities that funneled money to Joule including all of it's companies. And it then led to, John Podesta, who also received consulting fees from the Wyss Foundation, a group controlled by Swiss billionaire Hansjoerg Wyss. Wyss is an investor in Joule Energy.

The Russian government investment fund Rusnano, the Russian Corporation of Nanotechnologies, founded by Vladimir Putin in 2007, announced it would invest up to $35 million in Joule Unlimited, just two months after John Podesta joined the board.

Vekselberg, the Renova Group, the Skolkovo Foundation and Wyss all have ties to the Clinton Foundation, either as large donors or participating in the Clinton Global Initiative. It seems that Hillary, her staff, her campaign, and her family's Foundation's and the donors are all one big revolving door.Uranium One, which is Russian controlled, retained the

Podesta Group, run by the brother of Hillary Clinton's campaign chief, John Podesta in 2012, to lobby Hillary's State Department.

Bill Clinton received $500,000 for a Moscow speech from a Russian investment bank with links to the Kremlin that was promoting Uranium One stock, shortly after the Russians announced their intention to acquire a majority stake in Uranium One.

The Russian government now owns 20% of the Uranium in the United States. As the Russian government was procuring ownership of the company, Uranium One funneled millions to the Clinton Foundation.

But Hillary had said she had no reason to intervene in the decision and did not even know the Clinton Foundation was being enriched by its beneficiaries.

"I was not personally involved because that wasn't something the Secretary of State did."

A cable from U.S. representatives in the European Union's city had warned, "The strategy paper reflects concerns raised by industry reps and Ukrainian diplomats the past few months and is consistent with Russia's efforts to dominate the gas supply market in Europe."

"I have never seen a diplomatic cable that had as stark a description of one energy company trying to cheat," said Fred Fleitz, Center for Security Policy.

Sen. John Barrasso warned that the Uranium One deal "would give the Russian government control over a sizable portion of America's uranium production capacity."

Led by Rep. Peter King, and five other Republican members of Congress, wrote that the Uranium One deal "would pose great potential harm to the national security of the United States."

Hillary did not use her position on the Committee on Foreign Investments in the United States (CFIUS) to stop the Uranium One deal, despite warnings from her own diplomats and the lawmakers. It would mean a lot of money for Hillary.

Those who profited from the Uranium One sale donated more than $2.6 million to the Clinton Foundation. The giving from these donors to the Clinton Foundation took place at the same time that the CFIUS deliberations were taking place.

Frank Guistra gave $31.3 million to the Clinton Foundation. He would benefit immensely from the transaction.

In 2009, one year before the United States approved the deal, Hillary's State Department received an internal strategy document from Russia's nuclear energy firm, Rosatom, that warned of Moscow's intentions as it "flexes muscles" in uranium markets.

But Hillary continues to receive money from Russia due to their procurement of 20% of uranium in the U.S. And since she would not be able to continue accepting the money if she became president she wanted the money to go to John Podesta, her campaign manager which would surely be routed to her through her foundation.

*****

WikiLeaks revealed a 2009 cable by then-Secretary of State Hillary, "More needs to be done since Saudi Arabia remains a critical financial support base for Al Qaeda, the Taliban, Lashkar e-Tayyiba and other terrorist groups."

But Hillary's family foundation received millions of dollars from Saudi Arabia and she had given Saudi Arabia a sale of $29.4 billion in U.S. weaponry, including 80 F-15 fighter jets. So she armed Saudi Arabia who arms ISIS and other terrorist groups. And she was accepting money from the country who supported the terrorists of 9-11 in 2001.

In March 2016, The Podesta Group, (John Posta was Hillary's campaign manager) filed as a foreign agent which is required under the Foreign Agents Registration Act of 1938. They are a registered foreign agent on the Saudi Arabia government's payroll. The filing shows that Tony Podesta oversees the Saudi account. John and Tony Podesta receives $140,000 a month from Saudi Arabia. They are the Saudis advocates in D.C. due to the bad press over civilian casualties from its airstrikes in Yemen and its crackdown on political dissidents.

A leaked email shows that John Podesta is also getting paid $7,000 under a consulting contract with the Sandler foundation linked to a major Clinton donor.

John and Tony Podesta were also registered as foreign agents in 2012. They signed a $50,000 a month contract.

Tony Podesta's signature appears on agreements with the Republic of Kosovo disclosed under the Foreign Agents Registration Act (FARA).

According to the agreement, the Podesta Group will "research and analyze issues of concern to the principal; counsel the principal on U.S. policies of concern, activities in Congress and the Executive branch and developments on the U.S. political scene generally; and maintain contact, as necessary, with Members of Congress and their staff, Executive branch officials, members of the press, and nongovernmental organizations."

In the late 1990's, Prime Minister, Hashim Thaci, had been implicated in a human organ trafficking scheme as leader of the Kosovo Liberation Army.

Hillary's State Department approved of him attending the Clinton Global Initiative in 2011-2013.

An American diplomat investigated the claims and found that the Kosovo Liberation Army (KLA) murdered 10 Serbian and Albanian prisoners and sold their kidneys and livers on the black market.

Viktor Vekselberg, also owned Skolkovo, the Russian foundation set up to be a Russian Silicon Valley. It was designed to be the biggest player in the Russia's "reset" technology transfer engineered in 2011 by Hillary as Secretary of State. The Skolkovo Foundation money was deposited in Metcombank owned by Viktor Vekselberg.

Vekselberg is a large donor to the Clinton Foundation. But the biggest concern is that Vekselberg has close ties to Russian military intelligence.

The State Department assisted in a Moscow visit of 22 of the biggest names in U.S. venture capital. Weeks later the first memorandums of understanding were signed by American companies and Skolkovo. A report written in 2012 and issued in 2013, by U.S. Army Foreign Military Studies Program at Fort Leavenworth concerned the security implications of Skolkovo. In this report was shown that the purpose of Skolkovo was to serve as a "vehicle for worldwide technology transfer to Russia in the areas of information technology, biomedicine, energy, satellite and space technology, and nuclear technology."

Security expert and former National Security Analyst Agency analyst, John R. Schindler, stated, "Even worse is how Clinton, Inc., profited. Vice President of the Skolkovo Foundation, Conor Lenihan, who had previously partnered with the Clinton Foundation, recorded that Skolkovo had assembled 28 Russian, American, and European 'Key Partners.' The Russian 'reset', that was one of the big achievements of Hillary's tenure at Foggy Bottom. Never mind that the reset was a disaster, culminating in Kremlin aggression against Ukraine. Hillary's signature program at the State Department ended in unambiguous failure. Yet Clinton, Inc. did very well out of the temporary warming of relations with Moscow."

*****

As Secretary of State, Hillary's use of an non-secure email server will leave a legacy of lawlessness for our justice system and on the public's trust in government in every aspect.

And it looks like James Comey is so intertwined with Hillary, it is most likely the reason, or one of the reasons that he recommended no charges be brought against Hillary.

A source close to James Comey stated that "the atmosphere at the FBI has been toxic ever since Jim announced last July that he wouldn't recommend an indictment against Hillary."

"Some people, including department heads, stopped talking to Jim, and even ignored his greetings when they passed him in the hall. They felt that he betrayed them and brought disgrace on the bureau by letting Hillary off with a slap on the wrist."

CHAPTER 4

The night watchman of the government, Judge Napolitano, said that, "The NSA leaked the DNC emails so that Hillary will not become president. A former high-ranking official who developed the software that NSA now uses, this individual said the NSA hacked the DNC because members of the intelligence community simply do not want Hillary Clinton to be president of the United States. NSA must have everyone of her emails. They do not want her to be president because she does not know how to handle State Secrets because some of the state secrets that she revealed used proper, true names of American intelligence operating undercover in the Middle East. When they lost their covers they ran for their lives and some of them didn't run fast enough and they lost their lives. It's very telling that the intelligence community would feel so strongly about Mrs. Clinton that they would attempt to sabotage her campaign to prevent her from becoming their boss. It's also telling that these folks would break American law in order to, in their view, save it."

With the second FBI investigation on Hillary, Speaker Paul Ryan stated, "Yet again, Hillary Clinton has nobody but herself to blame. She was entrusted with some of our nation's most important secrets, and she betrayed that trust by carelessly mishandling highly classified information."

"This decision, long overdue, is the result of her reckless use of a private email server, and her refusal to be forthcoming with federal investigators. I renew my call for the Director of National Intelligence to suspend all classified briefings for Secretary Clinton until this matter is fully resolved."

Just after 8 days of reviewing 650,000 emails, found on Hillary's then deputy chief of staff, Huma Abedin's estranged husband, Anthony Weiner's computer, FBI director James Comey announced that he will not change his decision he had made in July 2016 concerning Hillary's email scandal.

Within the 650,000 emails were found Hillary's State Department emails.

Huma Abedin said she did not know how the emails were on her estranged husband's computer. She had told investigators that she had turned over all devices that she had State Department emails on. The emails were first discovered by NYC area field agents in October while investigating a complaint that Anthony Weiner was sending sexual images to a 15 year old girl. The agents could not read the emails because their warrants to search Weiner's computer did not include reading the emails. This made senior officials aware of the contents of Hillary's emails on his computer.

Huma Abedin had sworn in a deposition that she had turned over all of her State Department related devices to the FBI. Those included a Blackberry, two laptops, and other files. Her estranged husband's computer is now being reviewed to see if his emails have a connection to Hillary.

The FBI did not even ask Hillary's aides for all of their computers and devices initially.

"The more we learn about the FBI's initial investigation into Secretary Clinton's unauthorized use of a private email server, the more questions we have about the thoroughness of the investigation and the administration's conclusion to not prosecute her for mishandling classified information," House Judiciary Committee Chairman, Bob Goodlatte, of Virginia stated.

"If the FBI is denied the ability to gather evidence through compulsory means, Secretary Clinton and her aides have enormous leverage to negotiate extraordinary concessions in exchange for voluntary cooperation. It is critical for the public to know whether the FBI has requested from the Justice Department vital investigative tools such as grand jury subpoenas and search warrants and whether it has been denied access to them," Senate Judiciary Committee Chairman Chuck Grassley wrote James Comey.

The reason FBI Director James Comey reopened the investigation is due to a threat from agents.

"A few weeks ago, almost 100 agents were threatening Comey that they were going to resign, and that kind of pressure is what turned him around. It wasn't Comey or his integrity," Tom Delay said.

"I know he made a huge mistake when he indicted Clinton, though not indicting her, but now he's trying to turn that around.

"He had to do it now or have all these FBI agents resign. That would have probably been a bigger story than what Comey did.

"He got the pressure. He got the notice.

"He understood as far as his own job and being able to go forward in his own job and his reputation.

"If 100 FBI agents resigned before the election, he would have been toast.

"It's taken them this long, a few months, to get to this point. They didn't stop working.

"The investigation, he said it was closed, but as far as those FBI agents were concerned, it wasn't closed.

"They were going forward, because they knew that they had to come up with some new information or some new evidence in order to get Comey to open up, particularly when he has this kind of pressure coming from his own agents," Delay stated.

And now we know that senior agents within the FBI tried to stop the investigation into the Clinton Foundation.

"Senior law enforcement officials repeatedly voiced doubt of the strength of the evidence... sought to condense what was at times a sprawling cross-country effort and...told agents to limit their pursuit of the case," the Wall Street Journal reported.

The agents came up against officials who adamantly dismissed the case when they presented the Clinton Foundation case to Attorney General Loretta Lynch's Department of Justice in February.

"That was the weirdest meeting I've ever been to," an agent said.

The Department of Justice officials refused to allow actions which included subpoenas or convening a grand jury. Connections to the email scandal go to the highest levels.

"Banks, intelligence, arms companies, foreign money, etc. are all united behind Hillary Clinton. And the media as well. Media owners, and the journalists themselves," Julian Assange of WikiLeaks stated.

Also in the 650,000 emails were found, Erik Prince, retired Navy SEAL, and Blackwater USA founder, said, that he was told by a "high-placed" source that emails found on Anthony Weiner's computer shows that Hillary occasionally went on trips with Bill Clinton to a Caribbean Island where Bill had sex with young girls. Eric Prince's "high-placed" source referred to was in the NYPD.

"They found State Department emails, they found a lot of other really damning criminal information, including money laundering, including the fact that Hillary went to this sex island with convicted pedophile Jeffrey Epstein. Bill Clinton went there more than 20 times. Hillary Clinton went there at least six times."

Former President Bill Clinton went to the Caribbean island with Epstein 26 times. Epstein owns the island. Those flights were confirmed by flight logs.

"The amount of garbage that they found in those e-mails, of criminal activity by Hillary, by her immediate circle and even by other Democratic members of Congress was so disgusting that they (NYPD) gave it to the FBI and they said, "We're going to go public with this if you don't reopen the investigation and you don't do the right thing with timely indictments."

The NYPD would have went public with their investigation in a press conference, but the Justice Department pressured and prevented them from doing so.

The FBI who is also looking into the Clinton Foundation was ordered to Stand Down by the Justice Department.

Prince said about Huma Abedin and Anthony Weiner, "They both… See potential jail time of many years for their crimes, for Huma Abedin sending and receiving and even storing hundreds of thousands of messages from the State Department server and from Hillary Clinton's own homebrew server which contained classified information. Weiner faces all kinds of exposure for the inappropriate texting that was going on and for the other information that they found."

The new emails are separate from all of the previous emails that were leaked. Sources stated that a 99% of probability that Hillary's Secretary of State non secure email server was hacked by at least five foreign intelligence agencies and that they did obtain information from Hillary's non secure email server.

Because Hillary had exposed sensitive information to foreign government hackers, the Chairman of the House of the Homeland Security Committee accused Hillary of treason.

"The concern I've had all along is she had 7 special access programs on these devices. Those are the most classified sensitive secrets in the federal government, many of them covert operations. In my opinion, quite frankly, it's treason.

"She took those devices overseas against the State Department's wishes, and now we find out, and James Comey told me previously, that it's very likely that foreign adversary nations got into her private server."

Agents of the FBI were outraged when Comey had recommended no charges be brought against Hillary. An "internal chaotic climate" in the FBI was due to Comey's decision. The agents who leaked so much information consider Clinton to be the Antichrist personified.

Also one of the lies of Hillary was exposed by WikiLeaks. It was in a campaign memo, The Trans-Pacific Partnership. Wikileaks "reveals that Hillary Clinton told Rep. Eddie Bernice Johnson (D-Texas) that Clinton was only pretending to oppose TPP in order to get Union support but would sign it when she was president," advisors Peter Navarro and Curt Ellis stated.

The FBI and the Justice Department could not or would not prove Hillary guilty without proving President Obama guilty also. The FBI had shown Huma Abedin an email between Hillary and President Obama.

Abedin had stated, "How is this not classified?"

This was in reference to President Obama's and Hillary's emails on an unsecured server. President Obama had used a fake name to communicate to Hillary over an unsecured email.

Of course she had to already know about their correspondence over nonsecure email.

In an email from Huma Abedin to Hillary, Huma writes about Edward Snowden, "We view this not as a clever game of WikiLeaks but rather as a criminal act against the United States of America. He might think this is a clever game today but when he is prosecuted and if convicted he will move from being a clever cyber thief to a convicted criminal and will find out that's a whole different kind of game."

Huma Abedin sent emails to Hillary's nonsecure email. And she stored classified emails on a home computer. So she should move to be a convicted criminal and find out that's a whole different kind of game.

And on Edward Snowden, Hillary stated at a town hall meeting, "Because he took valuable information and went first to China and then is now under protection of Vladimir Putin I think that raises a lot of questions about everything else he did. So I do not think he should escape having to return and answer for what he has done."

Yeah right. Like she has a lot of room to talk.

But Edward Snowden told the American people that their government was spying on them. Unlike Hillary who allowed numerous foreign governments to attain classified and top secret information regarding the United States. So not only are Hillary and Huma Abedin guilty of serious crimes against the United States, but they also lied to cover it up.

*****

At the "Clinton Scandal Update – Emails and the Clinton Foundation" symposium held in Washington on September 29, 2016...

Chris Farrell, director of investigations, and Tom Fitton were joined by three experts: WND senior staff writer Jerome Corsi, author of Partners in Crime: The Clinton's Scheme to Monetize the White House for Personal Profit; Peter Schweizer, author of the New York Times best-seller, Clinton Cash; and Joseph E. diGenova, former United States Attorney for the District of Columbia.

Peter Schweizer stated that Hillary's pay-for-play sets "an extremely dangerous precedent. This is about more than the Clintons, if it is not dealt with in a legal manner, it's going to be imitated."

Schweizer noted that this scandal is "larger than anything seen before in efforts to hide what was going on and the amount of money involved."

Chris Farrell spoke of the FBI Director James Comey's negligence and his damaged reputation. "Mr. Comey is personally compromised. The institution won't get over it." Before joining Judicial Watch Chris Farrell worked in national intelligence. He pointed out that at least 22 emails crossing Hillary's unsecure server contained "sensitive compartmented information," a high level of classification. "This puts the United States at grave risk. Any first class intelligence organization would be looking for that kind of information."

Jerome Corsi spoke on the unaccounted money, millions, that flowed into the Clinton Foundation. "Tens of millions of dollars were diverted," he stated. There is a discrepancy between the amount of money the foundation reported and the amount people gave to the foundation. "The Clintons ended up with net worths of 100 million dollars each." And the money that they were paid for speaking fees cannot account for the discrepancy.

Joe diGenova stated, "I do not believe Comey is fit to continue in office. His arrogance and obfuscation should disqualify anyone with the power the FBI has. He violated his oath. It is very clear that from the moment he took control of this investigation he decided he was not going to recommend prosecution. It was a political decision.

"Congress is refusing to take steps to hold Mrs. Clinton accountable. Why isn't there a contempt citation pending now? Emails were destroyed after they were subpoenaed.

"It's a fundamental issue of government transparency.

"We depend on the good faith of government when we file a Freedom of Information Act (FOIA) request. We rely on civil servants to do the job they've been entrusted to do. Hillary Clinton tore that contract up. If Mrs. Clinton gets away with it, if there's no institutional accountability for her conduct, FOIA may end because you can't rely on the law being enforced.

"This, as you can see, is no longer just about Bill and Hillary Clinton. It's about the federal government generally, the FBI, the Department of Justice, the rule of law, national security, transparency and trust in government..."

Partners in Crime, author Jerome Corsi said, "Hillary was sending emails from Clintonemail.com to Huma Abedin at Yahoo.com. They were both involved, and they completely compromised the State Department security, because anybody that had the password or username could read, in unredacted form, all these emails in real time.

"That's obviously a major felony in violation of federal security laws for handling classified information. You can't do that."

"Clearly, sending these emails to Yahoo.com, and we know some of them had classified material because they've been marked classified, is a violation of the law, and it doesn't require intent," he said.

Hillary had told federal investigators that her use of a private server was not to avoid Freedom of Information Act requirements. She specifically denied using the server to avoid Federal Records Act requirements for storage and archiving. But in an email to Huma Abedin Hillary wanted to know who was seeing her emails or where they were going.

Asked if she was putting top secret information at risk by using her unsecured private server, Hillary answered "No, absolutely not. And you know what was announced on Friday is no different from what I've been saying for many months. I took the handling of classified materials very seriously. The State Department has the process for classifying material and then they mark it..."

But classified information does not have to be marked. Classified information is to be handled properly with or without being marked classified.

And one of Hillary's emails showed her telling Jake Sullivan, "If they can't, turn into non-paper w no identifying heading and send <u>non-secure</u>".

What was stated by FBI director James Comey, that he recommended no charges be brought against Hillary, is a conflict of interest in which James Comey should be disqualified from making that recommendation and from holding any government office.

Under a Freedom of Information Act obtained, it showed that in 2009 when she took office as Secretary, Hillary failed to complete the highest level of security training for the proper handling of the government's most secret documents. All of them should be thrown out and never be allowed to hold a government office again.

CHAPTER 5

As for Hillary's choice of Vice President, Tim Kaine, he was involved way too closely with radical Muslims.

"Kaine should move to put some distance between his administration and the Falls Church based Muslim American Society," said Delegates Todd Gilbert and Clifford L "Clay" Athey Jr.

Kaine had appointed Dr. Esam Omeish, the president of the society, to the Virginia Commission on Immigration. Gilbert wrote to Kaine and asked him to reconsider his appointment of Omeish after seeing online videos of Omeish accusing Israel of genocide against Palestinians and exhorting Muslims to the "jihad way".

Due to pressure that Kaine exerted on him, Omeish resigned less than a day later.

The delegates, after doing some investigating, said the connections between Kaine and MAS appear to be deeper than just his appointment of Omeish.

In October 2011, Tim Kaine spoke at an event where Jamal Barzinji was given a Lifetime Achievement Award. Dr. Barzinji was one of the founders of the U.S. Muslim Brotherhood. An important part of the Muslim Brotherhood, the International Institute of Islamic Thought (IIIT), stated, Dr. Barzinji had a role in help founding almost all of the organizations that comprise the US Muslim Brotherhood.

In June 2016, the Global Muslim Brotherhood Daily Watch reported that the Obama administration had appointed Zaki Barzinji, Dr. Barzinji's 27 year old grandson, as the liaison to the Muslim American community under the White House Office of Public Engagement.

Hillary's selection of Tim Kaine appears to be a continuation of democratic political leaders support for the Global Muslim Brotherhood.

The late leader of the Muslim Public Affairs Council (MPAC) Mater Hathout was invited to the White House in December 1995 to discuss the Bosnia peace agreement with senior Administration officials.

Kaine, when governor of Virginia, appointed Muslim American Society president Esam Omeish to the state immigration commission. According to Federal prosecutors in 2008, the American Muslim Society "was founded as an overt arm of the Muslim Brotherhood in the US".

In 2012, convicted terrorists Abdurradman Alamoudi confirmed this when he testified; "Everyone knows that the American Muslim Society is the Muslim Brotherhood".

Omeish was also the vice president of the Dar Al Hijrah Islamic Center, which had al-Qaeda operative Anwar al-Awlaki as an imam. Two of the 9/11 hijackers and the perpetrator of the Fort Hood shooting, where Major General John G Rossi was Colonel at that time, had attended services at the mosque. Omeish expressed extremism before Kaine appointed him. In 2004, Omeish praised the Hamas spiritual leader as 'our beloved Sheikh Yassin'.

A video from 2000 also surfaced where Omeish pledged to help Palestinians who 'understand that jihad is the way to liberate your land'.

Also Omeish's website shows that he served as president of the National Muslim Student Association which is another Muslim Brotherhood front group.

The US Justice Department had labeled the Islamic Society of North America a Muslim Brotherhood entity stressing that they were an unindicted co-conspirator in a Hamas financing trial. Omeish had served on that board.

"Many of Omeish's statements and activities in the past have in fact been a manifestation of political Islam and his attempt to use the Muslim Community as a tool in a specific Islamism political agenda. This not only violates the core principles of separation of religion and state which is a Cornerstone in our nation but is in fact the main mechanism of influence regarding transnational Islamism. His public advocacy of jihad in the Middle East by co-religionists implicitly via terror organizations like Hezbollah and Hamas against Israel, a U.S. ally should certainly highlight the toxicity of Islamism as a political ideology.

This becomes especially concerning in an individual appointed to contribute to a more sound immigration policy because it begs the question; will appointees point of view be one primarily of American nationalism and security or will it be one of transnational global Islamism? This inappropriate appointment and hasty resignation should yet again remind our elected officials across the country of the stakes in this global idealogical conflict in which we are engaged."

This statement was not made from any official in the US government. It was given by the moderate American Islamic Forum for Democracy due to Omeish's radical history.

The FBI had identified, Jamal Barzinji, as part of a group of individuals with the Muslim Brotherhood who sought to "institute Islamic Revolution in the United States".

In a sworn affidavit, Investigator David Kaine said in 2000, Barzinji was investigated because "he is not only closely associated with the Palestinian Islamic Jihad but also Hamas".

Counter-terror reporter David Poole said that Barzenji was almost prosecuted but the Obama Administration did not allow it. Obama had appointed Barzenji's grandson as the new liaison to the Muslim American Community under the White House Office of Public Engagement.

Kaine also supported Obama's Iran deal and played a big role in overriding Congressional opposition to it. Also, Kaine was one of the first to deliberately boycott Israel's prime minister Benjamin Netanyahu's 2015 U.S. Congressional speech on the dangers posed by the Iran deal.

Kaine's involvement with these radical islamists may have something to do with his embracing Marxism, and his adventures with radicals and revolutionaries in the 1980s in Latin America. As violence and Civil War erupted throughout Central America in September 1980, Kaine left Harvard Law School to volunteer with Jesuit missionaries in Northern Honduras. Reports claim that while in Honduras he embraced liberation theology. Liberation theology was a radical Marxist based ideology at odds with the church, the pope, and the United States. Kaine's political ideology was pro-soviet.

CHAPTER 6

THE OLD FLAG

H.C. Brunner

> ...Lift up the boy on your shoulder high, And show
> him the faded shred; Those stripes would be red as the
> sunset sky If death could have dyed them red. Off with
> your hat as the flag goes by! Uncover the youngster's
> head; Teach him to hold it holy and high For the sake of
> its sacred dead.

Carl von Clausewitz definition of war, "An act of violence intended to compel our opponent to fulfill our will. Violence, that is to say, physical force is therefore the means; the compulsory submission of the enemy to our will is the ultimate object."

"There's no such thing as al- Qaeda. I'm so sick of hearing that," Travis Lively, Navy Seal, and drone expert said. What? Well, then, who is al-Qaeda? The U.S. government? Or the shadow government which is composed of elements in our government?

Seymour Hersh, Pulitzer prize winning investigative reporter stated; "...The Senate Intelligence Committee released a report on the assault by a local militia in September 2012 on the American consulate and a nearby undercover CIA facility in Benghazi, which resulted in the death of the US ambassador, Christopher Stevens, and three others. The report's criticism of the State Department for not providing adequate security at the consulate, and of the intelligence community for not alerting the

US military to the presence of a CIA outpost in the area, received front-page coverage and revived animosities in Washington, with Republicans accusing Obama and Hillary Clinton of a cover-up."

The Benghazi debacle was one of the most horrendous acts of the American government.The 17 February Martyrs Brigade was hired to provide security and act as the Libyan "quick reaction force" to protect the US State Department's Special Mission Compound in Benghazi. But the diplomatic corps in Benghazi did not fully believe the loyalty of the 17th February Martyr Brigade. Among the 17 February militia, there were members who were suspected of very strong anti-American ideals.

At least six different incidents which included bombs, rocket propelled grenades, and improvised explosive devices occurred during the Spring and Summer of 2012 in Benghazi. A review of the events in Benghazi by the US Government during that same time period showed "a general backdrop of political violence, assassinations targeting former regime officials, lawlessness, and an overarching absence of central government authority in eastern Libya."

And to top it off, approximately one week before the 9/11 attacks in 2012, an intelligence cable was sent to the Special Mission Compound from Washington. The cable warned in approximate wording, "Be advised, we have reports from locals that a Western facility or U.S. Embassy/Consulate/Government target will be attacked in the next week."

And still Hillary tried to blame the attacks on an internet video.

And since they knew the Special Mission Compound was very likely to be attacked without having sufficient security forces or the basic security perimeter for the compound, the Obama administration and Hillary left them there willingly, knowing what very likely would take place.

A Government review in December 2012, proved that Washington knew that the compound "included a weak and very extended perimeter, an incomplete interior fence, no man traps, and unhardened entry gates and doors. Benghazi was also severely under-resourced with regard to weapons, ammunition, (non-lethal deterrent) and fire safety equipment, including escape masks."

But the actual cover up did not even have its beginnings in Benghazi. It started in Cairo. Officials knew that the protests in Cairo were not due to an internet video. The protests regarded the release of the Blind Shiek, according to Kenneth Timmerman in, Dark Forces. And since it has been proven that people from other countries were brought in to start the Arab Spring in these countries, and that they had State Department backing, was the protest in Cairo even a real protest? Or was it another orchestrated event by the U.S. government? Possibly to help propagate the cover-up of Benghazi? In Tripoli everyone at the U.S. Embassy had evacuated. But it was not attacked.

The GRS operators at the annex in Benghazi were repeatedly told not to go assist those at the Special Mission Compound even though they knew they were being attacked. Did Washington not want anyone at the compound to survive the attack to cover up the gun running operation to Syria that the Obama administration and Hillary were involved in? That makes sense more than anything else. Since Washington knew they were being attacked, and knew the compound did not have the proper security, and knew of the threat, and had repeatedly turned down requests for additional security, and even propagated, as Washington called it, "riots", in Cairo, while it was happening, their actions, or inactions made sure that at least some of the Americans got killed and possibly all of them. Colonel Andy Wood also specifically requested aid from a nearby C-130 aircraft that was meant for deep firefights like the one at the annex. Obama turned down this request.

Seymour Hersh also said; "A highly classified annex to the report, not made public, described a secret agreement reached in early 2012 between the Obama and Erdoğan (President of Turkey) administrations. It pertained to the rat line. By the terms of the agreement, funding came from Turkey, as well as Saudi Arabia and Qatar; the CIA, with the support of MI6, was responsible for getting arms from Gaddafi's arsenals into Syria. A number of front companies were set up in Libya, some under the cover of Australian entities. Retired American soldiers, who didn't always know who was really employing them, were hired to manage procurement and shipping. The operation was run by David Petraeus, the CIA director who would soon resign when it became known he was having an affair with his biographer. (But that most likely was a way to discredit Petraeus who was scheduled to testify before Congress.)

In Jack Murphy's and Brandon Webb's, Benghazi, The Definitive Report, they say that General Petraeus had little if any knowledge of the mission: "The nature of these operations remains highly classified. They were never intended to be known to anyone outside a very small circle in the Special Operations community and within Obama's National Security Council. Ambassador Stevens, the CIA chief of station in Tripoli and then-director of the CIA, Gen. [David] Petraeus, had little if any knowledge about these JSOC missions."

Petraeus was "was furious about being left in the lurch by the Obama administration."

They say that leading CIA figures allowed Petraeus' affair to be made public. The FBI had already known about the affair. Webb and Murphy say his fall was a "palace coup". They stated that during a 2011, New York Veterans Day parade, Petraeus' personal security detail lost contact with him for an hour. The Director of the CIA would be a highly prized target. Were they hoping someone would assassinate him? Some wonder, since they did not reveal their sources, if they should be believed. The importance of not revealing sources is that it could put their lives in danger and the lives of their families, also the life of the person who revealed the sources.

Seymour Hersh; "The operation had not been disclosed at the time it was set up to the congressional intelligence committees and the congressional leadership, as required by law since the 1970s. The involvement of MI6 enabled the CIA to evade the law by classifying the mission as a liaison operation. The former intelligence official explained that for years there has been a recognised exception in the law that permits the CIA not to report liaison activity to Congress, which would otherwise be owed a finding. (All proposed CIA covert operations must be described in a written document, known as a 'finding', submitted to the senior leadership of Congress for approval.) Distribution of the annex was limited to the staff aides who wrote the report and to the eight ranking members of Congress – the Democratic and Republican leaders of the House and Senate, and the Democratic and Republicans leaders on the House and Senate intelligence committees. This hardly constituted a genuine attempt at oversight: the eight leaders are not known to gather together to raise questions or discuss the secret information they receive.

"The annex didn't tell the whole story of what happened in Benghazi before the attack, nor did it explain why the American consulate was attacked. 'The consulate's only mission was to provide cover for the moving of arms,' the former intelligence official, who has read the annex, said. 'It had no real political role.'"

After Hillary's State Department paid a $9.2 million contract to the Blue Mountain Group, the guards were not even armed. And the 17 February Martyr Brigade had to supply their own weapons and ammunition. The unmanned drone overhead (but it was discovered that it was a predator drone but it was not armed) that arrived at approximately 11:10 p.m. Benghazi time, should have focused out around the annex to let the GRS operators know if anyone and how many and from which direction the attackers might be coming. When they were told, the operators already knew they were attacking. They could already see them. Why? Why was the drone not watching out for attackers and why had they not told the compound when the attackers were coming back and what areas they were in and approaching from? And since we know it was a predator drone, why was it not used to help the GRS shoot the terrorists. The team leader of the GRS guys at the annex was inside. He was not helping in the fight. There were other weapons guys there that were not fighting. Of those that came from Tripoli the only one that helped fight the terrorists was Glen Doherty. There were 2 Delta boys there also. Why, of all the people from Tripoli, did the Deltas not fight the terrorists?

One of the GRS operators had kept wondering why they had continued to be told to "Stand Down" before they went to the compound. They never got the okay to go. They were told to wait and were told to "Stand Down". No matter what any politician or anyone else says, They were told to "Stand Down." The GRS operators went anyway to help those at the Special Mission Compound.

"If you want to get down to the exact words, wait. Five minutes into it, stand down was told to us 15 minutes into it, then another wait, twenty-five minutes into it and that last one was when we, the team, made a team decision to say, 'Hey, we need to go,'" Kris "Tonto" Paronto said.

"The irony is that the CIA Chief of Base (COB) was too afraid to act, so Navy SEAL Ty Woods took charge of the situation, and later the COB got an award for it all," a confidential source within the CIA told SOFREP.

The chief of base knew who he would have to answer to.

Minutes after September 11th ended and the next day began, the White House received an email from the State Department's Operational Center in Washington. At 12:06 a.m. Benghazi time the email read, "Update 2: Ansar al-Sharia Claims Responsibility For Benghazi Attack. Embassy Tripoli reports the group claimed responsibility on Facebook and Twitter and has called for an attack on Embassy Tripoli."

A fellow at the Washington Institute for Near East Policy investigated and found no evidence that Ansar al-Sharia had ever made any statements on-line. And at approximately the same time State had sent the email to the White House, the reinforcement team, due to Greg Hicks, from Tripoli went to charter a private flight to Benghazi. But Hillary had emailed her daughter an hour earlier about the 2 officers lost due to an al-Qeada like group. Ansar al-Sharia was an al-Qeada like group. They were actually created in 2011 when Hillary and Obama backed the militia's in Benghazi. They are al-Qaeda's entity on the Arabian Peninsula. Also, Ansar al-Sharia denied responsibility for the attacks.

Thankfully, Greg Hicks, sent the Tripoli team to Benghazi. So why no attacks on the embassy in Tripoli? None of it adds up. If there were no statements made with Ansar al-Sharia claiming responsibility for the attack, and there was no protest due to the internet video, why were these reasons ever even given for the attacks at the compound and annex? Washington had known that Ansar al-Sharia had a safe house 200 meters from the Special Mission Compound. Was all of it a lie? And why did Hillary email her daughter approximately one hour before State emailed the White House about Ansar al-Sharia supposedly claiming responsibility for the attack?

And it is not even plausible that the "rebels" did not know where the compound and CIA annex were located. They were white guys, some with blue eyes and light colored hair, and one female coming in and out of the annex. If Hillary wanted to keep the compound and annex from being known, why did the 17 February Martyr Brigade have the responsibility of "guarding" the compound? The Blue Mountain Group was a relatively unknown Security Company based in Wales. The excuse of not renewing the contract with the company, which was thoroughly vetted by the U.S. before the Blue Mountain Group,was "said" due to the situation in Benghazi (which was one of the most dangerous places in the world). If the State Department left Benghazi, they would not need them and then would have to place them elsewhere. But they signed a years contract with the Blue Mountain Group so that voids that excuse. Hillary had fired the thoroughly vetted group and then hired BMG. It begs the question, Why? Also the State Department stated by law they had to go with the lowest bidder. But there were other, better known companies that were never even considered.

Representative Mike Rogers became chairman of the Intelligence Committee in January 2011. It was made known that Rep. Mike Rodger's wife ran a private military contracting firm, Aegis.

There have been links of Aegis to the Blue Mountain Group guarding the State Department's Benghazi mission.

A biographical profile of Mrs. Rogers was on the Manatt website; Ms. Rogers "obtained top-secret facility security clearance for Aegis, created the company's board of directors and positioned it for future growth and expansion."

What is most interesting is that two former senior CIA officials, Robert Reynolds, a leader in contracts and procurement for the CIA, and John Sano, a former deputy director of the CIA's clandestine services was on the board of Aegis.

An Aegis Advisory Intelligence Report directed toward corporate clients stated, "Aegis has been operating in Libya since February 2011."

Aegis Advisory, is an Aegis subsidiary. A "CONFIDENTIAL" report shows Aegis Advisory's capability of providing "proprietary information expert knowledge from our country team based in Tripoli.

"Aegis has extensive links in Libya which can be leveraged quickly to ensure safe passage." Or possibly leverage to ensure something deadlier.

A contract renewal "worth up to $475 million over two years" was won by Aegis through approval of the Pentagon to run security services for reconstruction projects in Iraq in 2007. According to the Project on Government Oversight, a $497 million State Department contract for embassy security in Kabul, Afghanistan was procured by Aegis in 2011.

Ambassador Stevens and Rep. Rogers both pursued efforts, that involved both the State Department and the CIA, to secure Gadhafi's arsenals, which included MANPADS.

Rep. and Mrs. Rogers tracked Libyan border security issues.

They were both also focused on the Libyan security and intelligence environment in the months that surrounded the Benghazi attack.This may play a part in that attack.

Mrs. Rogers left Aegis in 2012 and joined the law firm Manatt as a managing director for federal government affairs.

On March 14, after only a thirteen month tenure, she left Manatt. Oddly, her association with the firm was taken off its website and her leaving the firm had not been made known.

Rep. Rogers gave up his seat in Congress and his position as House Intelligence Committee Chairman.

Rogers had warned his colleagues in Congress about the upcoming investigation and was in opposition of the select committee on Benghazi being formed. It looks more and more likely that they both distanced themselves from Benghazi for a very good reason.

*****

The annex was still being attacked at the time Hillary emailed her daughter and told her they had lost two people to an al-Qeada like group, and also when State sent the White House an email stating that Ansar al-Sharia claimed responsibility for the attack. Why would Ansar al-Sharia take time to post on Facebook while they are trying to kill Americans? Well they did not post it. That was also a lie. Ansar al-Sharia denied on September 12, 2012, that they were responsible for the attack in a statement read on television.

Threat levels were assigned to each diplomatic compound based on six categories; International terrorism, indigenous terrorism, political violence, crime, human intelligence, and technical threats. The threat levels were designated, low, medium, high or critical. The high or critical threat levels were regarded as having serious or grave impact on American diplomats. More than half of all of the American diplomatic posts around the world were considered critical or high for threat of terrorism in 2012. There were fourteen diplomatic posts that were dangerous enough for the threat level to be designated critical or high in each of the six categories. Two of the fourteen diplomatic posts were in Benghazi and Tripoli.

In late August 2012, the State Department issued a severe travel warning for Libya which stated that "political violence in the form of assassinations and vehicle bombs has increased in both Benghazi and Tripoli...militia conflict can erupt at any time or any place in the country."

An intelligence cable warning came from from Washington as September 11th, 2012, approached, in approximate wording; "Be advised we have reports from locals that a western facility or U.S. Embassy/ Consulate/ Government target will be attacked in the next week." That was the approximate wording of the cable.

A government review issued in December, 2012, showed that the compound "included a weak and very extended perimeter, an incomplete interior fence, no mantraps and unhardened entry gates and doors. Benghazi was also severely under-resourced with regard to weapons, ammunition, (non-lethal deterrence) and fire safety equipment including escape masks."

A hole in one of the exterior walls of the compound blown out by an I.E.D. was approximately 30 ft. wide earlier in the summer. It was never repaired. Cameras were sent but never installed. The cameras had night vision.

In all, there were 600 security requests. Six hundred.

As early as June 2012, Ambassador Stevens had sent an email to a Washington State Department official requesting that two six-man mobile security detachments (MSD teams), of specially trained DS agents be allowed to remain in Libya through the national elections which were to be held in July and August. In his email Stevens wrote that the State Department personnel, "would feel much safer if we could keep two MSD teams with us through this period (to support) our staff and (provide a personal detail) for me and the (Deputy Chief of Mission) and any VIP visitors." Stevens request was denied and was told it was due to staffing limitations and other commitments.

But State has a total of 2000 DS agents with 800 in posts worldwide so that would leave 1200 agents in the U.S. to protect the Secretary of State and visiting dignitaries. Why did they at least not allow more DS agents? And Benghazi was one of the fourteen diplomatic posts that was categorized in every threat level as high, or critical. It was one of the most dangerous places on earth. But the State Department made those at the compound depend on the Libyans for security. This will become clearer later on.

In July, Stevens requested that the State Department extend the stay of the Site Security Team (SST). The team consisted of 16 active duty military special operators. That request was also denied by Hillary's State Department even though Colonel Andy Wood and General Carter Ham would have allowed the SST to stay. Everything was done to ensure the diplomatic compound was not protected. Why?

When the Libyan Shield Militia, who were loyal to Gaddafi, arrived at the annex to escort them to the airport, John "Tig" Tiegan's question encompassed the ambiguity of it all; "If these guys are friendly, why the f*** didn't they get called in to help us at the beginning?"

And to emphasize the absurdity of it all, after 3 mortars hit the roof of Building C where Dave Ubben, Tyrone "Rone" Woods, Glenn "Bub" Doherty, and Mark "Oz" Geist were firing at the terrorists, John "Tig" Tiegan, ran to the building and called on his radio: "Hey, guys on Building C, you guys OK? You guys OK?" "Yeah. We're fine in here, we're good," replied the Team Leader from inside of the building.

Tig's response, "Not you! The guys on top of the f****** roof!"

It might have been better if it was, "Not f****** you! The guys on top of the roof!"

Breaking down the events of the Benghazi attack; First, every attempt to get help from Washington went unheeded.

The base chief was on the phone with someone and would not allow the GRS operators to go. Thankfully they went anyway.

Approximately 2 hours after the attacks began, Hillary emailed her daughter at 11:12 p.m. telling her that they lost 2 officers due to an al-Qeada like group.

Approximately one hour later someone from the State Department emailed the White House.

No one from Washington sent reinforcements.

About that time, deputy chief of missions, Greg Hicks, in Tripoli heard from the embassy about the attacks and sent Glen Doherty and others.

Approximately 2 hours after the attacks began, the unmanned predator drone arrived overhead showing everyone in Washington, who was watching, what was happening. No help was sent.

Again, no reinforcements sent by Washington.

Wikipedia gives the specifications of the predator drone;

General Atomics MQ-9 Reaper (formerly named Predator B) is an unmanned aerial vehicle (UAV) capable of remote controlled or autonomous flight operations, developed by General Atomics Aeronautical Systems (GA-ASI) primarily for the United States Air Force(USAF). The MQ-9 and other UAVs are referred to as Remotely Piloted Vehicles/Aircraft (RPV/RPA) by the USAF to indicate their human ground controllers.The MQ-9 is the first hunter-killer UAV designed for long-endurance, high-altitude surveillance. In 2006, the then–Chief of Staff of the United States Air Force General T. Michael Moseley said: «We›ve moved from using UAVs primarily in intelligence, surveillance, and reconnaissance roles before Operation Iraqi Freedom, to a true hunter-killer role with the Reaper."

The MQ-9 is a larger, heavier, and more capable aircraft than the earlier General Atomics MQ-1 Predator; it can be controlled by the same ground systems used to control MQ-1s. The Reaper has a 950 shaft horsepower (712 kW) turboprop engine (compared to the Predator's 115 hp (86 kW) piston engine). The greater power allows the Reaper to carry 15 times more ordnance payload and cruise at about three times the speed of the MQ-1. The aircraft is monitored and controlled by aircrew in the Ground Control Station (GCS), including weapons employment.

In 2008, the New York Air National Guard 174th Attack Wing began the transition fromF-16 piloted fighters to MQ-9 Reapers, becoming the first fighter squadron conversion to an all–unmanned combat aerial vehicle (UCAV) attack squadron. In March 2011, the U.S. Air Force was training more pilots for advanced unmanned aerial vehicles than for any other single weapons system. The Reaper is also used by the United States Navy, the CIA, U.S. Customs and Border Protection, NASA, and the militaries of several other countries. The USAF plans to keep the MQ-9 in service into the 2030s.

General Carter Ham of AFRICOM was going to send reinforcements but was forced not to. Later he was relieved of command due to his actions.

No one would allow help to be sent.

Afterwards, some of the compound staff was given new names and sent to reside in unknown places.

By all accounts, every action and inaction from Washington, those at the compound were not supposed to leave Benghazi alive.

Interestingly, the FBI had identified one of the five main suspects as someone with who the U.S. government had a quid pro quo relationship. An intelligence source, when I asked if they just left them there (those at the compound), said, Yes. No one was coming for them. And there were special ops 2 hours away. All roads seem to lead down a very dark path. From all accounts it looks as if Libyan President Magariaf would have wanted the compound protected. So the excuse that they did not have approval to send their planes in is ridiculous. They dif not even attempt to get approvalAlso security was changed by the State Department from a group that was thoroughly vetted by the United States to the Blue Mountain Group who hired locals by placing an ad in a Libyan newspaper.

CIA Director, John Brennan, Obama's chief counterterrorism advisor at the time, was involved in the weapons shipment to Syria. He was in charge of U.S. covert operations in Libya which allowed 800 Russian surface to air missiles which were taken from Gaddafi's store of weapons to go to al-Qaeda groups which went to Africa and who knows where else. And our own U.S. combat helicopters in Afghanistan were shot down by these very missiles. Not surprisingly the tactics used in assassinations of Gaddafi associates were extremely similar to the tactics used by JSOC in the insurgency in Iraq.

In January 2014, the Senate Select Committee on Intelligence released a report showing the CIA briefed the U.S.Embassy in Tripoli on the equipping, funding, and training of militia terrorists in Benghazi by June, 2012. So they knew of that threat. Unless it was all part of Hillary's and the Obama administration's plan. Because the Obama administration and Hillary made sure militia terrorists were equipped, funded, and, trained. The CIA was involved, at least some of them were. They were going to use private security firms to coordinate buying and shipments of weapons. One was Mark Turi. But then Hillary decided to use her own people. Why? We will look at Mark Turi in a later chapter.

In January 2014, the Senate Select Committee on Intelligence report found that the attacks in Benghazi "were likely preventable." Intelligence "produced hundreds of analytic reports in the months preceding the September 11–12, 2012, attacks, providing strategic warning that militias and terrorist affiliated groups had the capability and intent to strike U.S. and Western facilities and personnel in Libya."

The NSA was at the annex before and while the attacks occurred. They had picked up chatter that there were militia groups lying in wait for the reinforcements the Americans would send in. How long before the actual attack did they know this? And what else did they know? Were the terrorists that knowledgeable on how to avoid NSA's surveillance. The most basic question points to the truth. Why were the GRS operators that were at the CIA annex, which was 5 minutes away, told not to go and told to "Stand Down"? And the Obama administration "did not convene its top interagency counterterrorism resource, the Counterterrorism Security Group."

At an embassy, the RSO reports directly to the Deputy Chief of Mission, who in turn reports directly to the Ambassador. Under the RSO's direct supervision are the following groups: U.S. Marine Security Guards, Assistant RSOs, local guards, foreign service national (FSN) investigators, an office management specialist and other secretarial and staff assistants, a Surveillance Detection Unit (with a mission of detecting hostile surveillance), security engineering officers, security technical specialists, as well as Navy Seabees assigned to post. This is stated from Wikipedia. Of course they were at the Special Mission Compound at the time of the attack but some of the same rules should apply.

The Chief of Missions was the head officer which was Ambassador Stevens. Stevens DS agent, Scott Wickland, had called for help and Stevens had called for help. The deputy chief of missions reported to Stevens so the deputy chief of missions should not have had to get permission from anyone else to send help. Who was he on the phone talking to while the operators were waiting to go? What this points to is that though they did not pull the triggers or shoot the mortars, Hillary, President Obama, and everyone else involved absolutely and undeniably, whether indirectly or directly, killed Ambassador Stevens, Sean Smith, Glenn Doherty, and Tyrone Woods. Death is an awful thing for families to go through. But when you know that your own government was responsible for these deaths, and could have prevented them but chose not to, it is unimaginable what these families went through. Just knowing someone who knew Glenn

Doherty makes it all much more real. And knowing people who could very likely have been in their place makes it much more disturbing.

In Ken Timmerman's book, Dark Forces, he gives insight into the types of weapons taken from Libya and shipped out on the Letfallah II;

Many questions about the Letfallah II shipment remain unanswered, despite an extensive investigation by the UN Panel of Experts appointed by the secretary general to report on the implementation of UN Security Council resolutions imposing an arms embargo and an assets freeze on Libya. The Turkish government initially rebuffed UN inquiries about the ship. Turkey's permanent representative to the UN, Ertug rul Apakan, sent an indignant letter to the secretary general and to the president of the Security Council, rejecting "unfounded allegations" that Turkey was conspiring with Libya to send weapons to the Syrian rebels. The Letfallah II "neither docked at any Turkish port nor has any affiliation with Turkey in terms of its registration or operator," Ambassador Apakan wrote on May 15, 2012. That turned out to be untrue. The Turkish government eventually admitted that the Letfallah II had docked in Turkey, and declared it was carrying three containers of "combustible engines" (sic) as its cargo, the UN inspectors reported in March 2014. An official inventory provided by the Lebanese government showed that the Libyans had scoured the local arms market for whatever they could find. The impounded containers included SA-7 and SA-24 MANPADS, French-made MILAN antitank missiles, AK-47s, Belgian -made FAL assault rifles, Dragunov sniper rifles, Soviet machine guns, RPG-7 launchers, antitank recoilless rifles, mortars, 40 kg of Semtex plastic explosive, and a wide variety of ammunition, grenades, rockets, and mortar rounds. (See appendix II for a full inventory.) The UN experts report insisted that the containers had been "sealed in Misrata and were still sealed when they were seized by the Lebanese authorities." However, photographs released by the Lebanese army showed half-empty containers stacked haphazardly with crates of weapons, as if they had been looted. "I would say certain items were removed by the Lebanese at the request of the U.S. government so we were not more embarrassed than we already were," a senior U.S. official with access to intelligence reporting on the Letfallah seizure told me. What items might have been removed? According to initial reports that surfaced in Arabic language newspapers in Beirut, the Letfallah II was carrying 100 Stinger missiles, and may have been intending to offload them at night onto dinghies on a deserted beach north of Tripoli in the rugged Akkar region of northern Lebanon bordering Syria. The Arabic-language reports estimated the street value of the weapons on board the Letfallah II at $60 million."

An anonymous former senior Defense Department intelligence official said, "The consulate's only mission was to provide cover for the moving of arms. It had no real political role."

A former CIA officer, Philip Giraldi, said that, "Benghazi has been described as a U.S. consulate, but it was not. It was an information office that had no diplomatic status. There was a small staff of actual State Department information officers plus local translators. The much larger CIA base was located in a separate building a mile away. It was protected by a not completely reliable local militia. Base management would have no say in the movement of the ambassador and would not be party to his plans, nor would it clear its own operations with the U.S. Embassy in Tripoli. In Benghazi, the CIA's operating directive would have been focused on two objectives: monitoring the local al-Qaeda affiliate group, Ansar al-Sharia, and tracking down weapons liberated from Colonel Gaddafi's arsenal. Staff consisted of CIA paramilitaries who were working in cooperation with the local militia. The ambassador would not be privy to operational details and would only know in general what the agency was up to. When the ambassador's party was attacked, the paramilitaries at the CIA base came to the rescue before being driven back into their own compound, where two officers were subsequently killed in a mortar attack."

Retired Lt. General William Boykin, stated that, "More supposition was that he (Ambassador Stevens) was now funneling guns to the rebel forces in Syria, using essentially the Turks to facilitate that. Was that occurring, and if so, was it a legal covert action?" He added that Ambassador Stevens was "given a directive to support the Syrian rebels" which the Special Mission Compound "would be the hub of that activity."

But it was found out that the ambassador was not willing to support this.

The United States Senate Committee on Homeland Security and Governmental Affairs released a report on December 30, 2012, "Flashing Red: A Special Report on the Terrorist Attack at Benghazi";

In the months [between February 2011 and September 11, 2012] leading up to the attack on the Temporary Mission Facility in Benghazi, there was a large amount of evidence gathered by the U.S. Intelligence Community (IC) and from open sources that Benghazi was increasingly dangerous and unstable, and that a significant attack against American personnel there was becoming much more likely. While this intelligence was effectively shared within the Intelligence Community (IC) and with key officials at the Department of State, it did not lead to a commensurate increase in security at Benghazi nor to a decision to close the American mission there, either of which would have been more than justified by the intelligence presented. ... The RSO [Regional Security Officer] in Libya compiled a list of 234 security incidents in Libya between June 2011 and July 2012, 50 of which took place in Benghazi.

In Benghazi, the CIA was monitoring Ansar al-Sharia and suspected members of Al-Qaeda in the Islamic Maghreb. And they were trying to distinguish the leadership and loyalty of the many militias in Libya.

So if it was Ansar al-Sharia that attacked the compound, it is likely that the NSA or CIA would have picked up something about the attacks beforehand. John Brennan said that they could not send in anyone because they did not know the situation. But one special forces operator said if the situation is unknown you send forces there to facilitate exfil for medical injuries. You send a. 130 for medical evacuation.

At the time of the attack, dozens of CIA operatives were in Benghazi.

American Joint Special Operations Command(JSOC) missions in the summer of 2012 had started targeting Libyan militias associated with the Al-Qaeda network of Yasin al-Suri. A combination of a U.S. Special Operations team with two JSOC members were already in Libya. Their mission was not part of the CIA and State Department operations.

US Embassies abroad are protected by an elite corps of US Marines. Known as the MSG (Marine Security Group), this elite group is pledged to protect US information and persons in Embassies and Consulates. According to the US State Department, "the MSG role is essentially defensive in nature. They serve as an in-house deterrent to limited acts of violence, as well as a defense mechanism to large scale riots. The Marines are expected to delay entry by hostile elements long enough to permit destruction of classified material and to assist in protecting lives of the mission staff until host government forces arrive. They are authorized, under the command of the senior Foreign Service officer present, to use weapons to protect their own lives or mission staff from direct and immediate danger. The specific use of force is outlined in the MSG post guard orders." The MSG was not in Benghazi. At the time of the attack, the MSG was guarding the US Embassy in Tripoli, although Ambassador Stevens was not inTripoli.

Al Qaeda's affiliate on the Arabian Peninsula, Ansar al-Sharia, was created in Libya during the Obama administration's and Hillary's State Department's backing of the militia's revolution of 2011. In an email, sent at 11:12 pm the night of the attack, Hillary wrote to her daughter: "Two of our officers were killed in Benghazi by an Al Queda-like group."

How did Hillary know that it was an Al-Qaeda like group?

Al-Qaeda is known to have deep and covert ties to the United States intelligence agencies. And the responsibility for the attack was supposed to have been stated on-line by Ansar al-sharia. But recalling the investigation, no posts by Ansar al-Sharia claiming the attack ever existed.

On June 18, 2012, 3 months before the Benghazi attack, the Tunisian consulate in Benghazi was attacked by individuals associated with Ansar al-Sharia, allegedly because of "attacks by Tunisian artists against Islam."

That seems to be a repeating theme. The "riots" in Cairo before the Benghazi attacks were supposed to be due to an offensive Internet video, offensive to Muslims. But the protests in Cairo according to, Kenneth Timmerman, were in regard to the release of the Blind Sheik.

A, D.C. Whispers source, stated about the relationship between the Obama administration, Hillary Clinton, and certain members of Congress;

"The real reason so little has been said regarding the Clinton email scandal is that some of those emails implicated some very powerful figures around here. From top Republicans, to Mrs. Clinton, to the most senior members of the Obama White House. By destroying the evidence, Hillary Clinton was not only protecting herself, but the White House and certain Republicans in both the House and the Senate. The Libya/Benghazi grave is very wide, very deep, and there's too much power vested in its continued cover-up. There were communications that made clear the links between the administration and the same Islamic militants who are now ISIS in Libya. Money and weapons continue to be funneled from Libya to Syria and Iraq. The word has gone out to anyone who makes a serious attempt to get to the bottom of this scandal – LEAVE IT ALONE or it might just be more than your career that is terminated." And they were exactly right, as we will find out in a later chapter.

Enormous pressure was put on CIA operatives not to reveal what the agency had been doing in Benghazi. CIA employees who had knowledge of the attacks had been forced to sign non-disclosure agreements and submit to regular polygraph tests.

Rep. Frank Wolf (R., Va.) had stated that his office was informed, anonymously, about a CIA employee, who was facing internal backlash due to the employee's refusal to sign a legal document which would disallow that person from publicly or privately discussing the events concerning the Benghazi attacks. The employee was suspended due to the refusal and forced to hire an attorney. Some in the State Department and CIA were threatened and hired attorneys, asking that they be allowed a security clearance to view classified documents. One attorney stated her client was threatened by the Department of State. The State Department would not provide process for the attorneys to obtain security clearances that would allow them to view classified documents.

On March,1, 2013, USAF retired Colonel Dick Brauer, co-founder of Special Operations Speaks, said that a gag order was put on 33 surviving Americans;

The FBI has interviewed the survivors, but they refuse to release that information to Congress, let alone the American people! And despite the efforts of Senators Lindsey Graham and Kelly Ayotte, who have been on the front lines of the Benghazi scandal, the Obama Administration is point-blank refusing to allow the representatives of "we the people" any access to those firsthand accounts. At this juncture, President Obama is hiding the injured survivors in a heavily guarded wing of Walter Reed National Military Medical Center. And those not currently needing medical treatment are supposedly legally barred by non-disclosure agreements from even admitting they were present during the attacks – something that should have been fixed by the Whistleblower Protection Enhancement Act of 2012.

CNN analyst and former CIA officer, Robert Baer told CNN that "agency employees typically are polygraphed every three to four years. Never more than that. If somebody is being polygraphed every month, or every two months it's called an issue polygraph, and that means that the polygraph division suspects something, or they're looking for something, or they're on a fishing expedition. But it's absolutely not routine at all to be polygraphed monthly, or bi-monthly."

Rep. Trey Gowdy (R-SC) said that the CIA is hiding those employees from the public, "changing names, creating aliases," and relocating them around the U.S. (Were they really relocated? Or something more sinister?)

Alan Clemmons stated;

I received the following email from a friend regarding Benghazi. What a shameful American moment…Paris (France), June 13, 2013, I would say every US fighter pilot, retired or on active duty, knows that Panetta and Dempsey both are full of crap when they said there was no time to send help to Benghazi. They claim it was a problem of "time/space." All my friends and I said, "Bullshit." We know they could have gotten F-16s there from Aviano. "Hands" Handley is a well-respected USAF fighter pilot. Here is his short resume and what he just wrote about Benghazi below that. If anything, Handley is pessimistic in his timeline of when F-16s could have reached Benghazi. I think they could have been airborne even sooner and turned quicker at Sig. The decision to not try was not based on capability. We had the operational capability in every way. I hope Handley's taxes are in order. His IRS audit is forthcoming.• • •

Eagle Biography, Colonel Phil "Hands" Handley;

Colonel Phil "Hands" Handley is credited with the highest speed air-to-air gun kill in the history of aerial combat. He flew operationally for all but 11 months of a 26-year career, in aircraft such as the F-86 Sabre, F-15 Eagle, and the C-130A Hercules. Additionally, he flew 275 combat missions during two tours in Southeast Asia in the F-4D and F-4E. His awards include 21 Air Medals, 3 Distinguished Flying Crosses, and the Silver Star.

Betrayal in Benghazi

Phil "Hands" Handley Colonel, USAF (Ret.);

The combat code of the US Military is that we don't abandon our dead or wounded on the battlefield. In US Air Force lingo, fighter pilots don't run off and leave their wingmen. If one of our own is shot down, still alive and not yet in enemy captivity, we will either come to get him or die trying.

Among America's fighting forces, the calm, sure knowledge that such an irrevocable bond exists is priceless. Along with individual faith and personal grit, it is a sacred trust that has often sustained hope in the face of terribly long odds.

The disgraceful abandonment of our Ambassador and those brave ex-SEALs who fought to their deaths to save others in that compound is nothing short of dereliction-of-duty.

Additionally, the patently absurd cover-up scenario that was fabricated in the aftermath was an outright lie in an attempt to shield the President and the Secretary of State from responsibility.

It has been over eight months since the attack on our compound in Benghazi. The White House strategy, with the aid of a "lap dog" press has been to run out the clock before the truth is forthcoming. The recent testimonies of the three "whistle blowers" have reopened the subject and hopefully will lead to exposure and disgrace of those responsible for this embarrassing debacle. It would appear that the most recent firewall which the Administration is counting on is the contention "that there were simply no military assets that could be brought to bear in time to make a difference" mainly due to the unavailability of tanker support for fighter aircraft.

This is simply BS, regardless how many supposed "experts" the Administration trot out to make such an assertion.

The bottom line is that even if the closest asset capable of response was half-way around the world, you don't just sit on your penguin ass and do nothing.

The fact is that the closest asset was not half-way around the world, but as near as Aviano Air Base, Italy where two squadrons of F-16Cs are based.

Consider the following scenario (all times Benghazi local): When Hicks in Tripoli receives a call at 9:40 PM from Ambassador Stevens informing him "Greg, we are under attack!" (his last words), he immediately notifies all agencies and prepares for the immediate initiation of an existing "Emergency Response Plan."

At AFRICOM, General Carter Ham attempts to mount a rescue effort, but is told to "stand down". By 10:30 PM an unarmed drone is overhead the compound and streaming live feed to various "Command and Control Agencies" and everyone watching that feed knew damn well what was going on.

At 11:30 PM Woods, Doherty and five others leave Tripoli, arriving in Benghazi at 1:30 AM on Wednesday morning, where they hold off the attacking mob from the roof of the compound until they are killed by a mortar direct hit at 4:00 AM.

So nothing could have been done, eh? Nonsense. If one assumes that tanker support really "was not available" what about this:

When at 10:00 PM AFRICOM alerts the 31st TFW Command Post in Aviano Air Base, Italy of the attack, the Wing Commander orders preparation for the launch of two F-16s and advises the Command Post at NAS Sigonella to prepare for hot pit refueling and quick turn of the jets.

By 11:30 PM, two F-16Cs with drop tanks and each armed with five hundred 20 MM rounds are airborne. Flying at 0.92 mach they will cover the 522 nautical miles directly to NAS Sigonella in 1.08 hours. While in-route, the flight lead is informed of the tactical situation, rules of engagement, and radio frequencies to use.

The jets depart Sigonella at 1:10 AM with full fuel load and cover the 377 nautical miles directly to Benghazi in 0.8 hours, arriving at 1:50 AM which would be 20 minutes after the arrival of Woods, Doherty and their team.

Providing that the two F-16s initial pass over the mob, in full afterburner at 200 feet and 550 knots did not stop the attack in its tracks, only a few well placed strafing runs on targets of opportunity would assuredly do the trick.

Were the F-16s fuel state insufficient to recover at Sigonella after jettisoning their external drop tanks, they could easily do so at Tripoli International Airport, only one-half hour away.

As for those hand-wringing naysayers who would worry about IFR clearances, border crossing authority, collateral damage, landing rights, political correctness and dozens of other reasons not to act," screw them". It is high time that our "leadership" get their priorities straight and put America's interests first.

The end result would be that Woods and Doherty would be alive. Dozens in the attacking rabble would be rendezvousing with "72 virgins" and a clear message would have been sent to the next worthless POS terrorist contemplating an attack on Americans that it is not really a good idea to "tug" on Superman's cape.

Of course all this would depend upon a Commander In Chief that was more concerned with saving the lives of those he put in harm's way than getting his crew rested for a campaign fund raising event in Las Vegas the next day. As well as a Secretary of State that actually understood "What difference did it make?", or a Secretary of Defense whose immediate response was not to the effect that "One of the military tenets is that you don't commit assets until you fully understand the tactical situation." Was he not watching a live feed from the unarmed drone, and he didn't understand the tactical situation?

Ultimately it comes down to the question of who gave that order to stand down? Whoever that coward turns out to be should be exposed, removed from office, and face criminal charges for dereliction of duty. The combat forces of the United States of America deserve leadership that really does "have their back" when the chips are down."

When asked, who gives such an order to stand down? Where does that come from? Congresswoman and former United States Ambassador to Luxembourg Ann Wagner (R-M0), answered, "The President of the United States."

A news agency had questioned Ambassador Steven's twice turning down offers of security assistance made by the senior U.S. military official in the region in response to concerns that Stevens had raised. He had already been turned down or ignored by the State Department. It was the State Department's call, not his. But the fact that he had been offered security assistance twice shows how dire the situation was in Benghazi.

The Accountability Review Board said there were no undue delays in responding to the attacks. They rejected allegations that the U.S. response was deliberately prevented by a "stand down" order;

"Quite the contrary: the safe evacuation of all U.S. government personnel from Benghazi twelve hours after the initial attack and subsequently to Ramstein Air Force Base was the result of exceptional U.S. government coordination and military response," Accountability Review

Board, Dec. 18, 2012, report. The major problem with the Accountability Review Board is Hillary was the person who selected the members.

Speaker of the House John Boehner resigned in October 2015.

No one has the answer as to why he resigned. But John Boehner was the one who proposed that a House select committee would be formed to further investigate the 2012 Benghazi attack. He would not call for one initially. He knew the road he was headed down. Several military leaders were forced to retire early over the Benghazi attacks. John Boehner most likely was also.

As was reported;

Obama is a long-time dirty trickster and has never shied away from using what he can against political opponents. They include Republican businessman Jack Ryan, whose divorce records were mysteriously unsealed during his race against Obama for an open U.S. Senate seat in Illinois; U.S. Sen. Robert Menendez, a Democrat from New Jersey who was suddenly brought up on corruption charges by the Justice Department after he became a top opponent of Obama's outreach to Cuba and the nuclear accord with Iran.

A statement made by Senator John McCain shows the real reason for no help being sent to Benghazi, particularly the 'massive coverup'; "You know, somebody the other day said to me this is as bad as Watergate. Well, nobody died in Watergate. But this is either a massive cover-up or incompetence that is not acceptable service to the American people."

"Benghazi and the operations in Libya are shrouded in a fog of lies, deceit, manipulation, threats, intimidation, coercion, abandonment, and worst of all, potentially treason," Former GOP Congressman and political commentator, Allen B. West wrote.

On a flight from Detroit, West said that he felt was God sent when the seat next to him was filled with a friend of one of the men at the Benghazi compound during the attack. He said that the friend drew maps and schematics of the Special Mission Compound in Benghazi and explained that men were ordered repeatedly to stand down and do nothing.

"Thank God two of them, Glenn Doherty and Ty Woods, lived up to their code of honor and ran to the sound of the guns, resulting in their loss of life — but the preservation of life for others, their fellow Americans," West wrote.

He also was told that Ambasador Chris Stevens had requested better security before the attack but was denied.

He said that those who know what happened in Benghazi have been threatened with pension cuts if they speak up. There was a covert weapons scheme happening under the radar in Benghazi.

"We had been supplying radical Islamists with weapons against Libyan President Moammar Gadhafi, effectively supplying the enemy and destabilizing that country. And it seems that there was a CIA weapons buy-back program, the aim of which was to ship the retrieved weapons out of Libya through Turkey, and to the Islamist forces in Syria.

"And to those Democrats appointed to the committee: if you seek to obstruct the revelation of the truth, you are complicit and guilty as well," Allen B.West wrote.

Retired Air Force Brigidaire General, Robert Lovell, spoke of the feelings in Africa Command (AFRICOM) during the attack: "It was desperation to gain situational awareness." He was the Deputy Director of Intelligence at U.S. Africa Command.

Brig. Gen. Lovell said that, "The military could have made a response of some sort," when asked if the military had been allowed to respond adequately.

"Four individuals died. We obviously did not respond in time to get there," he said.

When Rep. Jason Chaffetz of the House Select Committee was questioning the Brig. General, Lovell said that a predator drone was over Benghazi. All other accounts stated it was an unmanned drone, nothing about being a predator. But Brigidaire General Robert Lovell said that it was a predator drone.So the predator drone could have given air support to the compound and annex.

Below is the transcript of Chaffetz questioning Brigidaire General Robert Lovell;

CHAFFETZ: What was going on in the room General? Our people are under attack. There are people dying. What is the military doing? [Vice Admiral Leidig was also present].

LOVELL: Desperately trying to gain situational awareness in an area where we had a dearth of it.

CHAFFETZ: Were they moving to the sound of the guns? Were they doing what they were trained to do or where they sitting around waiting for the State Department and Hillary Clinton to call them up and say 'do something?' What did they actually do?

LOVELL: We sent a predator drone overhead to be able to...

(I have always held Rep. Jason Chaffetz in high regard, but I do not understand why he interrupted Brigidaire General Robert Lovell when he mentioned the predator drone. Well, I really do, but it is very disappointing.)

CHAFFETZ: Did we do enough, General?

LOVELL: Sir...

CHAFFETZ: You're a professional. You're retired. I know you care deeply about this. What was the mood in the room. What was the feeling? Was it to save our people?

LOVELL: It was desperation there, to be able to...

CHAFFETZ: It was what?

LOVELL: It was desperation there to gain situational awareness and to be able to do something to save people.

Chaffetz asks if other forces in Europe were called in.

LOVELL: No sir, those assets did not.

CHAFFETZ: Why not?

LOVELL: Basically, there's a lot of looking to the State Department for what it was that they wanted, and in deference to the Libyan people and a sense of deference to the desires of the State Department, in terms of what they'd like to have.

CHAFFETZ: Did they ever tell you to go save the people in Benghazi?

LOVELL: Not to my knowledge, sir.

CHAFFETZ: We didn't run to the sound of the guns. They were issuing press releases. We had American's dying. We had dead people. We had wounded people, and our military didn't try to engage in that fight. Would you disagree with that?

LOVELL: Four individuals died, sir; we obviously did not respond in time to get there.

CHAFFETZ: Could we have?

LOVELL: We may have been able to, but we'll never know.

Air Force Brigidaire General Robert Lovell retired in October of 2013.
Below is an interview by Bret Baier on Bret Baier's Fox News Channel program Special Report of Tommy Vietor, Former National Security Council spokesman.

BRET BAIER: People on the ground testified that they knew where the ambassador was, that they were military in their precision. It was not guys coming to protest. They had mortars and heavy weapons.

TOMMY VIETOR: Bret, a couple of things. I was in the Situation Room that night, okay. We didn't know where the ambassador was definitively.

BAIER: Was the president in the Situation Room?

VIETOR: No. And the fact that your network at one time reported that he watched video feed of the attack as it was ongoing is part of what I think is a pattern of inaccurate --

BAIER: Where was the president?

VIETOR: In the White House. Let me finish my initial statement. The notion that we could, you know, divine motives from a drone feed I think is wrong. And I also think this idea that the military had the capability to rescue those individuals but chose not to is I think extremely unfair to the military. And Admiral Mullen said basically the opposite.

BAIER: In the ARB report.

VIETOR: Right.

BAIER: Where was the president?

VIETOR: In the White House.

BAIER: He wasn't in the Situation Room?

VIETOR: At what point in the evening?

BAIER: Any point in the evening.

VIETOR: It's well known that when the attack was first briefed to him it was in the Oval Office and he was updated constantly. And during that briefing he told Tom Donilon and his Joint Chiefs and Sec Def to begin moving all military assets into the region.

BAIER: So when Hillary Clinton talks to him at 10:00 p.m., he's where?

VIETOR: I don't know. I don't have a tracking device on him in the residence.

BAIER: But you were in the Situation Room and he wasn't there.

VIETOR: Yes, I was in the White House.

BAIER: And the president wasn't in the Situation Room?

VIETOR: Not in the room I was in. Let's just be clear. You don't have to be in the Situation Room to monitor an intelligence situation. The PDB is in the Oval Office.

But monitoring is not the same as leading and being involved.
"When there is a lack of honor in government, the morals of the whole people are poisoned." Herbert Hoover.

Kris "Tonto" Paronto;
"I am a former Army Ranger, military contractor, and survivor of the September 11, 2012 terrorist attack in Benghazi, Libya.
For 13 hours that night, my teammates and I did everything in our power to save American lives. Two of us didn't make it home. Neither did Ambassador Christopher Stevens or Sean Smith. For some reason that I'll never understand.
But several months after being home, I hit rock bottom and started to have serious thoughts about taking my own life.
We were left behind, plain and simple, and I had lost complete faith in our leaders.
But I had also lost faith in my fellow Americans. What they were being told about that night, they seemed to believe, and it was killing me inside. I was doing everything I could to share the truth, but it didn't seem to matter.
Flying home for what may have been my last night, I was approached by a random stranger at the airport. She recognized me from a television interview and said three words that literally saved my life: "I believe you."
It may seem overly simple, but a light switched on, and I knew my next mission. It made me realize there were millions of people out there who knew they were being lied to – not just about Benghazi but about the severity of the threat that we are facing as a nation.

Radical Islam is at war with America. It's the defining national security challenge of our time, and we are slowly losing. When I look into my kids' eyes, it scares me because I know what kind of world they'll be facing if we don't get our act together."

At a conference in Maryland, Kris "Tanto" Paronto revealed that two AC-130H "Spectre" gunships were "on call" the night of the attacks, both were within range of Benghazi. One gunship was only 45 minutes away. He had also requested a predator drone. The gunship never arrived but Brigidaire General Robert Lovell said that a predator drone was sent. But it was not used in the fight. And there has been no information on the person that controlled the drone.

Below describes the AC-130 Spectre Gunship, courtesy of Wikipedia;

The Lockheed AC-130 gunship is a heavily armed, long-endurance ground-attack variant of the C-130 Hercules transport fixed-wing aircraft. It carries a wide array of anti-ground oriented weapons that are integrated with sophisticated sensors navigation, and fire-control systems. Unlike other military fixed-wing aircraft, the AC-130 relies on visual targeting. Because its large profile and low operating altitudes (around 7,000 ft) make it an easy target, it usually flies close air support missions at night.

The airframe is manufactured by Lockheed Martin, while Boeing is responsible for the conversion into a gunship and for aircraft support. Developed during the Vietnam War as 'Project Gunship II', the AC-130 replaced the Douglas AC-47 Spooky, or 'Gunship I'. The sole operator is the United States Air Force, which uses the AC-130U Spooky and AC-130W Stinger II variants for close air support, air interdiction, and force protection, with the AC-130J Ghostrider in development. Close air support roles include supporting ground troops, escorting convoys, and urban operations. Air interdiction missions are conducted against planned targets and targets of opportunity. Force protection missions include defending air bases and other facilities. AC-130Us are based at Hurlburt Field, Florida, while AC-130Ws are based at Cannon AFB, New Mexico; gunships can be deployed worldwide. The squadrons are part of the Air Force Special Operations Command (AFSOC), a component of theUnited States Special Operations Command(SOCOM).

The AC-130 has an unpressurized cabin, with the weaponry mounted to fire from the port side of the fuselage. During an attack, the gunship performs a pylon turn, flying in a large circle around the target, therefore being able to fire at it for far longer than in a conventional strafing attack. The AC-130H Spectre was armed with two 20 mm M61 Vulcan cannons, one Bofors 40 mm cannon, and one 105 mm M102 howitzer; after 1994, the 20 mm cannons were removed. The upgraded AC-130U Spooky has a single 25 mm GAU-12 Equalizer cannon in place of the Spectre's two 20 mm cannons, an improved fire control system, and increased ammunition capacity. New AC-130Js based on the MC-130J Combat Shadow II special operations tanker were planned as of 2012. The AC-130W is armed with one 30 mm Bushmaster cannon, AGM-176 Griffinmissiles, and GBU-39 Small Diameter Bombs(SDBs)."

The Spectre Gunship can "walk down" alleyways and hit an individual target. If a gunship would have been sent to Benghazi, that is all the help they would have needed.

Below is what Drew Dwyer of SOFREP.com had to say;

"What Kris Paronto and his team did that night was simply heroic. The world would be a better place if people emulated the selflessness and conviction demonstrated by a handful of men that night. They fought not for fame or medals, but for one another."

It is shameful the way that Kris, and everyone that fought that night, was treated.

To learn more visit www.kristantoparonto.com

In a two-part report, Rescue Interrupted, on the Emmy Award-winning journalist Sharyl Attkisson's show, Full Measure, a Commander of Green Beret Special Forces told her that there were Special Forces on their way to Benghazi and were ordered to turn back.

Colonel Andy Wood had commanded a Special Forces anti-terrorism team protecting Ambassador Chis Stevens and other diplomats in Libya. Col. Wood told Congress in October 2012, that one month before the Benghazi attacks his team had been removed from Libya by the Obama administration. Even though there were numerous warnings of impending terrorist attacks.

"Those individuals I know loaded aircraft and got on their way to Benghazi to respond to that incident. They were not allowed to cross the border as per protocol until they got approval from the commander in chief. That authority has to come from him or they're not allowed to enter the country," stated Woods.

Kris "Tonto" Paronto knew people in that unit. He had called them after he and his security team arrived back to the CIA Annex with the survivors from the compound where they had come under the first attacks. "They were loading their gear into their aircraft and ready to go," Paronto ssid.

His friends in the unit later told him that they had been shut down sometime after midnight.

In Part One of "Rescue Interrupted", Attkinson said that "the White House has refused to detail the involvement of President Obama, the Commander-in-Chief, while Americans were under attack on foreign soil."

Judicial Watch cited this email;

"They are spinning up as we speak." U.S. Department of Defense Chief of Staff Jeremy Bash Tuesday, September 11, 2012, 7:19 PM

Bash was offering "forces that could move to Benghazi" during the terrorist attack on the U.S. Special Mission Compound in Benghazi, Libya on September 11, 2012;

"We have identified the forces that could move to Benghazi. They are spinning up as we speak."

But the details of the email that had identified the milittary forces available had been redacted by the Obama administration and replaced with a Freedom of Information Act exemption that allows the withholding of "deliberative process" information. This email difinitely refutes Leon Panetta claim that "time, distance, the lack of an adequate warning, events that moved very quickly on the ground prevented a more immediate response."

Below is the email in its entirety, that is result of a Judicial Watch Freedom of Information Act (FOIA) lawsuit filed on September 4, 2014 (Judicial Watch v. U.S. Department of State (No. 1:14-cv-01511) From: Bash, Jeremy CIV SD [REDACTED]

Sent: Tuesday, September 11, 2012 7:19 PM

To: Sullivan, Jacob J; Sherman, Wendy R; Nides, Thomas R

Cc: Miller, James HON OSD POLICY; Wienefeld, James A ADM JSC VCJCS; Kelly, John LtGen SD; martin, dempsey [REDACTED]

Subject: Libya
State colleagues:

I just tried you on the phone but you were all in with S [apparent reference to then-Secretary of State (Hillary Clinton).

After consulting with General Dempsey, General Ham and the Joint Staff, we have identified the forces that could move to Benghazi. They are spinning up as we speak. They include a [REDACTED].

Assuming Principals agree to deploy these elements, we will ask State to procure the approval from host nation. Please advise how you wish to convey that approval to us [REDACTED].

Jeremy

"The Obama administration and Clinton officials hid this compelling Benghazi email for years.The email makes readily apparent that the military was prepared to launch immediate assistance that could have made a difference, at least at the CIA Annex. The fact that the Obama Administration withheld this email for so long only worsens the scandal of Benghazi," stated Tom Fitton, Judicial Watch President.

Many sources have stated the availability of help to the Benghazi compound but was not given the command to do so. One Special Forces Operator said that a C110 UCOM SIF was doing training in Europe and had the ability to react and respond. A C110 is a Commander's in extremis force, a 40 man Special Operations Force capable of rapid response and deployment, specixically trained for situations like Benghazi, in Croatia three and a half hours away. He also said that there are guys in specials operations command that would be decapitated if they came forward with information that would affect high level commanders. He said that there were two elite military assets that could have reached Benghazi. Decapitated? Has Sharia law already started in the US?

A former CIA operative asked some enlightening questions;

Is the United States secretly arming and supporting various factions of the Syrian Rebels with high caliber impact weapons from The United States arsenals? (Everyone now knows that they are.)

Is the United States little known Direct Commercial Sales Program, also known as "The Blue Lantern Report", being used as a "cutout" to secretly aid both sides of a Middle Eastern civil war? (To those who are familiar with the MIC and the BIS, most know that they are.)

Is America again playing both sides against the middle for corporate gain as previously demonstrated by the Cuban Project of the fifties and sixties, as well as the Iran Contra fiasco of the eighties and the South American—Mexican Drug Wars of the nineties? (And the Fast and Furious. YES.)

It has been established via some field reports from the Middle East and some isolated media reports that the Direct Commercial Sales Program (DCSP) an American international program, which legally allows the United States to sell weapons to a host of foreign countries without monitoring those weapons after leaving our arsenals, stockpiles, and jurisdiction, has shipped High Impact weapons to Syrian Rebels during the last two years. I have to ask. What happens to those weapons after legally being sold via this program and they leave our control? (Obama waived a ban on supporting terrorists to supply weapons to the Syrian rebels.)

Are they being monitored, traced, certified, and inventoried after arriving in other countries? (Most likely no.)

Will our troops one day again face these American made weapons on some foreign battlefield?

Is this Direct Commercial Sales program a secret cash cow for many US Corporations, International arms merchants, its insiders, or affiliates? (Remember President Eisenhower's warning about the Military Industrial Complex.)

Is it possible this could be another "off---the---books" secret covert operation ran by the CIA's Special Tactical Unit, similar to the Iran---Contra operations of the eighties and the old Cuban projects of the fifties and sixties, where we supplied both sides weapons and escalated the conflict for personal and corporate gain?

(It is actually more well known than at the time of the Iran contract operations, and the Fast and Furious operations.)

Could we be selling and supplying dangerous high impact weapons, while aiding and financing both sides of a Civil War in Syria? (Of course.)

69

Could we be escalating the Middle East conflict either knowingly or unintentionally providing weapons to both sides of the Syrian conflict? (Knowingly.)

These are simple questions. I'm just asking: Did our Ambassador and others, weeks before they were murdered, notify our State Department and CIA that Syrian Rebels had obtained US Weapons, including "Stinger missiles' from Jordan, Turkey, Pakistan, shipped from CIA safe houses? (YES.)

Were they told to "Stand Down? (That answer will be discovered later.)

*****

There have been many connections made to the government and mainstream media. To be fair to the media, not all want to be so biased. But when you are told what you can and cannot report on, this puts news reporting into an altogether different realm. In 2011, The Media Research Center reported how George Soros has ties to approximately 30 mainstream news outlets. He funds Clinton-leaning, Media Matters. The billionaire, George Soros, is a left leaning, anti-Israel advocate. Many members of the media have been on boards or advisory boards of George Soros' groups. Some of those report on news channels of ABC, NBC, CBS, the Vice President of the Washington Post, the New York Times, The Seattle Times, Heart Newspaper, the CBS News producer, and NPR (radio) which was given $1.8 million by George Soros.

George Soros created a "Shadow Party", that essentially controsl the Democratic Party,that are made up of leftist organizations. He also supported Democratic presidential nominee Hillary. Soros gave $9 million to pro-Hillary Super PACs. He "was able to dictate State Department policy in Albania."

ProPublica, which has won two Pulitzer Prizes, initially was given millions of dollars from the Sandler Foundation to "strengthen the progressive infrastructure". "Progressive" meaning very liberal. In 2010, it also received a two-year contribution of $125,000 each year from George Soros' Open Society Foundations. It is a network of more than 30 international foundations, mostly funded by Soros, who has contributed more than $8 billion to those efforts.

It is very important to remember the "Shadow Party" or otherwise the "Shadow Government".

*****

"One of things that I have learned about Hillary Clinton is that one of her heroes, her mentor was Saul Alinsky and her senior thesis was about Saul Alinsky, someone that she greatly admired and it affected all of her philosophy subsequently. He wrote a book called, The Rules for Radicals. On the dedication page it acknowledges Lucifer the original radical who gained his own kingdom. Think about that. This is a nation where our founding document the Declaration of Independence comes from our Creator. This is a nation where our Pledge of Allegiance we are one nation under God. This is a nation, this is a nation where every coin in our pocket and every bill... well it says In God We Trust. So are we willing to elect someone as president who has as their role model is somebody who acknowledges Lucifer? Think about that."

This was Ben Carson's thoughts on Hillary.

Hillary was ineligible to run for the president of the United States. Hillary has committed treason against the United States.

The State Department showed that Hillary discounted directives from State.

Hillary's unsecured email server and the classified information she sent over it broke federal laws. She could not use her email during a period in 2011 because it had been hacked. This information was from the Inspector General's report.

According to Federal law, Hillary was ineligible to run for President under, 18 U.S.C. § 2071(b) which states:

"Whoever, having the custody of any such record, proceeding, map, book, document, paper, or other thing, willfully and unlawfully conceals, removes, mutilates, obliterates, falsifies, or destroys the same, shall be fined under this title or imprisoned not more than three years, or both; and shall forfeit his office and be disqualified from holding any office under the United States."

So under Federal law, Hillary is disqualified from running for President of the United States. So why had Congress not acted on this?

Just like Comey, almost everyone in Washington D.C. is involved with the Clinton Foundation. Leaked emails show that Hillary's team wanted the focus to be on Benghazi, not her unsecured email server. This would lead to her foundation and all of the corruption and some of the people involved.

*****

At the beginning of the U.S. Libyan War, where Hillary's State Department armed militia terrorists, Muammar Gaddafi's assets were frozen. Gaddafi was one of the wealthiest men in the world worth over $200 Billion. So who has Gaddafi's assets?

Anatoly Egorin Russian expert in Eastern affairs said:

"The West most likely decided right after the very start of the anti-Gaddafi rebellion in Libya to do whatever possible to prevent Gaddafi from staying in power. His and his associates' bank accounts were immediately frozen. Or, it would be probably better to say that it was only officially announced that they were frozen, but in reality they were stolen. Nobody can say for sure precisely who stole this money and where it is now. There is only some vague information that it was allegedly pocketed by the bankers themselves and that these bankers allegedly tried to launder this money in offshore zones. Attempts to find this money are now under way, but I doubt that it will ever be found."

"However it would be wrong to say that only the West has stolen the money of the former Libyan regime. It is known that those people who fought against Gaddafi and who are now in power in Libya have conveyed many trucks literally stuffed with money abroad."

But who knows where it ended up being shipped to. Hillary and Obama's administration helped set up the Libyan government and armed the militias fighting against Gaddafi.

The Head of the International Association for Democracy in Libya, Fatima abu an-Niran stated:

"The chaotic situation in Libya enabled everyone to steal anything that lay in his or her temptation's way. The West was quite aware of that, but didn't try to stop it. I can back my words with facts, and the former head of Libya's Central Bank can also confirm this."

"The $150 billion in Gaddafi's and other former Libyan leaders' bank accounts is not the only money that was stolen during the period of anarchy in Libya. Lots of money was trafficked and is still being trafficked abroad by the Libyan "revolutionaries" themselves. To a large extent, the situation in Libya still remains chaotic. The new authorities seem to be incapable of controlling the situation in many of the country's provinces. These provinces are in fact controlled by groups of bandits who do whatever they want with those who try to resist them.

"When the West threw bombs on Libya, Western politicians said that this allegedly was done to help Libyans oust the tyrant and establish democracy in their country. Now, it has turned out that these words were mere demagogy. The real aim of the West was to try to steal Libya's riches."

*****

In September 2015, Geil Lundestad, the former director of Norway's Nobel Institute said that he regretted the committee's decision to give the 2009 Nobel Peace award to President Obama. The Institute's committee had unanimously decided to grant the Nobel Peace award to President Obama soon after his election in 2009. But it was not due to something that was accomplished by the president. The award was given in support of the president to achieve his goals on nuclear disarmament.

"We thought it would strengthen Obama and it didn't have this effect," Lundstedt stated.

He said that looking back over President Obama's presidency the granting of the award did not fulfill the committee's expectations.

Lundestad stated, "Even many of Obama supporters thought that the prize was a mistake."

In Geil Lundestad's memoir he expressed regret that the decision had been based in a hope for the future rather than recognition of past accomplishments.

President Obama has been the only second-term president in American history in which the United States has been continually at War. The misconception of civil wars in these countries is that the US has been involved in is propagated by the Obama Administration. They did not start out as civil wars. They were terrorist militias brought in to overtake the governments of these countries. And with the help of the Obama Administration and Secretary of State Hillary Clinton these terrorist organizations overcame the countries governments and hundreds of thousands of people have been killed. Now what they have are countries that have been destabilized and destroyed by terrorists. Citizens have been killed or made homeless. Women and children have been kidnapped, raped, and murdered by these terrorists. Hillary's constitution of women and children's human rights has been destroyed. In Bashar al-Assad's interview with Charlie Rose this glaring misconception of civil wars in terrorist ridden countries has been denounced. The U.S. government, the Obama administration, or Hillary's State Department never contacted Bashar al-Assad in the beginning. They supplied weapons to terrorists to overthrow Assad. They had no interest in negotiating anything.

The lies of the Obama Administration and Hillary Clinton is like photography. You have to search through all of the negatives to get the true picture.

*****

The Homeland Security Department had been allotting as many citizenship applications as it could to get as many people as possible to vote in this year's presidential election, an internal department document shows.

And a Texas immigration office made volunteers work weekends, to try and enroll as many people as possible before the end of September, which would allow them enough time to register to vote in November. And who are the people they are trying to register to vote? Illegal immigrants.

The Immigration and Customs Enforcement knew who they were releasing when they released over 100,000 illegal immigrants who had criminal convictions.

"Today there are over 350,000 known criminal aliens in the United States who are not detained by ICE, 350000. "According to ICE, those released have been convicted of more than 10,000 assaults, more than 800 sexual assault more than 400 homicide related offences, and more than 300 kidnappings."

And President Obama has made 72 more commutations. Requirements for commutation includes those who have a good behavior record with a non-violent background and non-violent, low-level offenders who have served at least 10 years of a federal sentence. They cannot have a significant criminal record. But some in Congress have stated that a good number of those whose sentences have been commuted do not fit the requirements for commutation.

Bob Goodlatte, House Judiciary Chairman, stated in a letter to Obama,

"An alarming number of offenders whose sentences you have commuted were convicted of possession of a firearm during the commission of a felony. These are clearly not low-level, non-violent drug offenders."

Reports from the Justice Department show that as of October 6, 2016, there were 11,253 commutation requests. A large number will likely be commuted before President Obama leaves the White House.

"The number of criminal aliens living in the United States, not in custody, not separated from society, is larger than the city of Pittsburgh, Pennsylvania. Larger than the city of Lexington Kentucky, larger than the city of Anaheim California," according to representative Trey Gowdy, at the opening of a hearing examining victims of illegal immigrant crime. "Can you imagine a city the size of Pittsburgh comprised solely of people who are here unlawfully who have also committed another crime?"

Trey Gowdy was presiding as chairman at the hearing.

He said, "Just yesterday the lawyer for the president was at it again this time at the United States Supreme Court arguing for the non enforcement of the law arguing for the wholesale failure to enforce the law. And he said this: 'The damage that would be reeked by tearing families apart'. If you want to see that damage, Mr. Solicitor General, if you want to see what tearing apart looks like, I hope you're watching this morning."

Many victims, present at the hearing, gave heartbreaking accounts of their experiences with violent criminals who were also illegal immigrants.

CHAPTER 7

THE AMERICAN'S CREED

"I believe in the United States of America as a
Government of the people, by the people, for the people,
whose just powers are derived from the consent of
the governed; a democracy in a Republic; a sovereign
Nation of many sovereign States; a perfect Union, one
and inseparable; established upon those principles of
freedom, equality, justice, and humanity for which
American patriots sacrificed their lives and fortunes. I
therefore believe it is my duty to my Country to love it;
to support its Constitution; to obey its laws; to respect
its flag, and to defend it against all enemies."

An agent with more than 10 years with ICE said, "This is a crisis situation that is not being acknowledged by the administration or the media. I know we had a crisis situation in 2014, but this has this by far surpassed that. Our officers are overworked and over run."

Due to the necessary amount of time to process the large number of arrivals, this massive number of illegal immigrants has not allowed agents the time to do background checks of those who enter the country illegally.

"Would-be perpetrators have much more of a chance to make it through the system and into our communities. That's a huge concern for us.

"In my book, if we miss one criminal alien who goes on to victimize one American citizen, that's one too many. But with the scale we're talking about here, it's likely lots of criminal aliens will be able to slip through the system. So many Americans could potentially be affected by this," the agent said.

"The surge is worse than it was in 2014. Our southern border is not secure. It's so porous. We have people working seven days a week just to meet the demand and workload that's being created by this administration's policies.

"Once they're processed, we have to either find placement for them or release them, and right now we don't have any place to put them… If we have nowhere to house them, they're going to be released into the public—hundreds of bodies will be released," he said.

And just two days before, ICE had 200 people they needed to place or release into the population.

Arrests of illegal immigrants crossing the U.S. southern border increased 23 percent at the end of the federal fiscal year, September 30, 2016.

Approximately 25 Americans are killed each day by illegal immigrants.

Charles Jenkins, Frederick County Maryland's Sheriff, testified before Congress. His testimony was on how President Obama's pro illegal immigration policies are causing a record amount of crime to break out in communities across the United States.

Sheriff Jenkins said that President Obama's changes in policy weakened and ruined secure communities and did not allow action by ICE when sheriff and police departments ignore detainers and allow criminal immigrants to be released into the population. And criminal immigrants that should have been deported have been allowed to stay and commit more serious crimes and become violent offenders.

Sheriff Jenkins also said criminal immigrant gang numbers and the number of serious crimes being committed by immigrants are growing.

Obama's DACA program (Deferred Action for Childhood Arrivals) allows unaccompanied minors to remain in the United States and then join gangs and then become hardened criminals.

Sheriff Jenkins stated, "Sixty four percent of the gang members encountered in 2015 were unaccompanied juveniles when they entered the US. They're now adults committing more serious crimes."

Chris Chrane, president of the National Immigration And Customs Enforcement Council, stated,

"ICE officers on the front lines are witnessing a deluge of illegal immigration unlike anything we have seen before.

"Our officers are being ordered to release recent border-crossers with no idea what their intentions are or what they are planning. Gang members, drug cartels, and violent smugglers are taking advantage of the situation and threatening American communities.

"The influx is overwhelming public resources, especially in poor communities including Hispanic communities and immigrant communities bearing the economic brunt of the illegal immigration surge.

"Hillary's pledge for 'open borders' will mean disaster for our country, and turn the present border emergency into a cataclysm. Hillary's plan would unleash violent cartels and brutal transnational gangs into U.S. communities and cause countless preventable deaths."

Multi-national gang activity in the United States has been rising which is shown in a report by the Center for Immigration Studies;

"Over a 10-year period (2005-2014) ICE arrested approximately 4,000 MS-13 members, leaders, and associates," the report read. MS-13 is a multi-national immigration gang.

"This represents about 13 percent of all gang members they arrested nationwide (31,000) during that period."

*****

Intelligence agencies say ISIS "hit squads" are operating in Germany acting as refugees. Bavarian intelligence agency BaLfV, said that other refugees are reporting the ISIS cells among them.

"We have to accept that we have hit squads and sleeper cells in Germany," Manfred Hauser, the vice president of the Bavaria region's intelligence gathering agency, BayLfV stated.

"We have substantial reports that among the refugees there are hit squads. There are hundreds of these reports, some from refugees themselves. We are still following up on these, and we haven't investigated all of them fully," said Hauser.

*****

Maines Governor, Paul LePage, is withdrawing his state from the federal refugee settlement program. Governor Lepage wrote a letter to President Obama in which he stated;

"I have lost confidence in the federal government's ability to safely and responsibly run the refugee program and no longer want the State of Maine associated with that shortcoming.

"The federal government has proven to be an unwilling partner with states in ensuring that refugee resettlement does not unduly put American lives at risk.

"I sincerely hope that the federal government will re-evaluate its current refugee policy — both the quantity and nation of origin of refugees it resettles and the vetting process they are subjected to — in order to best protect the safety and interests of the American people," LePage wrote.

Maine is now the thirteenth state to withdraw from the program. This year three other states have withdrawn from the federal refugee resettlement program, Texas, New Jersey, and Kansas.

Between 1990 – 2015 nine states withdrew from the federal refugee resettlement program, Kentucky, Idaho, North Dakota, South Dakota, Nevada, Tennessee, Alabama, Louisiana, and Alaska.

*****

President Obama nominated Abid Qureshi who was born in Pakistan with terrorist ties to sit on the District of Columbia's Federal bench.

President Obama did not mention Qureshi's involvement in numerous illegal activities which include arranging the issuance of fake Visas for suspected terrorists that include Mohammed Atta and Marwan Al Shehhi. These were two of the terrorists responsible for flying hijacked planes into the trade World Trade Center on 9/11. Qureshi also has ties to the Council on American Islamic Relations (CAIR) and the Islamic Society of North America (ISNA) which are fronts for the Muslim Brotherhood, and has connections to Saudi officials.

Qureshi is a devout student of Sayyid Qutb. Qtub was known for his strong disapproval of American society and culture. Qtub and other Muslim Brotherhood members orchestrated a plot to assassinate the Egyptian president Gamal Abdel Nasser in 1954 because his rule was not based on islamism. Nasser's secular nationalist ideology was incompatible with the Islamism of Qtub and the Muslim Brotherhood. But the plot to overthrow Nasser failed and Qtub was imprisoned. He was released in 1964 and was free for 8 months before being arrested again in August 1964, for plotting to overthrow the state. His trial culminated a death sentence for him and six other members of the Muslim Brotherhood. He was sentenced to death for his part in the plot to assassinate the president and other Egyptian officials. On August 29, 1966, he was executed by hanging.

Obama's appointment of Qureshi is not even reasonable because Qureshi has never been a judge. And with Abid Qureshi being a devout student of Sayyid Qutb, he is not someone qualified to sit on a federal bench in the United States.

But Obama stated, "I am confident he will serve the American people with integrity and a steadfast commitment to justice."

Nihad Awad, national executive director of the Council on American Islamic Relations, a terrorist group front acting as a civil rights group said, "The nomination of Abid Qureshi to fill a seat on the US District Court for the District of Columbia sends a message of inclusion that is welcomed by the American Muslim Community and by all Americans who value diversity and mutual respect at a time when some seek division and discord".

President Obama's support for the Muslim organizations do not support American values. The Muslim Brotherhood has approximately 25 FBI identified terrorist networks in our schools and communities across the United States.

The Obama Administration also allowed terrorist front organizations to change FBI anti-terrorism material that they believed to be offensive to Muslims. The Obama Administration helped Islamic activists stop an FBI internet program in which they were working to prevent the radicalization of youths. Muslims and Arab rights groups stated that the program discriminates against Muslims. So ridiculous. But this is another example Muslims wanting to 'assimilate' and then destroy our way of life.

And the Obama administration's civil rights chair has called to free illegal immigrants being detained. The US Commission on Civil Rights report calls for the release of illegal immigrants due to widespread "egregious human rights and constitutional violations".

But Peter Kirsanow, a member of the U.S. Commission on Civil Rights said that the goal of the commission was to allow illegal immigrant citizenship. And that would be at the expense of taxpayers.

Kirsanow stated in reference to the comission report, "The majority's Recommendation 13 urges that taxpayers pay for attorneys for illegal immigrants. Exactly why a nation that is 18 trillion dollars in debt should pay for attorneys for people who broke its immigration laws is unclear particularly given that most of those heavily burdened taxpayers want recent border-crossers packed off to their countries of origin post haste. Taxpayer funding for immigration attorneys would however be a boon to the immigration bar and to open borders advocates. This report is primarily motivated by the interests of those two groups and the need to provide political cover to the administration's lawlessness so perhaps that is the only explanation needed for a recommendation that would extend plundering of taxpayers and of gutting immigration enforcement into a new realm."

Kirsanow, who is African American, also said that, "Granting legal status to millions of people who are in the United States illegally will continue to depress the wages and employment opportunities of African American men and teenagers. It would depress the wages and employment opportunities of African Americans going forward."

Kirsanow also disagreed on allowing more special visas for high-tech workers.

"There is little evidence other than the protestations of tech Titans and politicians that there is a shortage of high-tech workers in the US.

"Such an increase in workers would have a deleterious effect on low-skilled American workers particularly black workers. Illegal immigration has a disparate impact on African-American men because these men are disproportionately represented in the low-skilled labor force."

Concerning the refugee crisis, any limiting on refugees coming into the U.S. is not something that Obama allows. "When I hear folks say that well maybe we should just admit the Christians but not the Muslims, when I hear political leaders suggesting that there would be a religious test for which a person who's fleeing from a war-torn country is admitted, that's not America. That's not who we are. We don't have religious tests to our compassion."

Of course he is way off the mark on that. It's not about a religious test of our compassion. It is an ideology test for our country's protection. Because not admitting Muslims at this precarious time in the US is not an erroneous idea. If it continues we will be like Europe and eventually much worse. An actual limiting of refugees who are men and accepting women and children would be the smartest way to approach the problem. At least until the refugee males can be very thoroughly vetted. President Obama may not be worried about radical Islamist terrorists coming into America and creating situations similar to Europe but he is worried about anti-Muslim xenophobia. What happened to not having religious tests to our compassion? Why not anti-Christian xenophobia? His compassion is most definitely with Muslims. Even his closest advisor, Valerie Jarrett, told him that Americans are worried that ISIS would soon take its beheading campaign to the US, which is a very real concern. But Obama dismissed this concern and said, "They're not coming here to chop our heads off."

Yes, President Obama, they are.

Colleen Hufford, from Oklahoma, was beheaded at Vaughan Foods, her place of employment by a Muslim. Alton Alexander Nolen had consistently attempted o convert co-workers to Islam.

Alton Alexander Nolen, the Islamist had recently been fired from Vaughan Foods. He was shot by an off-duty police officer. Nolen was hospitalized and survived.

"After conducting interviews with coworkers of Nolen information was obtained that he recently ... started trying to convert some of his coworkers to the Muslim religion," Jeremy Lewis of the Moore Police Department said.

The other victim attacked by Nolen, Traci Johnson, survived. Police believe she would have been killed if the off-duty police officer had not shot Nolen.

Generals and leaders from around the world have warned America of radical Islamists infiltrating the country and attacking citizens.

Here are other attacks and beheadings in the United States in the last decade;

Ariel Sellouk – Houston, Texas: August 2003: throat was slit and beheaded.

Hossam Armanious, Amal Garas, Sylvia Armanious, and Monica Armanious, – Jersey City, NJ: January 2005: necks, throats and bodies stabbed, mutilation of Coptic tattoo.

Aasiya Hassan – Buffalo, NY: 2009: Beheaded by her husband Muzzammil. HassanBrendan Mess, Erik Weissman, and Raphael Teken – Waltham, Massachusetts: September 2011: throats slit, probably by Tamerlan and Dzhokhar Tsarnaev, the Boston Marathon bombers.

Hany F. Tawadros and Amgad A. Konds – Jersey City, NJ: February 2013: shot, decapitated, hands severed.

Many people are under the misconception that Muslims can be integrated and assimilated into another society and culture. If they are radical this would be false. They bring their society and culture with them when they immigrate.

So yes the radicals are coming here to chop our heads off if we do not convert to Islam.

International criminal lawyer, Christopher Black, has good insight to the role the U.S. plays in the war on terror; "We are told, the world over, by every government, that we are in a "war against terrorism. How can there be a war against a method of war...

The War On Terror is in fact The American War Against The World.

Fighting against terrorism" in Iraq, the Americans "really mean they are fighting the resistance to their invasion and occupation… the Russians, when they say they are fighting terrorism in Syria, know that in fact they are fighting the United States and its allies and proxy forces. The bombings and shootings in Europe, Asia, the US, and Russia are all connected to the real war that is being conducted by the United States against the world it wants to control, and, in fact, can better be described as a war of terror being waged against the rest of us by the United States and its vassal states. Each set of 'terrorist" bombings from London to Madrid, to Paris to Boston and the shootings" always end up with the claimed attackers being dead instead of arrested. All the alleged attackers apparently have some connection to the intelligence services of the countries involved... Finally, terror is an act that is used by those that can't get what they want legitimately. Individual acts of terror, carried out by the lone terrorist or small groups are carried out because they have no other political power than to try to frighten the populace. But acts of terror carried out by those factions of society that hold state power proves that they know their objectives and methods are criminal. That is why they have to resort to the terrorism of their own peoples in order to maintain control and dominance. If we want to eliminate terrorism in this world then we have to eliminate the conditions that bring to power those willing to use terrorism to rule."

*****

Former CIA operative, Charles Faddis, summed up Hillary's email scandal;

"I have worked in national security my entire life. Most of that has been in the intelligence community surrounded by classified information.

For 20 years, I worked undercover in the Central Intelligence Agency, recruiting sources, producing intelligence, and running operations. I have a pretty concrete understanding of how classified information is handled and how government communications systems work. Nobody uses a private email server for official business. Period. Full stop. Classified and unclassified information do not mix. They don't travel in the same streams through the same pipes. They move in clearly well-defined channels so that never the twain shall meet.

"Mixing them together is unheard of and a major criminal offense. If you end up with classified information in an unclassified channel, you have done something very wrong and very serious. Every hostile intelligence agency on the planet targets senior American officials for collection. The Secretary of State tops the list. Almost anything the Secretary of State had to say about her official duties, her schedule, her mood, her plans for the weekend, would be prized information to adversaries. It is very difficult, in fact, to think of much of anything that the Secretary of State could be saying in email that we would want hostile forces to know. While serving in one of the most senior positions in the United States Government, Hillary Clinton was at a minimum, grossly negligent in the handling of classified information and when confronted with this practice, acted immediately to destroy information and prevent a full, fair, and complete investigation of any damage to national security. Anyone else who did such things in the government would long ago have been tried, convicted, and sent to jail."

On March 2, 2015, the New York Times first reported that while Secretary of State Hillary exclusively used a private email for government business. The emails were found during a House investigation into the Benghazi attacks.

The leaked emails show that Hillary's campaign wanted the main focus to be on the Benghazi 2012 terrorist attacks instead of on her unsecure private email server.

"My perspective is that we want the fight to be about Benghazi, not about servers in her basement," John Podesta, Hillary's campaign manager said.

In the emails, Nick Merrill stated;

"Specifically, we added some straight-forward language in the third paragraph that aims to do two things: give this guy some simple context for the emails he references, and nudge this ever-closer to putting it in the Benghazi box."

"Nick, Great job in fighting this to more or less of a draw. This story is smoke without even the warmth of a fire." This was stated by John Podesta.

Hillary's campaign staff decided to place ads on cable channels to take the attention away from the hearings on Hillary's unsecure email server and garner attention towards Benghazi.

Oren Shur, Hillary's director of paid media, stated in an email, "The trick, of course, is to connect Benghazi to emails in a way that's credible. But we discussed different ways to do it."

"The difficult part here is testing, if we want to ship something early next week, our testing options are very limited, and I feel like we really need to understand whether voters will believe that we can credibly conflate Benghazi and emails."

Discussing which states to buy ads in, Hillary's spokeswoman Jennifer Palmieri said," I am for IA and NH. I know the boss wants a national cable buy to reach the inside the beltway types, press and donors. But press will hate this. We will lose ground with them because of it. (I am still for doing it)."

"If the objective is purely to undermine the Benghazi hearings, I think these spots will certainly help do that," Oren Shur said.

"But if the objective is to connect emails-Benghazi and conflate the two in voters' minds (which consultants feel is an imperative here), I'm not sure we know whether we can credibly do that – we'll get a read from groups, but may need to just make a judgement call once we see rough cuts."

Hillary and her staff should have spent that much time and effort on the actual attack in Benghazi.

CHAPTER 8

There is a lot of misunderstanding about the Muslim religion of Islam. And those who propagate the Muslim religion such as President Obama do not want the real tenets of this religion understood. Most people believe the word Islam means surrender and that it is related to the Arabic, salaam, or peace. In the Qur'an 4:90 says, "thus if they let you be and do not make war on you and offer you peace God does not allow you to harm them."

But the translation must be correct. Some Muslim apologists claim that the root word of Islam is "al- salaam", which is peace in Arabic. But in Arabic a word has only one root. The root word for Islam is "al-selim", which means "submission" or surrender.

Arabic and Islamic scholars agree that "al-selim", submission, does not mean the same thing "al-salaam", peace.

The Koran calls Muslims to submit to Allah as it also orders them to subdue people of all of the religions until they are in a full state of submission to Islamic rule.

And that is what radical Islamists do.

"The theory that our religion is a peaceful and loving religion is a wrong theory." This was written by Shaykh Muhammed Said Ramadan al-Buti, and until his death he was the leading Islamic scholar in Syria, professor and a retired dean of the College of Islamic Law at Damascus University. He is the author of Jurisprudence of the Prophetic Biography regarded as one of Islam's best prophetic biographies written in the 20th century;

"The Holy War as it is known in Islamic jurisprudence is basically an offensive war and it is the duty of all Muslims of every age... because our prophet Muhammad said that he is ordered by Allah to fight all people until they say "No God but Allah," and he is his messenger. It is meaningless to talk about the holy war as only defensive, otherwise what did the prophet mean when he said, "from now on if they don't invade you, you must invade them".

Sayyid Qutb, the late Egyptian scholar, was a well-respected author whose works are quoted in the Muslim world and influenced the members of the Muslim Brotherhood. He wrote that Western democracy is infertile of life-giving ideas, that obedience to Sharia is necessary to achieve harmony and peace for mankind. He preached "when Islam strives for peace its objective is not that superficial peace which requires that only that part of the earth where the followers of Islam desires that the religion (the Law of the Society) be purified for God, that the obedience of all people be for God alone."

A specific claim by Qtub was the conquest of non-muslims States as "a movement to wipe out tyranny and to introduce true freedom to mankind. A true Muslim not only has no loyalty to any country 'where the Islamic Sharia is not enforced' but must be prepared to fight against such countries.

*****

For some reason President Obama's focus is on Asia. Ash Carter, Obama's Secretary of Defense, said that Obama maintains his focus on Asia even though several of the Middle Eastern countries are in conflict. Al-Assad of Syria is fighting the opposition which is ISIS.

Carter said that Obama believes that Asia "is the part of the world of greatest consequence to the American future and that no president can take his eyes off of this. He consistently asks, even in the midst of everything else that's going on 'where are we in the Asia-pacific rebalance?' He's been extremely consistent about that even in times of Middle East tension."

Why is that? What is his obsession with Asia? Does it have something to do with his giving the U.S. control of the Internet to China? Or possibly to Russia? Yes he did that. He gave away the U.S. control of the Internet.

*****

Former FBI Assistant Director, James Kallstrom has been outraged with the refugee movement throughout Europe. He feels that it has been an organized and orchestrated movement. After the terrorist attacks in Paris, Kallstrom called Obama's plan dangerous to import thousands of Syrian refugees. Kallstrom stated, "You know the fact that these folks travel from Europe and here in the United States and get training and then they come back to the countries, to me it is just crazy and preposterous. And I don't know how we are continuing to do this thing. When you look at pictures of them 90% males between the age of 18 and 30, it's crazy, it's phony. And we must end the sanctuary cities in the United States. What a farce. What a joke." According to Kallstrom a future attack on American soil is all but certain. And unfortunately we have seen this in San Bernardino and Orlando and now in New York and New Jersey.

Not only are the sanctuary cities that house immigrants, and some of them criminals, a serious subject, but also the Islamic Terrorist Network in the United States needs serious attention.

These are the states that have Islamic Terrorist Networks and the names of those networks;

Seattle Washington;

Hybrid Fundamentalist Group, Algerian Armed Islamic Group.

Portland Oregon; Al-Qaeda

San Francisco California; Islamic Liberation Party, Abu Sayyaf.

Santa Clara California; Al-Qaeda, Hamas.

Los Angeles California; Hamas, Al-Gama'at al-Islamiyya group, Algerian Armed Islamic Group.

San Diego California; American Islamic Group, Algerian Armed Islamic Group.

Tucson Arizona; Al-Qaeda, Hamas.

Denver Colorado; Al-Qaeda.

Oklahoma City Oklahoma; Hamas (groups and conventions)

Tulsa Oklahoma; Muslim Brotherhood, Hamas.

Arlington Texas; Al-Qaeda.

Dallas/Fort Worth Texas; Hamas, Islamic Jihad, Hezbollah.

Houston Texas; Al-Qaeda, Hamas, Muslim Brotherhood.

Detroit Michigan; Al Gama'at al Islamiyya, Hamas, Hezbollah, Muslim Brotherhood.

Chicago Illinois; Hamas, Islamic Jihad.

Kansas City Missouri; Hamas.

Columbia Missouri; Algerian Islamic Salvation Front, Al-Qaeda, Hamas.

Plainfield Indiana; ISNA, Muslim Brotherhood.

Roanoke Virginia; al-Fuqra.

Springfield Virginia; Hamas.

Herndon Virginia; Al-Qaeda, Islamic Jihad.

Charlotte North Carolina; Hezbollah.

Raleigh North Carolina; Islamic Jihad.

Orlando Florida; Al-Qaeda

Tampa Florida; Islamic Jihad,

Fort Lauderdale and Boca Raton Florida; Al-Qaeda.

New York Al Gama'at al Islamiyya, Al Muhajiroun, Hezbollah, Jamaat E-Islami, al-Fuqra, Hamas.

Cleveland Ohio; Islamic Jihad, Muslim Brotherhood.

Boston Massachusetts; Al-Qaeda, National Islamic Front.

Laurel Maryland; Al-Qaeda.

Potomac Maryland; Hezbollah.

Washington DC; Hamas, Hezbollah.

*****

The Muslim Brotherhood is a radical organization that originated in the Middle East as an ally to nazi-style fascism. The Muslim Brotherhood has infiltrated the US government at very high levels. They have also set up a U.S political party, U.S. Council of Muslim Organizations, and plans to elect islamists in D.C. Their objective is to institutionalize policies reflecting sharia law. During the brief time Obama and Hillary held power in Egypt after the overthrow of Mubarak, Egypt had charged the two with conspiring with the Muslim Brotherhood.

*****

This is what will happen to America if the refugee movement to the U.S continues. Over 1 million immigrants and unvetted refugees were admitted to Germany in 2015. Angela Merkel, Chancellor of Germany, is expecting approximately 1 million more in 2016. And Germany is now facing a migrant rape crisis. Instead of limiting or disallowing the immigrants from entering their country, German officials are teaching women how to flee from a pursuing immigrant rapist. They are now encouraging women to wear sneakers to outrun the immigrant rapists.

More than one million immigrants in the past year have invaded Germany. They are almost exclusively younger men. Now Germany is experiencing a historic rape crisis. Germany's Federal Criminal Police, BKA, advised German women on how to best protect themselves against rape;

– If a woman gets an unsafe feeling when she encounters a group of men, or perceives that a situation could pose a risk, she should always trust her intuition and avoid getting into such situations, says Markus Koth, spokesman for BKA.

"Women must continue, if necessary, to be ready "to take detours." In addition, women should see if there are "any policemen nearby that can be contacted," according to Koth.

If, despite all precautions, she is attacked by asylum seekers, nevertheless, it is very important to be able to protect one's self.

"Here you have to behave so boldly and decisively as possible. But even by shouting loud one could make passersby aware of what is going on," said the BKA.

"Every police officer knows he has to meet a particular political expectation. It is better to keep quiet (about immigrant crime) because you cannot go wrong," said Rainer Wendt head of the German police union.

The local leader of the Free Democrats (FDP), Wolfgang Kubicki, is dismayed by the situation in Kiel:

"It cannot be that girls and women, as well as their parents or spouses, should be afraid in public spaces. People are asking: If you are no longer safe in Sophienhof, where then?

"The perpetrators must be brought to justice. We must not create the impression that perpetrators will go unpunished for such assaults. ... Turning a blind eye to such incidents is the opposite of integration and ultimately leads to the creation of parallel societies.

"It starts with small things. Time and again I keep hearing from the police how disrespectful young migrants are towards the officers. We have to support our security forces and reverse the loss of confidence in the police and judiciary. Otherwise we risk citizens taking the law into their own hands. I do not want to see vigilantes patrolling our streets."

Kubicki was talking about his concerns that politicians in Kiel ordered the city police to overlook many of the crimes committed by immigrants.

A document leaked in January 2016, showed that the orders were given in October 2015, to police to be lenient toward criminal immigrants. Police in North Rhine-Westphalia and Lower Saxony where also instructed to be lenient to criminal immigrants when more than 10,000 immigrants were entering Germany each day. During New Year's celebrations in Germany sexual assaults and robberies showed that the ability to integrate large numbers of immigrants does not exist. The men that attacked dozens of women in Cologne were of "Arab or North African origin."

Chancellor Angela Merkel and other political leaders in Germany condemned the attacks. They then warned the public against making immediate decisions about the nationalities of the attackers. But Germans are not happy over the one million asylum-seekers that have entered their country.

"It's unacceptable that women are sexually molested and robbed by young migrants on the streets and public squares of German cities at night," said Andreas Scheuer, general secretary of the Christian Social Union. Scheuer is the Bavarian wing of Merkel's party.

"Whoever won't accept our rules for living together, including respect for women, can have no place in our society here in Germany," said Scheuer.

The Immigrant crime Rape Crisis has spread to Switzerland and Austria.

The head of the Austrian Police Union, Hermann Greylinger, estimates that in order to establish order in the capital, Vienna needs approximately 1,200 more police officers:

"If we are allowing in our country 111,000 migrants, few of whom have had background checks, then clearly the police must be massively increased. Almost all asylum claimants are moving to Vienna. We now have more migrants than the population of the city of Salzburg, the fourth-largest city in Austria."

"Austria's migrant crime problem is being exacerbated by an extremely lenient criminal justice system. On May 4, for example, a 21-year-old migrant from Kenya randomly killed a 54-year-old woman on a busy street in Vienna by hitting her over the head with an iron bar. It soon emerged that the Kenyan was well known to city police: since arriving in Austria in 2008, he had committed at least 18 previous crimes — including dealing drugs, attacking police officers and hitting someone over the head with an iron bar — but he has repeatedly been set free.

Because of the threat from the immigrant crisis, Austrian voters are changing their political views.

Sweden has become Europe's rape capital. Denmark and Norway also are having a rape crisis. But these countries admit that the crimes are committed by the immigrants.

In Norway, recent statistics show that 100 percent of violent street-rapes committed in the capital city of Oslo were committed by "non-western" immigrants. In Denmark, the majority of rapes are committed by immigrants, usually Muslim.

Tens of thousands of young British girls are beaten, raped and tortured, by organized gangs. These gangs are mostly Muslims. When the German Chancellor, Angela Merkel, opened the doors to a million migrants from the Middle East and Africa, she opened the door to the rape of German women. And not only women but children also.

"Never before in the course of our surveys have peoples' fears risen so drastically within a year as in 2016," said Brigitte Roemstedt, head of the R+V Info Center, which conducted the survey of 2,400 Germans.

Here are a few examples of the extreme amout of females being raped by immigrants. These are from a report by the Gladstone Institute;

On August 28, a 22-year-old Eritrean asylum seeker was sentenced to one year and eight months in prison for attempting to rape a 30-year-old Iraqi-Kurdish woman at a refugee shelter in the Bavarian town of Höchstädt. The reduced sentence was thanks to the efforts of the defense attorney, who persuaded the judge that the defendant's situation at the shelter was hopeless: "For a year now he sits around and thinks about — about nothingness."

On August 26, a 34-year-old asylum seeker attempted to rape a 34-year-old woman in the laundry room of a refugee facility in Stralsund, a city near the Baltic Sea.

On August 6, police revealed that a 13-year-old Muslim girl was raped by another asylum seeker at a refugee facility in Detmold, a city in west-central Germany. The girl and her mother reportedly fled their homeland to escape a culture of sexual violence; as it turns out, the man who raped the girl is from their country.

Australia and Italy are now refusing to take any more immigrants.

Germany's crime rate has increased 65% sine the large influx of immigrants flowed into the country. Below is part of a letter from four social work organizations and women's rights groups concerning refugee shelters;

The practice of providing accommodations in large tents, the lack of gender-separate sanitary facilities, premises that cannot be locked, the lack of safe havens for women and girls — to name just a few spatial factors — increases the vulnerability of women and children within the HEAE. This situation plays into the hands of those men who assign women a subordinate role and treat women traveling alone as 'wild game'.

"The consequences are numerous rapes and sexual assaults. We are also receiving an increasing number of reports of forced prostitution. It must be stressed: these are not isolated cases.

"Women report that they, as well as children, have been raped or subjected to sexual assault. As a result, many women sleep in their street clothes. Women regularly report that they do not use the toilet at night because of the danger of rape and robbery on the way to the sanitary facilities. Even during daylight, passing through the camp is a frightful situation for many women."

What these countries are doing, including the U.S., is importing ideals and values which are antithetical, opposite, of a free society. This is irrational at the least and it is dangerous. When a government does something that endangers it's citizens, it is treason.

President of National Citizenship and Immigration Services Council, Kenneth Palinkas, warned that the current immigration system can be very easily exploited by Islamic terrorist groups like ISIS:

Unfortunately – and perilously overlooked in Washington – our caseworkers are denied the urgent professional resources, enforcement tools, and mission support we need to keep out those who are bent on doing us harm. In fact, this Administration has widened the loopholes that terrorists could use to gain entry to the United States through our asylum system. The Administration has also blocked our partners in Immigration and Customs Enforcement (ICE) from enforcing visa overstays. The 9/11 hijackers got into the U.S. on visas and now, 13 years later, we have around 5 million immigrants in the United States who overstayed their visas – many from high-risk regions in the Middle East. Making matters more dangerous, the Obama Administration's executive amnesty, like S. 744 that he unsuccessfully lobbied for, would legalize visa overstays and cause millions additionally to overstay – raising the threat level to America even higher. There is no doubt that there are already many individuals in the United States, on visas, expired or active, who are being targeted for radicalization or who already subscribe to radicalized views.

Many millions come legally to the U.S. through our wide open immigration policy every year – whether as temporary visitors, lifetime immigrants, refugees, asylum-seekers, foreign students, or recipients of our 'visa waiver program' which allows people to come and go freely. Yet our government cannot effectively track these foreign visitors and immigrants. And those who defraud authorities will face no consequence at all in most cases. Our caseworkers cannot even do in-person interviews for people seeking citizenship, they cannot enforce restrictions on welfare use, and they even lack even the basic office space to properly function. Applications for entry are rubber-stamped, the result of grading agents by speed rather than discretion. We've become the visa clearinghouse for the world. This is a dangerous situation and a recipe for disaster.

CHAPTER 9

O bama's Department of Homeland Security did not want a 2015 study commissioned by the House and Senate Appropriations Committees "seeking to pinpoint the number of illegal immigrants who successfully sneak across the southern border" to be reported. The study had been finished as early as Nov. 2015 but the DHS claimed that the study was not completed.

Obama's DHS was keeping the findings from the public because they are in contradiction to what Obama has said.

John Lott, president of the Crime Prevention Research Center, stated: "The Obama administration knows that the number of illegal aliens successfully getting across the Mexican border is 158 percent higher than they are telling people."

"The administration has made fraudulent changes in the numbers to hide this," he added.

In 2015, President Obama began his program, The Task Force on New Americans. In early 2016, his administration gave the program $19 million to reach its main goal which is making sure new voters are registered who would vote Democrat in the election. The money was handed out by the US Citizenship and Immigration Services (USCIS), a department of Homeland Security that oversees lawful and most likely unlawful immigration. And naturally this flow of cash will cost American taxpayers a lot of money to provide immigrants with free 'citizenship preparation' programs the administration claims will 'strengthen civic, economic, and linguistic integration' and 'build strong and welcoming communities'.

Almost every Federal agency is participating in this effort in contributing resources and starting programs to help immigrants.

The Department of Labor (DOL) is implementing "new workforce programs" for the "new Americans". The Department of Education is promoting funding opportunities to assure that the immigrants "are provided the tools they need to succeed". The Department of Health and Human Services (HHS) will work with other agencies on "immigrant focused Career Pathways programs". Worker rights and protections for the 'new Americans' will be assured by the Department of Justice and USCIS. A two-year pilot program so that non-English speakers have "meaningful access to housing programs" which of course is paid by U.S. taxpayers, has been started by the Department of Housing and Urban Development HUD).

So what about those who already live in the United States? How come none of this money is going to help American's find better jobs, have meaningful access to housing programs, and be provided with the tools they need to succeed? After all, that is who is paying for it.

One thing that needs to be addressed, well actually several things, is that the refugees and immigrants who are coming in to all the other countries and the United States seem to be very well-dressed, seem to be very healthy, and they have cell phones. Who is paying for this? And what about charges for their cell phones to be used in other countries? Who is paying for this? And why is the majority of them younger males, 90-98%? Where are all the women and children?

And concerning refugees cell phones, at the Norway border the police check the immigrant's cell phones as they come through. And what they have found are pictures and videos of ISIS beheadings and executions.

*****

Hillary has no need to worry if Trump is president and has the nuclear codes because according to the Single Integrated Operational Plan;

In the United States, the decision to use nuclear weapons is vested in the National Command Authority (NCA), composed of the President of the United States and the United States Secretary of Defense or their duly deputized alternates or successors. The President alone cannot order an attack. The ordering of use, communication of orders, and the release of nuclear weapons is governed by the two-man rule at all times.

No one person ever can take such an action. All military personnel that participate in loading, arming, or firing weapons, as well as transmitting launch orders, are subject to the Personnel Reliability Program (PRP).

But President Vladimir Putin is worried about Hillary becoming the President. He feels if it's Hillary, it's war.

There is no other office in the US government used to promote the Permanent War Economy like the Secretary of State. The State Department officials were carrying out black operations Syria, and Libya while Hillary was Secretary of State from 2009 through 2013. Some have said that they were running their own government. And Putin is aware of the part Hillary has played in these wars.

Russia's President Vladimir Putin fears that if Hillary is elected as the president of the United States in the upcoming election that war will be the result. He has warned his military Commanders, "If it's Hillary, it's War." His fear is based on Hillary being a war hawk adherent to the Permanent War Economy that was instituted near the end of World War II, In 1944. The Permanent War Economy was instituted to sustain global economic power. But all of these wars have led to the deaths of hundreds of thousands if not millions of innocent people in so many areas of the world. This institution of the Permanent War Economy has left nations in abject poverty and some in ruin. Millions have been made homeless and displaced. President Putin has decided to launch the Angara class heavy carrier rocket from the Plesetsk Spaceport by the end of December 2016. These early missile attack warning system next-generation satellites are being launched before the next U.S. President takes office in January 2017. These early warning system missile attack Next Generation satellites are in direct response to the Obama regime activation on the Western Front, in Romania, of the European Phased Adaptive Approach (EPAA) missile system. Putin warns that this EPAA is a direct threat to Russia.Russian officials say that the system violates the 1987 treaty that ended the Cold War. The placing of weapons increases the risk of nuclear war and directly threatens Russia. Vladimir Putin's spokesman, Dmitri S. Puskov, said the Kremlin feels imperiled by the presence of these weapons located in nearby Romania.

"We have been saying right from when the story started that our experts are convinced that the deployment of the... system poses a certain threat to the Russian Federation. Measures are being taken to ensure the necessary level of security for Russia. The president himself, let me remind you, has repeatedly asked who the system will work against."

The Obama regime and NATO continue to pour troops into Eastern Europe and conduct overtly hostile military maneuvers on the Federation border. This action has forced President Putin to order the Ministry of Defense (MoD) to form three new divisions to counter Obama's and NATO's troops. The three Russian military divisions that Putin was forced to implement equals approximately forty thousand troops. And the U.S. keeps provoking Russia.

An article from The Free Thought by Justin Gardner October 23rd 2016;

While mainstream media has dutifully echoed the U.S. government narrative that Russia is to blame for increasing tensions, we at the Free Thought Project have reported on the numerous ways in which the U.S. has actually been the provocateur.

Earlier in 2016, a U.S. military official said the U.S. "needs and wants Russia as an enemy," which was followed by a litany of falsehoods about Russian threats from elected and appointed officials. A hacked email showed a NATO general plotting conflict with Russia, as American and NATO military forces amass along Russia's borders.

U.S. intervention in Syria has provided the perfect context for escalating tensions. In its effort to topple the Assad government, the U.S. nurtured the Salafist fundamentalist sect in Syria, which went on to become a major part of ISIS. As U.S. military operations get dangerously close to Syrian or Russian forces (invited there by Assad), any "accidental" strike could be the spark for World War III.

Emails show the Revolutionary Forces of Syria (RFS) media office, a major Syrian opposition media outfit and frequent source of information for Western media, is funded by the British government. And is managed by Westerners operating out of Turkey, according to emails provided to AlterNet by a Middle East reporter RFS tried to recruit.

****

What Libya, Syria, Lebanon, Iran, Iraq, Somalia, and Sudan have in common; None of these countries are listed among the 56 member banks of the Bank for International Settlements (BIS). This means that they are not under the regulations of the central bank in Switzerland.

Iraq had decided to accept euros instead of dollars for oil six months before the U.S. went into Iraq. This threatened the domination of the dollar globally as the reserve currency. And also its domination as the petrodollar.

Gaddafi also decided to refuse the dollar and the Euro. He called on Arab and African nations to use the gold dinar. Gaddafi wanted to create a United African Continent. And the 200 million people would only use the gold dinar.

The Central Bank of Libya was owned solely by Libya. The Libyan Central Bank made its own money, the Libyan dinar. So for all banking cartels to do business in Libya they must go through the central bank where they would have no power brokering ability. This would have put Libya in the globalist agenda for absorbing Libya into their compliant Nations.

A lot of questions are answered when you follow the money.

Robert Wenzel wrote;

I have never before heard of a central bank being created in just a matter of weeks out of a popular uprising. This suggests we have a bit more than a rag tag bunch of rebels running around and that there are some pretty sophisticated influences.

Alex Newman wrote;

In a statement released last week, the rebels reported on the results of a meeting held on March 19. Among other things, the supposed rag-tag revolutionaries announced the "[d]esignation of the Central Bank of Benghazi as a monetary authority competent in monetary policies in Libya and appointment of a Governor to the Central Bank of Libya, with a temporary headquarters in Benghazi."

Gaddafi had wanted to nationalize the oil reserves. Nationalization of a country's resources is often a cause for invasion.

After becoming acquainted with the Libyan people and their way of life, a group of medical professionals from Belarus, Russia, and Ukraine wrote in an appeal to Prime Minister Vladimir Putin and Russian President

Dmitry Medvedev that it was their view that in few nations did people live in such comfort as the Libyan people did.

"[Libyans] are entitled to free treatment, and their hospitals provide the best in the world of medical equipment. Education in Libya is free, capable young people have the opportunity to study abroad at government expense. When marrying, young couples receive 60,000 Libyan dinars (about 50,000 US dollars) of financial assistance. Non-interest state loans, and as practice shows, undated. Due to government subsidies the price of cars is much lower than in Europe, and they are affordable for every family. Gasoline and bread cost a penny, no taxes for those who are engaged in agriculture. The Libyan people are quiet and peaceful, are not inclined to drink, and are very religious.

In 2008 Gareth Porter said, "Three weeks after the September 11th 2001 Terror attacks, Former US defense secretary Donald Rumsfeld established an official military objective of not only removing the Saddam Hussein regime by force but overturning the regime in Iran as well as in Syria and four other countries in the Middle East, according to a document quoted extensively in then - under secretary of defense for policy Douglas Feith's recently published account of the Iraq war decisions. Feith's account further indicates that this aggressive aim of remaking the map of the Middle East by military force and the threat of force was supported explicitly by the country's top military leaders. Feith's book, War and Decision, provides excerpts of the paper Rumsfeld sent to President George W Bush on September 30th, 2001, calling for the administration to focus not on taking down Osama Bin Laden's al-Qaeda network but on the aim of establishing "new regimes" in a series of states..

The new regimes were in countries who have their own central banks. They are not regulated by the Swiss bank.

Gaddafi had proposed nationalizing Libya's oil reserves. Hundreds of thousands of Libyans gathered to discuss the proposal by their leader Muammar Gaddafi to disband the government and allow the country's oil wealth to flow straight to the people.

"Libyans this is your historic opportunity to take over your oil wealth, power and full freedom. Why do you want to let the chance slip away from you?" stated Gaddafi. Three years later Gaddafi was overthrown and murdered.

The UN's Human Development Index shows that prior to the invasion, Libya had the highest levels of well-being, the best economic policies for the quality of life, the lowest infant mortality and the highest life expectancy of any country in Africa.

*****

Hillary shares an address at 1209 North Orange St. in Delaware with 285,000 companies. She had condemned Trump for not having to pay $900,000 in taxes. But at this address is where she received more than $16 million in speaking fees and book royalties. Although Hillary has consistently stated that she would crack down on "outrageous tax havens and loopholes that super-rich people across the world are exploiting in Panama and elsewhere", she avoids paying a lot of money in taxes due to the 'Delaware loophole' which has caused Delaware to be described as "one of the world's biggest havens for tax avoidance".

CHAPTER 10

Some of the things that Hillary Clinton has stated makes one wonder exactly what her ideals and goals are.

"We must stop thinking of the individual and start thinking about what is best for society." "We just can't trust the American people to make those types of choices... Government has to make those choices for people," Hillary to representative Dennis Hastert in 1993 discussing her health care plan.

"I am a fan of the social policies that you find in Europe."

"God bless the America we are trying to create."

"You know I'm going to start thanking the woman who cleans the restroom in the building I work in. I'm going to start thinking of her as a human being."

"I want to get this s*** over with and get these damn people out of here!" Hillary on the governor's mansion intercom as preschoolers posed for photographs on the lawn.

And she is supposed to be a fighter for children.

Hillary attacked Trump on calling women pigs, dogs and slobs. But what she said was much worse.

"When are they going to get those f- - - - - - retards out of here?!"

These were Hillary's words in 1984 when handicapped children were at the Arkansas governor's mansion and not collecting their Easter eggs quickly enough for Hillary.

*****

The Obama Administration has told a federal judge that they cannot turn over any documents on the Iran lie cover-up until November 8, Election Day.

Leaked emails show that the White House was in contact with Hillary's campaign. In concocting lies for their pro-Iran talking points, they were trying to defend the earlier nuclear agreement. Leaked emails also show that both gave information about the Iran deal in which they knew that information was lies. Officials called this a pro-Iran "echo chamber" to mislead Congress and the public about the lies of the agreement.

After the email leaks, the Obama Administration deleted footage from a State Department press briefing where it admitted it had in fact lied to the American people about the Iran nuclear deal. ACLJ filed a Freedom of Information Act (FOIA) Request.

ACLJ wanted to know who authorized the deletion, how it was accomplished, and why it was covered up. By law, the Administration is required to comply with FOIA request. The State Department, five months later, had not sent any documents to ACLJ.

ACLJ then filed a federal lawsuit. The Obama Administration, on September 27, filed a statement with the court. They stated that it would produce some of these documents to ACLJ. Although, until Election Day, Obama's administration would not produce any related documents.

The Obama Administration's statement;

This case involves The American Center for Law and Justice's ("Plaintiff") request under the Freedom of Information Act ("FOIA") seeking records from the U.S. Department of State regarding a video of a daily press briefing that took place on December 2, 2013. Defendant has identified documents potentially responsive to Plaintiff's FOIA request and is in the process of reviewing those documents to determine the volume of responsive records that will need to be processed. Accordingly, Defendant is unable at this time to state with certainty when it will be able to complete production of responsive, non-exempt records. However, based on the results of its review to date, Defendant anticipates that it will be able to release responsive, non-exempt records to Plaintiff on a rolling basis, with the first production to occur on November 8, 2016, and a final production to occur by December 6, 2016.

And not surprisingly, the federal court's date was set at November 11, in which the administration has to produce a status report on the production of the documents.

And now Congress is fighting through legislation to prevent the Obama administration from giving Iran any more money. Iran had previously received $1.7 billion from the Obama administration. Now Iran wants billions of dollars more before they release any of the six American hostages that they have detained in Iran.

*****

The U.S. District Court Judge, Reggie Walton, refused an FOIA request in the release of drafts of a criminal indictment prosecutors had prepared for Hillary's indictment for the 1990's Whitewater investigation. Judge Walton wrote, "The fact that information about the independent counsel's investigation and potential indictment of Mrs. Clinton is readily available to the public does not extinguish Mrs. Clinton's privacy interest."

"Although an individual's interest in privacy fade when the information already appears on the public record... the fact that an event is not wholly private does not mean that an individual has no interest in limiting disclosures or dissemination of information," Judge Walton said.

Judicial Watch spokesman Chris Farrell did not agree with the ruling; "It's difficult to imagine how a person running for the presidency enjoys the form of privacy concerning their near indictment on criminal charges that somehow supersedes the public's right to know. Judicial Watch will continue to fight to make the facts public."

Deputy Idependent Counsel, Hickman Ewing, said that he felt a need to draft them because he had doubted then first lady Hillary's statements in 1995 interviews. And also doubted Hillary's testimony before a grand jury in 1996. Some of Hillary statements about her law firms work for the Madison Guaranty Savings and Loan were not consistent with those of other statements at the law firm, according to Ewing. At the time there was a 2% chance the Judge would throw out the case, according to prosecutor Paul Rosenzweig. In Rosenzweig's memo was written; 18%=acquittal; 70%=hung jury, 10%=conviction. Judge Walton said that since Hillary was the first lady of the United States at the time of the investigation that she was either part of a government agency nor a government oficial when the events that were the subject of independent council's investigation occurred which led to the drafting of the proposed indictments. The judge said the disclosure of the draft of the proposed indictment would not shed light on any agency's performance of its statutory duties but potentially shed light solely on the character of Hillary, independent to her position as a public official. But the American people do not care about the law firm in 1995 that Hillary worked for at that time. When the judge said that the draft of the indictments solely shed light on the character of Hillary he hit it right on target. That is what the American people want to know about. And had a right to know since she was running for the highest office in America. But once again Hillary is not held accountable for her actions.

And a way to avoid any more light shed on Hillary is the deal that the Obama Administration is working on to dismiss charges against an arms dealer, Mark Turi, who was accused of selling weapons that were in route to militias in Libya.

In 2014, Mark Turi, an American, was indicted on four felony counts. Two of those indictments were for arms dealing in violation of the Arms Export Control Act and two indictments for lying to the State Department and official applications. His lawyers defended Turi saying that the shipments were part of the U.S. government authorized effort to arm Libyan rebels. Also the government decided not to use Turi. So he did not even ship any weapons. The U.S. government through Hillary's State Department supplied rebels with weapons in Libya, Syria, and Tunisia. And most likely every Arab Spring revolt.

Mark Turi's attorney demanded documents, during discovery, and told prosecuters that he had substantial evidence, that though they did not use Turi for the weapons transfer, another weapons supplier was hired by the U.S. Government. These are the documents Turi's lawyer demanded;

"Any documents or other evidence relating to instances in which the United States assisted or considered assisting in any way, overtly or covertly, in the transportation, provision, acquisition, transfer, or transport of Defense articles to or from any person, entity, group of people, quasi-governmental entity, or government within the territory of Libya, Syria, Qatar, the United Arab Emirates, Turkey or Jordan (these countries collectively here the 'Covered Countries') within the timeframe of 2010 to the date of the request."

If this case would go to trial it would bring Hillary's email scandal to light again. It would bring disclosure of the illegal weapons supply because the Justice Department lawyers filed in a federal court to drop the case against Mark Turi. This case cost the government approximately $10 million and lasted for five years. A friend of Mark Turi's said the Justice Department dropped the case because, "They don't want this stuff to come out because it will look really bad for Obama and Clinton just before the election."

The U.S. Federal Government requested that the court dismiss the indictment of Mark Turi;

The Obama administration is moving to dismiss charges against an arms dealer it had accused of selling weapons that were destined for Libyan rebels.

Lawyers for the Justice Department on Monday filed a motion in federal court in Phoenix to drop the case against the arms dealer, an American named Marc Turi, whose lawyers also signed the motion.

The deal averted a trial that threatened to cast additional scrutiny on Hillary Clinton's private emails as Secretary of State, and to expose reported Central Intelligence Agency attempts to arm rebels at that time fighting Libyan leader Moammar Gaddafi.

Government lawyers were facing a Wednesday deadline to produce documents to Turi's legal team, and the trial was officially set to begin on Election Day, although it likely would have been delayed by protracted disputes about classified information in the case.

All of the terrorists including al-Qaeda, Ansar al-Sharia, and ISIS received these weapons.

Mark Turi lost everything because of the Obama Administration trying to put the blame on him.

Emails about the illegal shipments of weapons were most likely deleted by Hillary or her staff because they would have ended up going to an organization in the Bureau of Political Military affairs. But Julian Assange nost likely has them. And one leaked email shows that Hillary emailed aide Jake Sullivan on April 8, 2011, "fyi. the idea of using private security experts to arm the opposition should be considered." This most likely had to do with Mark Turi.

Robert Stryk of the government relations and consulting firm SPG is the advisor of Mark Turi. Stryk accused the government of trying to make Turi the scapegoat. This action would help to protect Hillary's disastrous, absolutely disastrous, handling of Libya. Regarding the attack on the SMC in Benghazi in 2012, Stryk stated, "The U.S. government spent millions of dollars, went all over the world to bankrupt him, and destroyed his life, all to protect Hillary Clinton's crimes."

Mark Turi is now working on book and movie deals to tell his story and his views on the Benghazi attack in 2012.

And if the four brave souls that left the CIA annex and came to the rescue of the Benghazi Special Mission Compound had not come to protect them most likely all 35 people would be dead.

This is not about Democrats and Republicans anymore. This is about America and her enemies. All of these revolutions and killings of the Arab Spring have been backed by the US. So is the U.S. government America's enemy? They are if they let the terrorists who they backed to revolt and cause all of the destruction and death and then allow the people of those regions into the US with the enemy infiltrated among them. Some generals and intelligence officials believe these asylum-seekers coming into the U.S. are orchestrated by the U.S. government. When looking at the immigrants they do not image people who have been forced from their homes by destruction and death.

And not surprisingly, the Justice Department is silencing Mark Turi;

In the dismissal motion, prosecutors say "discovery rulings" from U.S. District Court Judge David Campbell contributed to the decision to drop the case. The joint motion asks the judge to accept a confidential agreement to resolve the case through a civil settlement between the State Department and the arms broker.

"Our position from the outset has been that this case never should have been brought and we're glad it's over," said Jean-Jacques Cabou, a Perkins Coie partner serving as court-appointed defense counsel in the case. "Mr Turi didn't break the law....We're very glad the charges are being dismissed."

Under the deal, Turi admits no guilt in the transactions he participated in, but he agreed to refrain from U.S.-regulated arms dealing for four years. A $200,000 civil penalty will be waived if Turi abides by the agreement.

CHAPTER 11

The human rights organization has proven that Gaddafi was not killing his people. And his regime was not assaulting females or raping them. Libya is a hive of terrorists now. Mubarak of Egypt stepped down because he did not want any more of his people to die. Bashar Assad of Syria is not stepping down because he knows if ISIS takes complete control of Syria all of his people will suffer immensely.

Even Kurdish leader Saleh Muslim said that overthrowing Assad's regime would be a disaster for the entire world.

"The Syrian armed opposition is almost wholly dominated by ISIS and it's Al Qaeda equivalents."

"Our main goal is to defeat Daesh (ISIS). We would not feel safe in our home so long as there is one Daesh left alive."

*****

Instead of getting additional security, on July 1, the Libyan employees in Benghazi received a raise in dangerous pay from 25% to 30%. If it wasn't so awful, it would be laughable.

Not only is Hillary responsible for the deaths of the four Americans in Benghazi it has been alleged that she may also bear responsibility for the deaths of 21 children who died at the Branch Davidian compound in Waco Texas in 1993. There had been a long standoff between members of the Branch Davidian "cult" and federal authorities over alleged trafficking and possession of illegal firearms. The standoff eventually led to an all-out assault on the compound with armored vehicles, weapons, and tear gas eventually starting an inferno of fire that killed 74 members including 21 children. It had long been thought that Janet Reno, attorney general at the time, had ordered the assault. But now a Freedom of Information Act shows that it possibly came from the Clinton White House and perhaps from Hillary herself. The evidence that suggests this, is the transcript of the FBI's interview with Lisa Foster, Vince Foster's wife following his death which was ruled a suicide. She had described how guilty her husband had felt due to the Waco raid. This is supported by comments made by FBI agents that were involved in the Waco raid. The Freedom of Information Act request suggests that the agents knew that the order to conduct the assault was "made in the White House". The transcript of an interview on CNN 15 years ago from the Larry King show between King and former White House staffer Linda Tripp, further confirmed this. She was a friend of Vince Foster's before his death. Remembering Foster's reaction to the Waco assault, Linda Tripp stated to King, "I was with him, well we had CNN all the time, not to plug, but it was always on in the White House. And a special bulletin came on showing the atrocity at Waco and the children.

"And his face, his whole body slumped, and his face turned white, and he was absolutely crushed knowing, knowing the part he had played. And he had played the part at Mrs. Clinton's direction.

"Her reaction, on the other hand, was heartless. And I can only tell you what I saw," Tripp said.

A folder that Foster kept on Waco vanished from his office after his death.

So Hillary may have been supporting arms trafficking even at that time and tried to place the blame on someone else.

*****

Hillary Clinton has been lauded as a brave crusader for all women, especially for women and children living in poor countries and controlled by extremism.

Hillary was the first Secretary of State to declare the subjugation of women a threat to the US National Security. At an appearance at the TEDwoman in Washington DC Hillary stated:

"The United States has made empowering women and girls a Cornerstone of our foreign policy because women's equality is not just a moral issue, it is not just a humanitarian issue, it is not just a fairness issue, it is a security issue. It is a prosperity issue and it is a peace issue... Give women equal rights and entire nations are more stable and secure. Deny women equal rights and instability of Nations is almost certain. The subjugation of women is therefore a threat to the common security of our world and to the National Security of our country."

She was somewhat right about that, but she is the one who has caused so much of the instability and terrorism in other countries.

So Hillary's desire for women's and children's rights conflict with her actions also in regard to Saudi Arabia. Ranking 145 of 158 countries in the UN Development Programs Gender Inequality Index, Saudi Arabia is among the worst countries in the world in which to be born female. This is a country in which the subjugation of women and children is undeniable. And sickening. There is no legal minimum age required to marry. Consent does not have to be given by the intended bride whether a woman or child. The only person to require anything is the male guardian and the groom.

An eight year old little girl from Yemen died on her wedding night from internal bleeding. Her name was Rawan and she was married to a man who was forty years old. Her death was due to uterine rupture and extensive bleeding. She was taken to a hospital but the medics could not save her.

Her husband or parents had no actions taken against them by authorities.

She had been taken to a clinic but the medics could not prevent her death.

This child marriage happens often in the Middle Eastern countries. Fawzan the Grand Mufti of Saudia Arabia states that no where does Sharia or Islamic law set an age limit for marrying girls. Fawzwan's belief is based on the Koran 65:4 which discusses marriage to females who have not yet began menstruating. Muhammad, Islam's role model, married Aisha when she was six or seven consummating the marriage when she was nine.

The point of the Saudi fatwa is that there is no legal age limit whatsoever. The only question is whether the girl is physically capable of handling her "husband". Fawzan quoted Ibn Battal's authoritative exegesis on Sahih Bukhari:

The ulema (Islam scholars and interpreters) have agreed that it is permissible for fathers to marry off their small daughters even "if they are in the cradle". But it is not permissible for their husbands to have sex with them unless they are capable of being placed beneath and bearing the weight of the men. And their capability in this regard varies based on their nature and capacity. Aisha was six when she married the prophet but he had sex with her when she was 9.

There is a staggering amount of pedophilia in Islam. The lives of so many young girls are devastated because of this teaching. The eight-year-old girl who died on her wedding night, the 12 year old girl who died giving birth to a stillborn, the 10 year old who hid from her 80 year old husband. ...The grand Mufti Abdul Aziz is the highest Islamic authority in the land of Islam dismisses placing an age restriction for marriage. Saudi Arabia has the highest number of child marriages in the Middle East and there has been no International outrage or objection directed at that practice. The US government for the most part has been indifferent to the plight of Child Brides in Saudi Arabia.

Saudi Arabia is a signatory of the United Nations Convention on the Rights of a Child which considers those under the age of 18 children. But the UN also seems to ignore the actions of Saudi Arabia.

In Hard Choices, Hillary's memoir, she tells when she "learned about an eight-year-old girl whose father forced her to marry a 50 year old man in exchange for about $13,000. Saudi courts rejected pleas from her mother to stop the marriage and it did not look like the government was going to intervene. I knew that embarrassing governments with Public condemnation can backfire, making them dig their heels in deeper. Instead of calling a press conference to condemn the practice and demand action, I looked for a way to persuade the Saudis to do the right thing and still save face. Quietly reaching out through diplomatic channels I offered a simple but firm message. Fix this on your own and I won't say a word. The Saudis appointed a new Judge who quickly granted a divorce... there's time to get on a soapbox and I've been on quite a few but sometimes the best way to achieve real change in diplomacy and in life is by building relationships and understanding how to use them."

She was Secretary of State at the time. She should have used the relationship that she had built with Saudi Arabia and demanded change in policy regarding child marriage. She should not have allowed them access to purchase weapons from the U.S. Hillary should have been working on a call to arms to protect little girls instead of working on an arms deal.

Even though Saudi Arabia including other Middle Eastern countries has the horrifying record concerning women's and children's rights, in 2011, Hillary and her staff celebrated a $29.4 billion arms deal with Saudi Arabia. The Clinton Foundation received millions of dollars from Saudi Arabia. Saudi Arabia received up to 84 F-15 SA advanced fighters manufactured by Boeing along with upgrades to preexisting Saudi fleet of 70 F-15 aircraft, and munitions, spare parts, training, maintenance, and logistics.

How can someone who propagates the global problem of undervalued women and children work on a deal with a government who undervalues women and children? And who sets no age requirements on marriage where children can be made to marry while still in the cradle.

In Egypt, under Mubarak's rule, he set the age limit at 18 for marriage. Yet Hillary and Obama helped to have him overthrown.

Muammar Gaddafi had set the age limit for marriage at 20 years old.

But after Gaddafi's overthrow and death, women's and children's rights do not exist.Libyans women's rights activist, Asmaa Syed, has been collecting data on girls being forced into marriage with Isis fighters in Libya. "The clinics where the girls are being taken to have been taken over by ISIS members. This complicates establishing how many girls are being married at a very young age. Just in the clinics that we were able to monitor we are seeing four to five cases of underage brides every week and it's getting worse. There is also the spread of STDs and the growing problems of miscarriages, premature, and still births," she said.

One local gynecologist said girls are so young they often have no idea what is happening to them. "We still see girls who are bleeding heavily from their genital area. Some of them don't know what sex is, they come into the clinic playing with their dolls."

Earlier in Hillary's run as Secretary of State, she had proclaimed an allegiance with the Libyan regime under Gaddafi, during a time when some of the major U.S. corporations doing business in Libya were also donating very large sums to the Clinton Foundation. That is where her allegiance was, with the companies. Hillary had met with Gaddafi's son, Mutassim Gaddafi, then-national security advisor in April of 2009. Hillary told Mutassim, "We deeply value the relationship between the United States and Libya." That did not last long or was not even true from the beginning.

In 2010, approximately one year before the overthrow of Gaddafi Libya ranked 53rd in the U.N.'s Human Development Index among 163 countries. With life expectancy at Birth at 74.5% and 88.4% adult literacy rate and gross enrollment ratio of 94.1%, Libya was classified as a high human development country in the Middle East and North Africa region. This rating was established by the United Nations.

Unlike many other Arab Nations, women in Gaddafi's Libya had the right to education, hold jobs, divorce, hold property, and have an income. The United States Human Rights Council had even praised Gaddafi for his promotion of women's rights. Libya was one of the most modern and secular states in the Middle East and North Africa with the highest regional women's rights and standard of living.

Before the overthrow of Gaddafi, Libya enjoyed a higher standard of living than two-thirds of the world. But now Libya is a terrorist stronghold ruled by competing radical Islamic groups. And who kidnap rape and murder women and children.

Human rights organizations discovered that there was no evidence for several highly publicized atrocities supposedly carried out by Gaddafi's forces. And that included the story of the mass rape by Gaddafi's troops. Amnesty International exposed that idea as being without foundation. But now Libya is plagued with assassinations, torture, and widespread rape. Women and children have suffered immensely. In the 2014 UN Development Report it was stated that, "the steepest decline in living conditions during 2013 occurred in Central African Republic, Libya, and Syria --three countries targeted by U.S. and French imperialism for military intervention and political subversion".

In 2003, then-senator Hillary Clinton was adamant that Saddam Hussein was giving sanctuary to terrorists. But the invasion actually transformed Iraq into a radical terrorist hive. A top military adviser to General David Petraeus stated that, "there undeniably would be no ISIS if we had not invaded Iraq. We have to recognize that a lot of the problem in the Middle East is of our own making."

The overthrow of Gaddafi had the same affect. Hillary Clinton stated that the United States had a moral duty to intervene in Libya.

Due to a claim that Qaddafi was handing out free Viagra to his soldiers, a rumor started by Al Jazeera, Hillary stated that she was "deeply concerned" that Gaddafi's troops were using rape as a weapon. Although she knew that was a lie.

But after Amnesty International went to Libya, they published a report stating: "Not only have we not met any rape victims, but we have not even met any persons who have met victims. As for the boxes of Viagra that Gaddafi is supposed to have had distributed, they were found intact near tanks that were completely burnt out."

Amnesty International also reported that they had, "failed to find evidence for these human rights violations. And in many cases has discredited or cast doubt on them. It also found indications that on several occasions the rebels in Benghazi appeared to have knowingly made false claims or manufactured evidence."

And now ISIS controls large areas of Libya. American intelligence officials estimated that ISIS in Libya had grown to 6,500 fighters, more than doubling since the fall. ISIS established their control in Libya, in 2014, and continued attacks ever since.

During Hillary's Democratic presidential debate in Manchester, New Hampshire, Hillary stated, "We have to continue to do what is necessary when someone like Gaddafi, a despot with American blood on his hands, is overturned. But I'll tell you what would have happened if we had not joined with our European partners and our Arab partners to assist the people in Libya, you would be looking at Syria."

Libya is worse off than Syria.

CHAPTER 12

CIA director John Brennan stated that, "ISIL has a large cadre of Western fighters who could potentially serve as operatives for attacks in the West". He feels that ISIL is working to smuggle them into countries among refugee flows or by using legitimate travel means. The director called IS a "formidable adversary".

"Unfortunately despite all our progress against ISIL on the battlefield and in the financial world our efforts have not reduced the group's terrorism capability and global reach. In fact as the pressure mounts on ISIL we judge that it will intensify its Global Terror campaign to maintain its dominance of the global terrorism agenda."

They generate tens of millions of dollars in revenue monthly from taxation and from the sale of crude oil.

ISIS had taken control of at least 2 oil fields in Libya and attacked the Dhahra oil field according to oil and government sources. An article in Times stated that... "ISIS is more than a network of terrorist cells or even a militia: it's almost a nation."

According to a report by The Institute for the study of War, "ISIS safe haven in Libya will allow it to survive even if it is defeated in Iraq and Syria. Isis will use its Libyan base to exacerbate Regional disorder and attack Europe."

"Conflict zones and failed states necessarily attract the violent extremists and Libya is the perfect candidate for a new safe haven for jihadist fighters. The phenomenon of foreign fighters has enhanced this threat as young extremists are provided with an ideal destination for waging violent jihad. Given geography, expansive territory, extensive oil reserves, and its history with violent jihadist networks a failed State in Libya could be disastrous for North Africa and Europe as well as the broader International community," according to a report by the Soufan Group an intelligence and risk consultancy. Isis has been governing by Sharia law in some areas carrying out executions and arrests according to the institute for the Study of War.

A research fellow at the American Enterprise Institute stated, "I see what ISIS is doing in Libya as a direct extension of what it has done in Iraq and Syria in terms of securing a piece of terrain and then moving its critical infrastructure which is of course the oil facilities in Libya."

In Dabiq, the Isis online propaganda magazine, Libyan ISIS leader Abdul Mujhirah al-Qahtani said, "The control of the Islamic State over this region (Libya) will lead to economic breakdowns especially for Italy and the rest of the European States."

*****

At the time of his retirement two years ago, retired US Air Force General Norman Ham, he had major misgivings concerning the armed forces under President Obama.

General Ham stated, "Now that I don't have to be politically correct anymore, it was demoralizing to work for Obama.

"Sequestration severely handicapped our military training-wise readiness equipment facilities. It was demoralizing. Your whole job as a general is to take care of people; because when you take care of people, you get the mission done. We weren't allowed to take care of the people the way we needed to take care of the people."

Ham, said the current administration has went through military leaders because many disagreed with Obama's policies.

"We're on our fourth secretary of defense. There's a reason for that. None of them gave Obama the answer that he wanted."

"When we're trading, you know, traitors for terrorists. We're paying ransom to the largest state sponsor of terrorism in the world."

"This country needs a leader. We need a leader with integrity, a leader that sees goodness in all Americans that can bring us together and lead us forward," Ham said.

*****

Libya has been in a state of chaos since the fall of Muammar Gaddafi. ISIS and other terrorist organizations have used Libya's environment of lawlessness to take a stronghold in parts of the country. Thanks to Hillary and Obama.

And now, Wikileaks has proven that Hillary is one of the chief architects behind the attempted Turkey coop, along with Fetullah Gulen. A file from Congress reveals there are strong ties between Hillary and high members of the Islamic cleric in Turkey. The documents also show that an email from a Gulen follower, Gokhan Ozkok, had asked deputy chief of staff, Huma Abedin, on April 2009 for help in connecting one of his allies to President Obama. The documents also proved that Ozkok is a founding member of the Turkish Cultural Center. He is part of a large business complex closely tied to the Gulen movement also known as Hizmet. And Ozkok served as the national finance co chair of the pro-Clinton Ready PAC and had contributed $10,000 in 2014. He contributed $2,700 to Hillary's campaign in 2015. Also Ozkok is a member of the Clinton Global Initiative and has contributed between $25,000 - $50,000 to the initiative. There is also a connection between Gulenists and Hillary. A Gulen aligned group, The Alliance on Shared Values, hired the Podesta Group which is connected to the Clinton's, to lobby Congress on its behalf.

Companies that no longer exist or may have never existed have donated to Hillary's campaign. Adil Oksuz, who was accused by the Turkish government of coordinating the coup attempt, is part of a group of 2014 suspicious contributions to a super PAC supporting Hillary.

CHAPTER 13

The Department of Homeland Security's statistics show that far more than double the numbers of immigrants from Muslim nations than from the European Union were admitted by the U.S. government. During a five year period, the Obama Administration issued approximately 680,000 green cards to those from Muslim nations from 2009 to 2013. Only 270,000 green cards were issued to immigrants from the EU.

"A green card entitles recipients to access Federal benefits lifetime residency work authorization and a direct route to becoming a US citizen," according to the Senate Judiciary Committee subcommittee on immigration.

The Department of Homeland Security's statistical breakdown of immigrants shows that 83,000 came from Iraq. Pakistan 83,000, Bangladesh 75,000, Iran 7,300, Egypt 45,000, Somalia 31,000, Uzbekistan 24,000, Morocco 22,000, Turkey 22,000, Albania 20,000 Jordan 20,000, Lebanon 16,000, Yemen 16,000, Indonesia 15,000, Syria14,000, Sudan 13,000, Afghanistan 11,000, Sierra Leone 10,000. The rest of the immigrants came from Algeria, Kosovo, Saudi Arabia, and a few thousand from Libya during the five-year period. Only 65,000 green cards were granted to immigrants from the EU (United Kingdom) during the five-year period.

The statistics for 2015 and 2016 have not been released yet. The numbers of illegal immigrants started dropping in late 2014 and early 2015. But when Homeland Security Secretary Jeh Johnson announced new relaxed rules for detaining illegal immigrants, illegals are streaming across the border again.

Judicial Watch, a government watchdog group, reported that the DHS met secretly with a group of extremist Arab Muslim and Sikh organizations to discuss National Security matters. This may be in violation of the Logan Act. And the State Department had sent an anti-American Imam, Feisal Abdul Rauf to the Middle East to gain better understanding and outrage among Muslim majority communities. And President Obama had hired a special Homeland Security adviser, someone who openly supports a radical Islamist theologian and renowned jihadist ideologue, Mohamad Elibiary. They also sent a special Islam envoy that condemns U.S. prosecutions of terrorists because they believe they are "politically-motivated persecutions". The Islam envoy has radical Islamic ideals.

A warning was given concerning workplace discrimination "against individuals who are or perceived to be Muslim or middle eastern" by Obama's administration after the San Bernardino's terrorist attacks. This warning was also issued to American businesses to accommodate the religious needs of Muslims and to ensure that they are not being harassed or intimidated. Obama's administration should have concerned themselves with the victims families and taken action to try to prevent that type of situation ever happening again.

*****

Saif al-islam Gaddafi, the son of Libya's former president, the late Muamar Gaddafi, was sentenced to death in 2015. The trial which started in April 2014 was mired in controversy after human rights groups and the International Criminal Court questioned its standards. The trial which included former regime figures was widely criticized by human rights groups and observers. The International Criminal Court (ICC) indicted Gaddafi, along with Senussi, for war crimes and crimes against humanity. Although The Hague refused Libya permission to try Gaddafi, the ICC gave permission for Senussi to be tried in Libya.

Amnesty International, Human Rights Watch, and the International Bar Association had issued statements criticizing the proceedings. Dr. Mark Ellis, the IBA director, had stated that several trial monitors were arrested and questioned by security forces. John Jones, Gaddafi's ICC appointed lawyer, had condemned the trial process.

"It's a complete show trial of farce. This trial is effectively being run by Libya Dawn militias," Jones stated.

Not attending the trial, Gaddafi, had been held in Zintan since he had been caught trying to flee Libya in the aftermath of the 2011 Revolution. The militia was opposed to Libya Dawn and had refused to hand him over to Tripoli.

Saif al Islam Gaddafi was accused during the trial of recruiting mercenaries, attacking civilian targets from the air, forming armed groups, and shooting into crowds of demonstrators. Among the charges that he was convicted of were incitement to murder and rape. But that sounds eerily familiar for the overthrow of his father, Muammar Gaddafi. Amnesty International had found no evidence of the charges of rape against Muammar Gaddafi's troops. What they did find contradicted those claims. Pristine unopened boxes of Viagra were found next to the burned out trucks which shows they were planted.

In 2015, the death sentence of Saif and others, given by the ICC, in Muammar Gaddafi's government started the most support and demonstrations for Gaddafi's government. Protests were held across the country even in Sirte which was ISIS held at the time. There can be no denying the support by the Libyan people of the Gaddafi government.

During her campaign Hillary Clinton had stated American blood being on Gaddafi's hands. That led to the Lockerbie bombing which Gaddafi had been blamed, and also charged was Senussi, Gaddafi's former intelligence chief. Looking into the bombing so many different scenarios could have been the reason. And it is very probable it had nothing to do with Libya.

So why the death sentence be given to Saif al Islam Gaddafi? He naturally would have been the successor to his father. And that would not work in the scheme of things.

In contrast to Western thought, Gaddafi was loved by his people. It is not possible for one person to stay in power for 42 years without most of the populations support. When Muammar Gaddafi was murdered in 2011, NATO hoped the 'Jamahiriya' movement which was led by Gaddafi would also die. In 2011, Gaddafi's son, Saif, had been captured by the Zintan militia after his father and brother were killed by NATO. The Zintan who were fiercely patriotic to Gaddafi refused the International Criminal Court when it demanded Saif be handed over to them. On France 24 news agency in an interview, Kazim Khan, lawyer of Saif Gaddafi revealed to the world that Saif had been given his liberty on April 12, 2016. This was in accordance with the amnesty law passed by the Tobruk parliament the previous year. The Tobruk parliament, the elected government, never even recognized the trial.

This was a major story but of course the Western media chose to ignore it. Five years after the NATO bombing campaign began, Libyans came out onto the streets in massive demonstrations in support of Saif and of their government in Tripoli, Sirte, Zintan and other cities.

"There is no discounting the genuine support that exists. 'Muammar is the love of millions' was the message written on the hands of women in the Square." This was stated by the BBC.

But after the US-UK-Qatari invasion of Tripoli in June with the reign of terror by NATO's death squads they made the supporters aware that their public show of support could get them killed. NATO's militias rounded up tens of thousands of 'suspected Gaddafi supporters' putting them in detention camps where torture and abuse abounded. Approximately 7000 are still there. Hundreds have been executed.

In particular, black people, were targeted as symbolic of pro African policies that Muammar Gaddafi had held and pursued.

"The forced displacement of roughly 40,000 people, arbitrary detention, torture, and killings are widespread, systematic, and sufficiently organized to be crimes against humanity." This was stated by Human Rights Watch in 2013. But this was not in reference to Gaddafi and his government. This statement made by Human Rights Watch was made in reference to the opposition that Gaddafi was fighting. The statement was made specifically about the brigades, in August 2011, that were centered in Misrata. The opposition brigades forced all 40,000 Tawergha-who are mostly descendants of black slaves, to flee the city that bears their own name.

Dan Glazebook summarizes his findings of Maximilian Forte's, Slouchinging Towards Sirte:

50 sub Saharan African migrants were burnt alive in Al-Bayda on the second day of the Insurgency. An Amnesty International report from September 2011 made it clear that this was no isolated incident. "When Al-Bayda, Benghazi, Derna, Misrata, and other cities first fell under the control of the NTC in February, anti Gaddafi forces carried out house

raids, killings, and other violent attacks" against sub-Saharan Africans and black Libyans and "what we are seeing in Western Libya is a very similar pattern to what we have seen in Benghazi and Misrata after the city fell to the rebels" - arbitrary detention, torture, and execution of black people.

Opposition figures claimed that the blacks were mercenaries hired by Gaddafi. This was just an attempt to cover up their racist violence. But of course this was also a lie. And Hillary also laid claim to the lies.

Muammar Gaddafi had proposed a 72-hour truce.

In, Lemond Diplomatique, Jean Ping of Gabon asked the question, "Why were we not given a chance to implement our plan that Gaddafi had accepted?"

The plan that Jean Ping, the African Union commission chairperson, spoke of was for Gadaffi to go into exile. But he said that the effort was thwarted by Western intervention.

An analyst on African Union Affairs, Mehari Taddele Mane, said, "The chances that Gaddafi would have left Libya for one of the African countries were high."

Using military intervention to solve what it considered a political problem in Libya, the African Union strongly opposed using military intervention to solve what it considered, Libya's political problem. Hillary had instructed the Joint Chiefs of Staff not to negotiate with the Libyan government. In the U.S. Pentagon officials were extremely frustrated with Hillary's Libya policy that even after she had ordered them to cease contact with Gadaffi the officials continued their own communication with the Gaddafi regime.

Former representative Dennis Kucinich was also in contact with Libyan officials. But he was also ignored by the State Department and the White House. Pentagon audio tapes proved that Gaddafi's son, Saif, called a U.S. general to try to negotiate a ceasefire. A Pentagon official asset told Gaddafi's son, Saif, in a telephone call "Everything I am getting from the State Department is that they do not care about being part of this. Secretary Clinton does not want to negotiate at all".

Remember Saif wanted a democracy for Libya but Hillary was not interested in that objective.

The Libyan government later made another attempt to negotiate through an intermediary. The intermediary was American businessman and former U.S. Navy officer Charles Kubic.

According to Kubic, General Carter Ham, head of AFRICOM, agreed to participate in the effort to stop the war. But Hillary's staff was closely monitoring the effects that the Obama's illegal bank seizures were having on the Gaddafi government.

Gaddafi still proposed a 72-hour truce. He said then he would step down to allow for a transition provided that NATO agreed to maintain the Libyan Army, lift sanctions against him and his family, and provide them safe passage. Sadly murder was desired instead of Gaddafi's safe passage out of Libya.

Gaddafi's motorcade was traveling under the White Flag, the flag of surrender. They were driving to a site designated by Hillary's State Department where Gaddafi would turn himself over to US and NATO authorities. But with the approval of Hillary, his motorcade was attacked and he was killed, shot to death. And arresting Saif and the giving of his death sentence ensured that he could not take over control of the Libyan government.

After the opposition controlled Tripoli in August 2011, Sidney Blumenthal urged Hillary to make the most of the victory. In his email to Hillary, Blumenthal wrote; when Qaddafi himself is finally removed you should of course make a public statement before the cameras... This is a very big moment historically and for you. History will tell your part in it. You are vindicated...

Odd that he would add that last part. Hillary had forwarded this email to Jake Sullivan and wrote; "Sid makes a good case for what I should say, but it's premised on being said after Q (Qaddafi) goes, which will make it more dramatic. That's my hesitancy, since I'm not sure how many chances I'll get."

Will make it more dramatic? They are planning on killing Muammar Gaddafi who they have lied about and made out to be an absolute monster and Hillary is concerned about dramatics. How sad.

Hillary had also laid claim to the line of attack in which Susan Rice claimed that Gaddafi was giving his troops Viagra to encourage rape. But it was discovered to be not true by Amnesty International. Sid Blumenthal had emailed Hillary the Viagra allegation in March. But he did stress that it was not confirmed.

So what it comes down to is that Hillary, Obama and other American officials lied about the humanitarian threat posed by Gaddafi. They also armed the opposition knowing that they were a force with Al-Qaeda allies and other terrorist groups.

Testifying before a grand jury investigation CIA officer David Manners stated; "It was then and remains now, my opinion that the United States did participate, directly, or indirectly, in the supply of weapons to the Libyan Transitional National Council."

Among its Western allies, the United States leads the war against any nation that stands in the way of it's total domination.

Experts say that Muammar Qaddafi was one of the wealthiest men in the world who ever existed. He was worth approximately $200 billion. He had his own central bank of Libya. His country had no debt. Before Gadaffi's assets were frozen and 8 days after the Libyan revolt began, Executive Order 13566 was executed. In part Executive Order 13566 reads;

"I, Barack Obama the President of the United States of America find that Colonel Muammar Gaddafi, his government, and Close Associates have taken Extreme Measures against the people of Libya including by using weapons of war, mercenaries, and wanton violence against unarmed civilians. I further find that there is a serious risk that Libyan State assets will be misappropriated by Qaddafi members of his government members of his family or his Close Associates if those assets are not protected."

The Treasury Undersecretary for Terrorism and Financial Intelligence Stuart Levey, who drafted the order, began the orders directives and froze billions of Gaddafi's assets that were held in banks across the United States. This was a coordinated effort. After all of the U.S Embassy Personnel had been evacuated from Libya, the bank personnel, who were waiting through the night, carried out Obama's plan. Around $30 billion in liquid assets and cash were seized. Gaddafi's assets in the amount of $60 billion, as of the summer of 2015, had been seized by banks in the United States, Germany, and United Kingdom. Hillary and her staff were closely monitoring the effects the bank seizures were having on Gaddafi's government. One of

Hillary's emails, April 1, 2011, just after President Obama seized upwards of $60 billion;

"On April 2, 2011, sources with access to advisors of Saif al Islam Gaddafi stated in strictest confidence that while the freezing of Libya's foreign bank accounts presents Muammar Gaddafi with serious challenges, his ability to equip and maintain his armed forces and intelligence services remains intact. According to sensitive information available to these individuals Gaddafi's government holds 143 tons of gold, and a similar amount in silver. During late March 2011 the stocks were moved to SABHA (southwest in the direction of the Libyan border with Niger and Chad); taken from the vaults of the Libyan Central Bank in Tripoli."

Phil Butler, policy investigator and analyst, a political scientist and expert on Eastern Europe, gives his opinion and interesting facts on the overthrow of Gaddafi;

"The overthrow of Gaddafi by the American Administration with the help of the United Nations will go down in history as the kindling of the most catastrophic foreign policy scheme in history. The evidence surfacing now can only lead us to one conclusion. Take the fact the former head of the LIFG, Norman Benotman, is currently the president of Quillam Foundations in London, and the fact he was in Tripoli working with the British government at the time of Gaddafi's demise attest to the dastardly and deep game of subterfuge affecting us all. Benotman tweets today in prolific and cryptic 140 characters that appear insane or at best unbalanced. Without delving into this character's mysterious past suffice it to point out that Quillam was established in 2007 by Ed Husain, Maajid Nawaz, and Rashad Zaman Ali, three former members of the islamist group Hizb ut-Tahrir. Named for the controversial William Quillam, the society is based on the concept of a global caliphate its namesake having sworn allegiance to the Ottoman Empire. Though the Quillam Organization appears outwardly to be a real puppet of Britain's anti extremist Islam operation some experts wonder if the organization is not operating in a "duality" of purpose.

Either way the intended goals of LIFG have been well-served by Benotman and other assets. From my perspective as a dissenter to the mainstream propaganda simply discovering Quillam's founding father is Maajid Nawaz, Op Ed master of the ubiquitous tabloid The Daily Beast is enough to categorize the organization as part of the problem and not the solution to world chaos. Ties between Nawaz the Next-Gen Foundation, Quillam shares offices within the US and ultimately former Secretary of State Hillary Clinton, they whisper "double agent" to me. This is only speculative on my part though. I won't start connecting the dots that lead to Google the Clinton Foundation and the neoconservative life lines holding up Clinton for President either. Our world system becomes suspect, as certainly it must."

CHAPTER 14

"The future does not belong to those who slander the prophet of Islam."

This statement was made by President Obama at the 2012 UN General Assembly. That may be part of the reason the Obama administration tried to have the "Innocence of Muslims" the film that was blamed for the attacks on Benghazi, removed from YouTube. The U.S. State Department spent $70,000 on a Pakistani television advertisement rebuking the film. $70,000 of taxpayers money was used to remove an advertisement in Pakistan to remove an anti-muslim video. Even though they knew from the beginning the film had nothing to do with the Benghazi attack. The Obama administration had the maker of the film arrested on charges that were unrelated to the film. But. The US government funded an inflammatory piece of art depicting Christ in a blasphemous way which was on display in New York. That artist was not arrested. If the artist had used Mohamed instead of Christ there would have been outrage. The U.S. would never be allowed to display artwork entitled "Piss Mohammed". But the Obama Administration allowed Christ to be depicted this way. President of the Catholic League, Bill Donahue, said that there is a "protected" class for Muslims. "I would like to find out what my government is going to say about this," he said.

The Obama Administration said nothing in condemning the artwork.

Muslims, the Muslim Brotherhood, even ISIS seems to be either protected, elected, or ignored.

These are some of the directions of the ISIS Manifesto: The Management of Savagery/Chaos, a tract which was written more than a decade ago by Abu Bakr Naji, for the Mesopotamian wing of al-Qaeda which would become ISIS;

"Diversify and widen the vexation strikes against the Crusader-Zionist enemy in every place in the Islamic world and even outside of it if possible, so as to disperse the efforts of the alliance of the enemy and thus drain it to the greatest extent possible."

"If a tourist resort that the Crusaders patronize... is hit, all of tourist resorts in all of the states of the world will have to be secured by the work of additional forces which are double the ordinary amount, and a huge increase in spending."

"Capture the rebellious youth, use their energy and idealism and their Readiness for self-sacrifice while fools preach 'moderation' (twasatiyyah), security and avoidance of risk."

"Work to expose the weakness of America's centralized power by pushing it to abandon the media psychological war and the war by proxy until it fights directly."

ISIS organization's strategy is finding, creating, and managing chaos. Islamic State says that it's "the first of the storm". And they have a framework for recruitment which is called the Grey Zone. It is a 10 page editorial in Dabiq, ISIS online magazine, in early 2015.

The attacks in Paris, Belgium, Turkey, San Bernardino, and Orlando are installments in ISIS' strategic storm.

Dabiq quoted Osama bin Laden; "The world today is divided. Bush spoke the truth when he said, "Either you are with us or you are with the terrorists, with the actual (terrorists) being the Western Crusaders."

"The time has come for another event to bring division to the world and to destroy the grey zone."

The grey zone Bin Laden spoke of is the nonexistent world where most Muslims feels exists between good and evil, the caliphate (good) and the Infidel (evil).

More attacks will continue to create ISIS "storm", and to fill a void wherever a state of "chaos" or "savagery" exists. And where there is insufficient chaos in the "House of War," (the lands of the Infidel), ISIS will create it.

And the atrocities committed by ISIS are so abominable.

This is an email received from Chief Counsel for American Center for Law and Justice, Jeff Sekulow;

Christians face catastrophic persecution like no other time in history... Christian Asia Bibi has been on death row in Pakistan over 2,100 days (Her punishment was for offering a Muslim a drink of water. Christian's, any non-muslims, are infidels). Christian attorneys in Kenya face corrupt killings as they protect girls from sexual slavery. Christian children in the Middle East are cut in half, others crucified. It's mind-numbing. (Children are also raped and tortured in front of their parents so that they will conform to Islam.) Our offices across the globe in Pakistan, Africa, Europe and the Middle East are aggressively battling to defend persecuted Christians from torture, imprisonment, and death. We've helped free Christian pastors facing death in Iran and Sudan. We're actively fighting for Asia Bibi's freedom.

And, Obama is denying Christian Refugees safe passage to the United States but allows illegal criminal immigrants. It looks as if only Muslims are allowed in. As in other countries. Does this not seem odd to anyone else?

In 2008, in Murfreesboro Tennessee the Islamic Center of Murfreesboro denied a court order to cease Construction of a 52,960 square foot Mega mosque. It was supposedly meant to accommodate a couple hundred families. Billions of dollars with questionable finances had been spent to build this mosque. Mosaad Rowash, board member of the Islamic Center of Murfreesboro is associated with the Muslim American Society (MAS) which is a front group for the Muslim Brotherhood.

The Muslim Brotherhood is the largest Islamic organization in the world that is designated as a terrorist group. The Muslim Brotherhood is the forefathers of Hamas and Al-Qaeda.

In the US the Muslim Brotherhood is represented by the Muslim Student Association, Muslim American Society, Islamic Society of North America, Islamic Circle of North America, North American Trust International, Institute of Islamic Thought, and many other organizations.

All of these organizations are listed in the Muslim Brotherhood, "Explanatory Memorandum on the General Strategic Goal for the Brotherhood of North America" This memorandum proclaims: The process of settlement is a Civilization Jihadist Process. The Muslim Brotherhood must understand that their work in America is a kind of grand Jihad in eliminating and destroying the Western civilization from within and "sabotaging" it's miserable house by their hands and the hands of the believers so that it is eliminated and allah's religion is made Victorious over all other religions."

Notice that the memorandum states that it is trying to destroy and sabotage its miserable house by their hands. Not just by the Muslim Brotherhood's hands but by the Western, America's hands. This is done through the infiltration of the American government.

The Islamic Center of Murfreesboro spokesman, Dr. Selah M. Sbenaty, is one of the original founders of the mosque. Sbenaty studied in Syria and then left Syria when the Muslim Brotherhood was expelled in 1982. One of his brothers fears for Sbenaty's safety in the US. He feels that Bashar al-Assad could reach him here and harm him. Why would he be afraid of Bashar al-Assad? Unless of course he knows that Bashar al Assad fights against radical Islamic terrorists.

Often stated about the ISIS recruits is that they are desperate, uneducated, and poor. But the World Bank released a study on the recruit's country of origin, education level, skills, and marriage status who joined ISIS between early 2013 and late 2014. No facts were found to connect a low education level or poverty and joining ISIS.

The documents, smuggled out by a former ISIS member, referenced the interviewing and vetting process of 331 foreign recruits between 2013 and 2014. The study found that wealthier countries were a source for recruitment more often than poorer ones.

The study also found that 69% of the recruits had received a high school education and many from North Africa and the Middle East attended a university. The study also compared the education levels of the recruits to the average education levels of citizens in their country of origin. And the recruits were significantly more educated than the country's citizens.

From their entry-interviews, the recruits who showed a desire to become suicide bombers were found to be the most financially established.

The World Association of Muslim Youth (WAMY) was created through the collaboration of the Wahhabist and Muslim brotherhood-led by Said Ramadan. Ramadan was the son-in-law of Hassan al-Banna the founder of the Muslim Brotherhood which included Abdullah Omar Naseef and Ahmed Bahefzallah, the Abedin's (Huma Abedin's family) immediate boss.

The founders of the institute for Muslim Minority Affairs which the Abedin's ran in the west was the same as the leader of the founders of the world Association of Muslim Youth. The World Association of Muslim Youth coalesced when Muslim leaders and Scholars came to Mecca to create and launch it worldwide.

The Muslim Manifesto which is translated from Arabic to English tells us; "The Muslim Societies in all continents of the world exist in either a Muslim Nation or Muslim minorities. The assessment to determine what constitutes state from a minority state is done based on a number of measures. First the number scale which is if a nation has Muslims who exceed half the population and its Constitution states that Islam is it's official religion or that Islamic Sharia is it source of law, this state is then considered an Islamic State."

"Since the number of Muslims has risen greatly in the last year where they became 1.3 billion Muslims from these we have 900 million already and Muslim nations. The 400 million with communities and as Muslim minority.... So according to the statistics it is expected that the number of Muslims will reach 2,000,600,000 (2 billion) within a short span of time. The Muslims will then become a mighty and effective power in the world, of course, due to the increase in their numbers, then shift the demographic balance in their favor."

Lt. Gen. (ret.) William G. "Jerry" Boykin, former head of Special Operations Command, said the "Explanatory Memorandum," a jihadist document, shows the radical Islamists plan to "infiltrate every element of our society, including the church."

"It's a five step phase plan to take over America. It's unfolding right now. Now there are more specific plans that they have for how they are going to take over. And as Kamal Saleem said they're going to infiltrate every element of our society, including the church."

The Explanatory Memorandum was found during a federal investigation covering fundraising for the terrorist group Hamas and the Holy Land Foundation.

"It's called the Explanatory Memorandum. It was found in 2004 in Annandale, Virginia, in the basement of the guy that ultimately was discovered was – what would you say? – operations officer for the Muslim Brotherhood. They found this Explanatory Memorandum.

"In the book, that John [Guandolo] was part of writing that book, the book is called Sharia: The Threat, and there's a copy of it [Explanatory Memorandum] in there. It lays out a five-phase plan."

John Guandolo exposes the 'Explanatory Memorandum', in his book, Sharia, The Threat.

"It's a five-phase plan to takeover America. Now, it's broad in nature but if you'll look at it you'll say, 'Holy mackerel, they're doing this.' It's unfolding right now."

"Now there are more specific plans that they have for how they're going to take over. And as Kamal said, they're going to infiltrate every element of our society, including the church."

"They're infiltrating every element of our society while we are trying to believe that there is a big separation between the radical Muslims and the moderate Muslims. And the reality is, John [Guandolo] said it, the moderate Muslims are just simply Muslims that have chosen not to follow the teachings of the Quran and the hadith. And there are a lot of them, and God bless them. I wish that more of them would refuse to follow it."

Lt. Gen. William G. 'Jerry' Boykin, one of the original members of Delta Force which he later commanded, also commanded the Green Berets and the Special Warfare Center and School. Lt. Gen. Boykin was Deputy Undersecretary of Defense for Intelligence in his last 36 years in the military.

To support retired Lt. Gen. Boykins, the information below shows the Islamists plan to subdue America.

Huma Abedin, Deputy Chief of Staff for Hillary when she was Secretary of State, worked for the Muslim Brotherhood magazine, The Muslim Minority Affairs (IMMA). So mostly her connections seem to be her and her family's relationship to the magazine. But it goes much deeper than that. Even more so than Huma's mother, Saleha. She was not only a member but also a leader, one of the 63 leaders, of the Muslim Brotherhood Sisterhood branch. For decades the Abedins have been affiliated with Abdullah Omar Naseef, an al-Qaeda financier. Naseef had appointed the

Abedin's to start the Institute of Muslim Minority Affairs. Working with Abdullah Omar Naseef was enough to raise many red flags. President Obama paid tribute to Huma Abedin and showed strong support for her at a Muslim Iftar dinner stating that she had been "nothing less than extraordinary in representing our country and the Democrat values that we hold dear". She was Hillary's deputy chief of staff who stored top secret and classified information on a home computer.

She may have represented these values due to her position at the time but how could she hold these values when having been associated with a Muslim Brotherhood organization. It is important to remember President Obama bowing to the king of Saudi Arabia. A former Muslim Brotherhood member had researched, in Arabic, Huma's father, Syed Zaynul Abedin. In his research he found the Wahhabist plans for Saudi Arabia commissioned by the House of Saud and this plan included the Abedins Institute for Muslim Minority Affairs. One of the books included in his research was titled, The Effects of the Servant of the Two Holy Places, King Fahd bin Abdul Aziz to Support the Muslim Minorities. This book was approved by the king.

The house of Saud had another Alliance which was the Muslim Minority Affairs which the Abedin's played a major role. Huma's father, Syed Abedin's work, Muslim Minority in the West, was used by the house of Saud as part of 29 works to construct a plan to conquer the world with Islam. The Muslim Minority Affairs in the West was a major discussion in which the US was mentioned throughout. Through this work and the internet the former Muslim Brotherhood member, who speaks Arabic, found more unknowns about the Abedin family. This work explains that the Muslim Minority Affairs was not just a title but a Saudi foreign policy and commandment from the highest of authorities commissioned by the Saudi Ministry of Religious Affairs. This is an entire management system. And it is using the Muslim Minority Affairs as the main vehicle to bring victory against an infidel world. And that defines anyone who is not Muslim. This management system speaks of recruiting Muslims in non-Muslim lands and transform them as a collective unit. It also states the educational programs, mosques, and organizations already established in the US as ISNA and MSA which are all focused toward hindering any Western plan for Muslim assimilation in a non-muslim host nation. It lists key agents to protect Muslims assimilation such as the Muslim Society of North America (ISNA) and the Muslim Students Association (MSA) established in the US in 1962. It also listed centers and mosques in the major cities in the US that were established to carry out this mission. It is a mission which is more of a political system which runs parallel with their religion. When those who are not fluent in Arabic speak of Muslims they usually talk about the assimilation of Muslims into US culture. But that is covert assimilation, to enter into a cultural system and blend in without being influenced by that culture. Billions of dollars were spent to procure that Muslims would be an unassimilated group. This is to ensure the Muslims can influence the non-muslim host nation and other nations even if the number of Muslims is small. This is done by shifting the demographic scales in favor of the Saudi agenda due to their population growth. A gradual change would occur that would eventually become a major revolutionary power which would move the host nation whether the US, Europe, or wherever to their population growth. It's plan is to transform a nation from within with the intention of implementing the Wahhabist plans. This was not expected to be revealed, discussed, or translated. But in becoming an ex-Muslim Brotherhood member he was able to find and translate it. Another document that he discovered and translated was an official testimony which discusses how during the Haji (Pilgrimage) in 1965, the parent Organization for the Abedin's Institute for Muslim Minority, the World Association of Muslim Youth (WAMY) was created. Muslim leaders and scholars came to Mecca to create it and implemented it worldwide. The World Association of Muslim Youth was created by the Wahabbist and Muslim Brotherhood led by Said Ramadan who was the son-in-law of Hasan al-Banna the founder of the Muslim Brotherhood and financiers as the wealthy Abdullah Omar Naseef, and Ahmed Bahefzallah who is the Abedin's immediate boss.

This alone should remind us not to allow the Muslim population through illegal immigration in America to grow. Their Constitution states that Islam is the official religion or that Islamic Sharia is its source of law if a nation has Muslims who exceed half the population. Then that state has been considered an Islamic State. And that is exactly their plan. They want every nation to be Islamic and for its law to be Sharia. They want to conquer the United States and the rest of the world and their Quran tells them that peace exists only when non-believers convert to Islam. And if not converted, then peace exists when non believers are dead, and in the Qur'an tenets Muslims are commanded to kill nonbelievers.

CHAPTER 15

Huma Abedin and other Muslims in American government are part of the Wahabbist plan. Muslim's plan for covert assimilation into non Muslim lands includes transforming that country from within and gradually implementing the Wahabbist (religious movement or branch of Sunni Islam) plans created by the house of Saud. That is how they are using Huma, from within our own government. This assimilation into the non-Muslim host Nations is to be a gradual change ensuring a major revolutionary power that will tilt the host nation in favor of Muslims due to their increased population. How much power would Huma Abedin attain if Hillary Clinton was elected president of the United States? That is a frightening thought.

Consider the Nations that have had or are having uprisings. Who are the rebels that are taking control? Radical islamists. The demographic balance is certainly shifting in Islam's favor.

Allen B. West asked an important question. West asked, "I do have a question for all of you folks out there with a "Coexist" bumper sticker on your Prius; How many churches and synagogues are in Saudi Arabia?"

In answer to his own question West said, "We have more mosques than Saudi Arabia has synagogues or churches."

He then said, "When intolerance becomes a one-way street, it leads to cultural suicide."

His meaning by that statement was exactly what the Muslim Brotherhood's Memorandum is exhorting. They want to destroy our way of life and replace it with their own.

Of the minorities in America, Muslims supposedly embrace the secular American way. And they overall earn more money than non-Muslim's. Really? A 2007 Pew poll represents American Muslims are comfortable when viewing themselves as part of America. According to the poll just five percent of American Muslims express any support for Al-Qaeda. And mostly condemned suicide attacks for any reason. They have an overall positive view of America and its promise for Muslims. But that is the way the Muslim Brotherhood Memorandum works. They immigrate and covertly assimilate into our culture only to influence our ways with theirs until their ways are tolerated and then accepted. And then our customs are replaced with their customs and our way of life in America is "eliminated" and eventually the religion of allah is victorious which dictates Sharia law. And that is their plans for our "miserable" house to be destroyed by our own hands because we have accepted it. Most feel that it would be impossible for them to do this. When the radical islamists overtake foreign governments, Sharia law is instituted. If the people do not accept Islam they are then murdered. Of course, that does not as a whole represent all Muslims. Some Muslims do not support the Quran's Sharia law.

Looking back over the last 6-8 years the US has seen a great change happening across the country. Some Muslims demand some cities and states implement Sharia Law here in America.

*****

When top Isis leader Al- Salafi was captured, he told Pakistan's officials that the Obama Administration had allowed the US banking system to filter funds to make sure ISIS was funded. Obama's appointee for Director of the Defense Intelligence Agency, General Michael Flynn, had accused Obama of knowingly and willingly arming Isis.

Four star Navy Admiral James "Aa" Lyons, former commander-in-chief US Pacific Fleet also accused Obama of treason and of deliberately disarming the military, colluding with the enemy, providing arms to the enemy, and allowing the Muslim Brotherhood to infiltrate every level of our government. Admiral Lyons also stated that he believes Obama has been acting as a foreign agent who deliberately orchestrated a massive infiltration of the US government. Many believe this but have not been so upfront in stating it. Even the US CIA has accused Obama and Hillary of funding ISIS. Retired US Force Lieutenant General Thomas Mcinerney and also retired US Army General Paul had claimed that Obama has allowed terrorists from within the Muslim Brotherhood to infect the whole government. President Obama said himself that he was raised and surrounded by communists his whole life. Radical Islam has been equated with Nazi fascism.

General Michael Flynn was appointed by President Obama to key national security jobs including Department Director of National Intelligence and later as Director of the Defense Intelligence Agency. General Flynn stated that President Obama had never once met with him. He was never asked for his assessment of ISIS in the Middle East or during the political meltdown of Libya and Egypt. Nor on Iran's efforts to build a nuclear bomb.

Flynn stated, "Here is the crux of my relationship with Obama. Here I am running one of the largest intelligence agencies in the world. He appoints me twice, one as the Assistant Director of National Intelligence and one as the Director of the Defense Intelligence Agency. I'm also his senior intelligence officer. And I had almost 5 years in combat. I never met with him once."

General Flynn, along with Iran and Middle East expert, Michael Ledeen, has written a book about the threat of terrorism, The Field of Flight-How We Can Win the Global War Against Radical Islam and Its Allies.

General Flynn described his feelings on Hillary; "She is somebody that you get the impression that she's got some other hidden agenda. I always felt where there were interactions, there is some other hidden agenda there that doesn't necessarily have the best interest of the country. Something else is going on."

He said that one of Hillary's biggest failures was the Russian reset. The reset was an initiative of Hillary's in an effort to restore a congenial relationship with Russian President Vladimir Putin.

"The Russian reset was a complete failure. That was her sort of baby. She lacked the understanding of how Russia deals on the global stage and how Russia deals with people, personalities, and also on nation on nation, and the way they see us. She went into it with a level of arrogance and a lack of understanding. That Russian reset actually could have turned into something that resulted in some sort of military mutual respect. But in fact under her leadership it completely collapsed," General Flynn stated.

On Hillary's acceptance of foreign money to the Clinton Foundation, Flynn said, "The fact that she takes $1 from Saudi Arabia as any kind of a donation is a disgrace. Any of these countries destroy women's (and children's) rights. And then she stands there and claims that she's for women."

Flynn said, "Hillary should give back every red penny that she gets from these guys. Then she can talk about women's rights."

*****

The Boycott Divestment and Sanctions Movement is all about undermining Israel's legitimacy as a Jewish state and destroying the Jewish people politically and economically. These enemies are taking their hatred of Israel to the US federal court. They are suing numerous organizations that support Israel. Also their suit is against citizen's businesses, and nonprofit groups and a long list of major US companies and individuals who dare to do business in, or support Israel. The biggest federal court case ever with Israel's legitimacy as a Jewish State on the line is Tamimi vs. Adelson. This is the biggest attempt in US legal history to delegitimize the state of Israel and to strip the Jewish people of the right to live on Israeli land. Palestinian activists have filed a billion dollar lawsuit against numerous entities who support or do business with Israel. They are charging them with conspiracy to war crimes and other charges. They are using American courts to assault Israel legally. But the American Center for Law and Justice is fighting against the Palestinian activists who have filed this lawsuit. The ACLJ is representing one of the many Israel-based charities, the Gush Etzion Foundation, which is dedicated to preserving one of the most historically significant regions of Israel.

The Jews of Gush Etzion were massacred by the Arab Legion before the state of Israel came into existence in 1948. But after the 1967 Six Day War, the Jews returned and started rebuilding their country. Those 450 Jews and four villages have become 90,000 Jews in 22 cities and towns. Israel's enemies are accusing the Gush Etzion Foundation in American federal courts of arms trafficking, war crimes, conspiracy, violence, and more. But the Gush Etzion Foundation is a peaceful organization dedicated to building schools and libraries, providing food for the needy, security for residential towns, and emergency medical services after terrorist attacks.

It is absolutely absurd that the Palestinians are bringing this case against Israel in American courts. Israel has been in the crosshairs of their enemies with rockets, and violence aimed at the Jewish people, the Palestinian Authority partnering with Hamas terrorists, President Obama threatening to use the UN to divide Jerusalem, war crimes charges at the ICC, the BDS movement aiming to delegitimize the Jewish state, and now the case against Israel by the Palestinians in American courts.

And other country's leaders have turned Benjamin Netanyahu's words into something completely opposite of what he was saying.

Benjamin Netanyahu had made a plea in 2015 for Jews to leave Europe due to anti-Semitic terror attacks. He said that Israel is the only country in the world where Jews can feel safe. Denmark's Chief Rabbi, Jair Melchior, said he was "disappointed" in Netanyahu. And European leaders were angry at his plea for Jews to leave Europe.

French president Francois Hollande stated, "I will not just let what was said in Israel pass, leading people to believe that Jews no longer have a place in Europe and in France in particular."

But that is not what Netanyahu had stated. He feels that his people would be safer in Israel.

German Chancellor Angela Merkel said her government is doing everything possible to protect Jewish sites. But Merkel has allowed radical Islam to spread throughout Germany. And no one can deny radical islamists hatred of Jews. The joint chair of Britain's parliamentary Committee Against anti-Semitism, attacked Netanyahu's statement, "Mr. Netanyahu made the same remarks in Paris. It's just crude electioneering. It's no coincidence that there is a general election in Israel coming up. The comments are not helpful and I think people will ignore them... We're not prepared to tolerate a situation in this country or in any country in Europe where any Jews feel they have to leave."

Why the contempt from these people? Netanyahu had made the plea to Jewish people to protect them. His statement was made after a deadly terror attack in Copenhagen and one month after four hostages were killed at a Paris kosher deli. Since 2012, French terrorists had been accused of deadly attacks on Jewish sites that include a school in the southern city of Toulouse, and at a museum in Brussels, and at a Kosher deli.

Benjamin Netanyahu's cabinet approved $46 million plan to encourage Jewish emigration from France, Belgium, and Ukraine. These countries have large numbers of Jews that have expressed their desire to move to Israel. A prominent Jewish MP in British Parliament, Louise Ellman, also had stated her opinion of Netanyahu's call to Jews. "I just cannot agree with what he has said... It is the responsibility of all governments to look after their citizens and that includes Jewish citizens."

But that is exactly what Benjamin Netanyahu is trying to do, protect the Jewish people. Netanyahu has also repeatedly warned of the danger to the International Community of allowing Iran to develop nuclear weapons. The European Jewish Association had called for round-the-clock security at Jewish institutions. And they have demanded more action by national governments. Jewish communities in France and Belgium have experienced deadly attacks in recent years. Netanyahu's idea of Jews coming to Israel does not sound so outrageous as these leaders have stated.

Danish Prime Minister, Helle Thorning Schmidt, told reporters, "They belong in Denmark, they are a strong part of our community and we will do everything we can to protect the Jewish community in our country."

Although Denmark, known for Islamic extremism, does not charge jihadists who return to the country with terrorism. They are offered rehabilitation. The Danish government enrolls them in a program of counseling and mentoring, education, or vocational training. How ridiculous.

This program was strongly opposed by Maria Krupp an MP for the conservative Danish People's Party. She said, "The project is misconceived. It rewards for violence."

"This wave of attacks is expected to continue. Jews deserve Security in every country but we say to our Jewish brothers and sisters Israel is your home," Netanyahu told his cabinet. The migration of French Jews to Israel has increased. In 2014, seven thousand French Jews left. And in 2013, more than double that number had left. This movement to Israel increased after the March 2012 attack by Mohammad Merah who killed three children and a rabbi at a Jewish school in Toulouse.

Netanyahu's other statements on the Jewish return to Israel included, "To the Jews of Europe and to the Jews of the world, I say that Israel is waiting for you with open arms."

"Extremist Islamic terrorism has struck in Europe again... Jews have been murdered again on European soil only because they were Jews."

Netanyahu's concern for the Jewish people should be commended, not held in contempt by other countries.

In one of Benjamin Netanyahu's meetings with President Obama he discussed the dangers of the region of Israel in which he lives. Obama interrupted Netanyahu, "Bibi you have to understand something I'm the African American son of a single mother and I live here in this house. I live in the White House. I managed to get elected President of the United States. You think I don't understand what you're talking about, but I do."

Living in the White House even though he was the son of a single mother does not give understanding of the problems Israel and Benjamin Netanyahu faces more recently in the past decade, but also years before that. Obama has been heading in the direction of anti-Israel when America has always been and should be pro-Israel.

CHAPTER 16

Obama stated, "ISIS is not an existential threat to the United States. Climate change is a potential existential threat to the entire world if we don't do something about it."

He is saying that a threat to the U.S. from ISIS does not exist. How preposterous.

Obama also said that very little is accomplished in international affairs without U.S. leadership. This has been proven by the backing, financially and politically, to overthrow democratically elected governments of other countries.

President Obama equated the protesters in Tunisia and Tahrir Square with Rosa Parks and the "Patriots of Boston".

"After decades of accepting the world as it is in the region we have a chance to pursue the world as it should be," Obama had stated in a speech during that time. But as it should be according to whom?

"The United States supports a set of universal rights. And these rights include free speech, the freedom of peaceful assembly, the freedom of religion, equality for men and women under the rule of law... Our support for these principles is not a secondary interest," he said.

But his support is only given with concern to Muslims. And the remark of equating the protesters of Tunisia with Rosa Parks is not equal or even close. It is disgraceful.

In Tunisia, a 27 year old man, Mohamed Bouazzi, set himself on fire after pouring gasoline over himself. He was supposedly protesting because of the payoffs police officials demanded from him after selling fruits and vegetables to provide for his family. But if he was protesting to be able to provide for his family why would he be willing to commit suicide? What would happen to his family then? Knowingly, radical Islamists commit suicide and this was the action that supposedly set off the Arab Spring. Almost with every revolution in the middle east and Africa, they have been instigated by radical islamists.

Obama also stated speaking of Libya, "So we actually executed this plan as well as I could have expected we got a UN mandate we built the Coalition it cost us $1 billion which when it comes to military operations is very cheap."

They spent $1 billion of taxpayer's money to kill a man who did not commit the crimes he was accused of and left that country in ruins, and then left Americans in Benghazi to die. Also $1 billion is a mere penance to pay for the amount of money that Muammar Gaddafi was worth which someone has.

He was slated as one of the wealthiest men in the world. He was worth over $200 billion. And the American government and other countries froze his assets. This money did not go to help the Libyan people.

Obama said, "We averted large-scale civilian casualties we prevented what mostly would have been a prolonged and bloody civil conflict. And despite all that, Libya is a mess."

Large-scale civilian casualties were not prevented. The US intervention caused large-scale civilian casualties by allowing the Islamic terrorists to take control. And Libya is a prolonged and bloody conflict. And Libya is "a mess".

But Libya is not a large-scale civilian conflict. It is a conflict between terrorist groups.

He went on to lay blame on French President Nicolas Sarkozy and British Prime Minister David Cameron "because he became distracted by a range of other things".

"Sarzoky wanted to trumpet the flights he was taking in the air campaign despite the fact that we have wiped out all of the air defenses and essentially set up the entire infrastructure" for the intervention in Benghazi.

The US. did set up the entire infrastructure for the intervention in Benghazi and it funded and allowed it to be led by the radical islamist groups.

He also laid blame on the internal Libyan dynamics. "The degree of tribal division in Libya it was greater than our analysts had expected. And our ability to have any kind of structure there that we could interact with and start providing resources broke down very quickly." That's because they had no interest in Libya afterwards.

And that's because that's what happens when dealing with terrorists.

"There is no way we should commit to governing the Middle East and North Africa. That would be a basic fundamental mistake," he said.

Too late, they have already been governing these areas. And they are fighting against Bashar al-Assad and supporting the opposition, ISIS.

Obama told the New Yorker that the many jihadist groups in Iraq and Syria are terrorist's "jayvee team".

ISIS - A jayvee team?

In contrast to what President Obama says about ISIS not being a real threat to the United States, CIA director John Brennan stated that, "ISIL has a large cadre of Western fighters who could potentially serve as operatives for attacks in the West."

He feels that ISIL is working to smuggle them into countries among refugee flows or by using legitimate travel means. The director also called IS a "formidable adversary".

"Unfortunately despite all our progress against ISIL on the battlefield and in the financial realm, our efforts have not reduced the group's terrorism capability and Global reach. In fact as the pressure mounts on ISIL we judged that it will intensify its Global Terror campaign to maintain its dominance of the global terrorism agenda."

Isis had taken control of at least two oil fields in Libya and attacked the Dhahra oil field according to oil and government sources. ISIS is far more than an "existential threat", or militia, or network of terrorist cells; it's practically a nation.

CHAPTER 17

When asked by Juan Gonzalez why Wikileaks' Julian Assange "did this and what the importance was of being able to create a searchable base," Assange stated;

"Well, Wikileaks has become the rebel Library of Alexandria. It is the simple most significant collection of information that doesn't exist elsewhere in a searchable, accessible, citable form, about how institutions actually behave. And it's gone on to set people free from prison. We can't possibly hope to reform that which we do not understand.

"So those Hillary Clinton emails they connect together with the cables that we have published of Hillary Clinton creating a rich perfect picture of how Hillary Clinton performs in office, but, more broadly how the US Department of State operates.

"So, for example, the disastrous, absolutely disastrous, intervention in Libya, the destruction of the Gaddafi government which led to the occupation of ISIS of large segments of that country, weapons flows going over to Syria, being pushed by Hillary Clinton, into jihadists within Syria, including ISIS, that's there in those emails. There's more than 1,700 emails in Hillary Clinton's collection that we have released just about Libya alone.

Investigators that went to Benghazi to track down the suspects in the Benghazi attacks spent months on taking audio, video, and photos of the suspects. In November 2012, the investigators had identified the suspects and their whereabouts and gave that information to be passed on to Libyan chief of mission William Roebuck in January of 2013. But no action was taken. These investigators had risked their lives and the lives of Libyans to collect the evidence and were angry when they were told that they were being pulled out of Libya.

"We put American Special Operations in harms way to develop a picture of these suspects and to seek Justice and instead of acting we stalled. We just let it slip and pass us by and now it's going to be much more difficult. It's already blowing up. Daily assassinations, bi-weekly prison escapes, we waited way too long."

One of the team leaders angry, and frustrated, yelled at chief of mission Roebuck asking him, "So you're willing to let these guys get away with murder?" Roebuck had no answer, only silence.

And to add more disgrace to the way the Benghazi attack was treated the Pentagon claimed that these investigators were not charged with tracking down the suspects. And that when Congress authorized a counterterrorism in Libya they were specific as to what the money was to be spent on. Audio, video, and photos of the Benghazi suspects cost too much? The Pentagon said that the soldiers out of Fort Bragg were responsible for tracking down the suspects. But the investigators disagreed with the Pentagon's statement and accused the Pentagon of using this as a reason to justify foregoing the operation.

An unidentified investigator told Fox News that the training is partly a cover and some of these guys... Provided the information on suspects directly to US military commanders and the US State Department last November and again in January. "They are there and trying to find, fix, and finish."

An unidentified man said that General Ham who was in-charge of AFRICOM at the time told Lawrence Pope Libya chief of mission that he could have planned a mission to capture or kill the suspects. Politics prevented him from doing so.

General Ham stated, "Politics and fallout kept us from acting. To do an operation we have to have Chief of Mission and State approval. We didn't get it... They sat on it."

The suspects went on to aid the terrorist groups the Muslim Brotherhood and Ansar al-Sharia.

Then U.S. officials allowed the Libyan government to occupy the camp where the US operators had spent a year and a lot of taxpayers money training a Libyan force that would be capable of fighting the terrorists. This was a counter effective measure the US officials took by allowing the camp to come under Libyan government control.

This group of men who were to leave Libya soon had briefed the acting US ambassador and the senior CIA representative in Libya. The men were told that the Secretary of State Hillary Clinton and an under secretary were briefed. But no one in the US government would authorize the action of either arresting or killing these particular terrorists who were either suspected or known to have participated in the murders of four Americans. Disgraceful beyond imagination.

According to Darrell Issa, chairman of the house oversight committee which investigated the Benghazi attack, Hillary chose to normalize the situation in Benghazi in order to make the appearance that the US was winning the war on terror.

"We know from Hillary Clinton on down there was a policy of normalization to make it appear as though we had won the war on terror. I was in Libya just the other day and one thing that I came back with was a strong opinion that that stand down had everything to do with the fight between Department of State headed by Hillary Clinton and the Defense Department and that ultimately State was willing to put their assets in and it did not want any military assets in because they did not want to escalate what ultimately should have been escalated to a real Rescue Mission." Issa laid the blame for what happened that night in Benghazii on Hillary.

"The investigation really is not about what we know but about how we can prevent abuse of security before the fact, how we respond during the fact, and how we hold people accountable after the fact, for deliberate misinformation if you want to be kind, outright lies if not," stated Issa.

*****

The Sate Department's internal audit found Hillary guilty of violating Federal protocols. In 2011, her IT chief completely shut down her server to prevent classified data from being compromised. Hillary had said that there were no attempts to hack her private server. The IG report proves that Hillary lied when she said she was unaware of any attempts to hack her private server. A former National Security Agency analyst stated that his Source who is "privy to some of FBI's findings" is certain Hillary's server was breached several times which jeopardized National Security.

"We know her email server was hacked numerous times, it's that simple. If I were Vladimir Putin I'd fire the head of the SVR (Russia's

Foreign Intelligence Service) if he didn't get a good look at Hillary's emails when they were sitting in plain sight online."

An Iranian nuclear scientist, Shahram Amiri, helped the United States obtain information about the Islamic republic's covert nuclear program. He was later executed for treason in Iran. He had been discussed in emails on Hillary's server, according to the Washington Examiner.

Did Iran's discovery of Shahram Amiri, whose body was returned to his family with rope marks around his neck, have anything to do with the "reckless" lack of security on Hillary's private server?

"I'm not going to comment on what he may or may not have done for the United States government, but in the emails that were on Hillary Clinton's private server, there were conversations among her senior advisers about this gentleman," Republican senator Tom Cotton said during a Sunday appearance on CBS' "Face the Nation."

"That goes to show just how reckless and careless her decision was to put that kind of highly classified information on a private server. And I think her judgment is not suited to keep this country safe," he added.

A spokesman for Iran's judiciary stated,

"This person who had access to the country's secret and classified information had been linked to our hostile and No. 1 enemy, America, the Great Satan. He provided the enemy with vital and secret information of the country."

During a 2009 religious pilgrimage to Saudi Arabia, Amiri disappeared. A year later he showed up in the United States at the Iranian interest section of the Pakistani embassy, demanding to be sent home to his country. Amiri's claim was that he had been abducted by the CIA, but U.S. officials said he had cooperated willingly, according to the BBC.

The Examiner reported that nine days before Amiri's return to Iran is when the email exchange began about Amiri on Hillary's server.

An email from Richard Morningstar, a former State Department special envoy for Eurasian energy stated, "We have a diplomatic, 'psychological' issue, not a legal one. Our friend has to be given a way out. Our person won't be able to do anything anyway. If he has to leave so be it."

Amiri may have very well lost his life due to Hillary's unsecured server.

*****

In one of her speeches, Hillary declared that "if you vote for me I will fight for you". But she did not fight for Ambassador Christopher Stevens, Sean Smith, Glenn Doherty, or Tyrone Woods. The only fight she was involved in was for a way to protect herself from being held accountable for the severity of the Benghazi attack and the deaths of four American citizens.

Hillary testified that she was never informed concerning the susceptibility of the Benghazi diplomatic compound was to attack or about requests for more security officers. US ambassador to Libya Chris Stevens and his security officers assigned to protect him repeatedly sounded alarms to their superiors in Washington about the lawlessness and violence in eastern Libya where Stevens and three other Americans died.

Before the House Select Committee on Benghazi, Hillary had said that none of their requests for additional security had reached her.

Republican representative Mike Pompeo from Kansas stated, "That's over 600 requests. You've testified here this morning that you had none of those reach your desk, is that correct also? Hillary's response was, "That's correct."

But for some reason an email that shows a request for humanitarian aid that had been sent by Ambassador Chris Stevens did reach Hillary's desk. The email from Stevens on August 26th 2011 was circulated among Hillary's staff and was delegated for action in under 1 hour.

"Can we arrange shipments of what is requested?" Was Hillary's response only 17 minutes after the request was received.

But Hillary emphasized to the committee, "Chris Stevens communicated regularly with the members of my staff. He did not raise security with the members of my staff. I communicated with him about certain issues. He did not raise security with me. He raised security with the security professionals."

In March 2011, British Prime Minister, Tony Blair, advocated for a no-fly zone over Libya in an email to Hillary.

"Please work on the non fly zone or the other options I mentioned. Oil prices are rising markets are down. We have to be decisive."

What was this about? Was this all about the oil? Was oil and business deals for contractors the reason for all of the deaths including four

Americans? It would not be surprising. Most likely though it was partly due to stealing Gaddafi's billions.

But no one knew how long the assault on the Diplomatic Mission Compound and CIA Annex would last. But President Obama's Administration has maintained that nothing, nothing could have been done to save the four Americans killed in the Benghazi attack on September 11th 2012. But since no one knew how long the attacks would last, how can that statement even be considered as truth? Many different sources have stated that forces could have been deployed and arrived in time to help in the fight. An unidentified member of the US Air Force stationed in Italy at the time said that assets were ready but they were left waiting for the "go" command which they never received. Also a source in intelligence said that a group of men comprised of special forces were two hours away from the attack in Benghazi. But they were never given the "go" command either. An unidentified member of the US Air Force told Fox News special report, "I definitely believe that our aircraft could have taken off in a timely manner maybe 3 hours at the most in order to… at least stop the second mortar attack and have those guys running for the hills, and basically save lives that day."

Sadly and so upsetting, a source in intelligence said that the people at the compound were left there, no one was coming for them.

The US Air Force member dismissed the reason given that help could not be sent because there was no refueling plane in the area and said that there were multiple opportunities to help those in Benghazi, opportunities that were allowed to pass.

And Hillary never gave the order to mobilize the State Department's Foreign Emergency Support Team (FEST) which would secure the compound. The Pentagon refused to send a C-110, a 50 Man team of Special Operations troops on a training mission in Croatia, to immediately fly to Benghazi just a few hours away. Who ordered the Stand Down? It is classified.

CHAPTER 18

B arack Obama will leave the office of President leaving the U.S. in a weakened state and its enemies growing in influence and power. Even Bill Clinton's stated that the past 8 years have left Obama with "an awful legacy". Not only will the president leave an awful legacy, Obama has shown that the forces that are in opposition to liberty and embrace tyranny will stop at nothing until the people of the United States are under their control completely. They have both proven this by acting illegally without Congress' approval of illegal immigration and supporting the oppositions radical movements to overthrow other countries governments.

In Egypt President Obama and Hillary supported a corrupt Muslim Brotherhood regime in Egypt led by Jew and Christian hating Mohamed Morsi. Egyptian people eventually overthrew the radical Islamic theocracy and made way for General el-Sisi who is a secular pro military leader who is waging war against ISIS.

But their support for rebel and radical Islamic group revolutions against foreign governments has hurt the United States.

Mischael Modrekamen, president of the Belgium People's Party stated that, "Hillary Clinton is the kind of politician we have here in Western Europe; weak, globalist, obsessed with multiculturalism, despising ordinary people but bending to elites and corporate interest."

The Obama administration's Department of Health and Human Services wants $167 million to be redirected to pay for unaccompanied minors until the current temporary spending bill expires. This money would be used for housing, health care, schooling, recreation, and other services for unaccompanied minors.

Director of policy studies for the Center for Immigration, Studies Jessica Vaughan, said that these youths are often being smuggled into the U.S. from from Central America paid by the youths parents.

Vaughan stated in a report;

"They don't have any basis for staying here.

"We should not be rewarding that by paying for these children to stay."

The Department of Heath and Human Services already had $171 million and a $90 million surplus which amounts to $267 million currently available for illegal immigrant youths.

The health programs that the money would be taken from are;

Health Resources and Services Administration - $14 million

Ryan White HIV/AIDS Program - $4.5

Maternal and Child Health program - $2 million

Centers for Disease Control and Prevention, for contagious disease prevention and treatment and other critical public health program - $14 million

National Institutes of Health, for research on cancer, diabetes, drug abuse, mental health, infectious diseases, and much more - $72 million

Substance Abuse and Mental Health Services Administration, for treatment and prevention programs - $8 million

Centers for Medicare and Medicaid Services - $8 million

Children and Families Services Program - $39 million

Aging and Disability Services Programs - $4 million

Public Health and Social Services Emergency Fund - $3 million, including more than $1 million from the Pandemic Influenza and BioShield Fund.

"The responsible thing to do is to change the policy. HHS is not picking the pockets of people on Wall Street. These are important programs," Jessica Vaughan stated.

*****

The first steps in opposing liberty and embracing tyranny until the people are under their control completely and absolutely is to take away First Amendment rights.

155

Citizens United is a non-profit organization which sought an injunction against the Federal Election Commission's action which blocked the release of a documentary titled, Hillary; The Movie. It was highly critical of Hillary while she was seeking the Democratic nomination. The FEC blocked its release on the grounds that the movie violated the rules regarding "electioneering communications" in the Bipartisan Campaign Act (BCRA). Citizens United sought an injunction against the FEC's action. The District Court refused to grant the requested injunction by Citizens United. It held that the statutes regulations of "expressed advocacy" during election was not unconstitutional. So Citizens United appealed to the Supreme Court which held the First Amendment does not allow the government to so regulate independent political messages. Hillary was adamant about the case because she said "she knows firsthand what it does to our democracy". What Citizens United did do was to allow the competition of candidates and ideas to escape complete federal control. The movie should have been free to be shown as it was accorded by the Supreme Court. This is a very important aspect in regard to not limiting the First Amendment. But Hillary favors a constitutional amendment that would allow the federal government to control free speech in political campaigns and in whatever she so deems necessary to fit her agenda. And that includes other countries as well.

Just as she had shown in her condemnation of Muammar Gaddafi and her attempts to sway the American's opinions of Gaddafi and his regime, claiming that they had committed atrocities. Evidence had proven that those claims were false. Actually the misinformation campaign had provided evidence that the Pentagon knew Gaddafi had ordered his generals not to attack civilians. But in her words Gaddafi was a creature who "will destroy anyone or anything in his way". Quite ironic.

"We came, we saw, he died," Hillary stated as she laughed about Muammar Gaddafi's death. It is more along the line of we came, we saw, we murdered him.

Gaddafi's motorcade had been traveling under the White Flag the flag of surrender. They were driving to a site designated by Hillary's State Department where Gaddafi would turn himself over to US and NATO authorities. But with the approval of Hillary, Gaddafi's motorcade was attacked and he was killed, shot to death.

In an interview, Hillary again, tried to create a situation to fit her agenda, "Imagine we were sitting here and Benghazi had been overrun the city of 700,000 people and tens of thousands of people had been slaughtered hundreds of thousands had fled... The cries would be, 'Why did the United States not do anything?' But this situation she spoke of was not thought of as a probability.

This was the rationale of a warmonger not of a serious Diplomat of the United States. There was no intelligence that suggested the impending massacre that she wanted people to imagine. And there were no negotiations in place between the State Department and the Gaddafi government. And that was because Hillary told the generals that there would be no negotiations.

Alan Kuperman had challenged the officials suggesting an impending massacre stance at that time. Kuperman had pointed out that Gadaffi had not targeted civilians in other cities his regime had recaptured. There was no evidence suggesting an impending massacre according to Sara Leah Whitson who was Human Rights Watch executive director of the Middle East and North Africa division. She had stated, "Our assessment was that up until that point (when NATO intervened militarily) the casualty figures around 350 protesters killed by indiscriminate fire... didn't rise to the level indicating that a genocide or genocide like mass atrocities were imminent."

Intelligence assessments contradicted almost everything that was stated by Hillary and the Obama administration about Gaddafi at the time of the Libyan coup. U.S. officials stated that the Pentagon believed, "Gaddafi was unlikely to risk world outrage by inflicting large civilian casualties as a crackdown on the rebels based in Benghazi". It became evident that the threat of mass atrocities came not from the government but from the opposition of terrorist groups which was supported by the Obama administration and Hillary.

The intelligence community was not the only one concerned that Hillary was selling the war on lies. In 2011, secretly tape-recorded conversations, an emissary sent by the Pentagon and Democratic Rep. Dennis J. Kucinich openly discussed with Gadhafi regime officials concerns that there was a false narrative being used to sell the war.

Some of the lies Hillary was touting;

"We had a murderous dictator, Gadhafi, who had American blood on his hands, as I'm sure you remember, threatening to massacre large numbers of the Libyan people.

"We had our closest allies in Europe burning up the phone lines begging us to help them try to prevent what they saw as a mass genocide, in their words. And we had the Arabs standing by our side saying, 'We want you to help us deal with Gadhafi.'

"Our response, which I think was smart power at its best, is that the United States will not lead this. We will provide essential, unique capabilities that we have, but the Europeans and the Arabs had to be first over the line. We did not put one single American soldier on the ground in Libya."

No American soldiers. They just armed jihadists to kill Gaddafi and a lot of civilians were murdered also.

Florida Sen. Marco Rubio, said in an interview with Charlie Rose of PBS in May that "the result in Libya was a protracted conflict that killed people, destroyed infrastructure, and left behind the conditions for the rise of multiple militias who refused to lay down their arms."

Hillary and her cohorts armed the militias with terrorist affiliations and then expected them to willingly lay down their weapons.

"What was decided was to declare Gaddafi guilty in advance of a massacre of defenseless civilians and instigate the process of destroying his regime and him (and his family) by way of punishment of a crime he was yet to commit and actually unlikely to commit, and to persist with this process despite his repeated offers to suspend military action." This was written by a scholar at Tufts University Robert Hughes. Hughes was head of the ICDG North Africa Project at the time.

Gaddafi had not committed the crimes he was accused of and he was very unlikely to commit them, yet Hillary would have nothing to do with negotiations that could have avoided the absolute abysmal situation in Libya.

Hillary "does not want to negotiate at all."

It is absolutely unacceptable that our State Department and our government did not negotiate a peaceful resolution. There was no proof that Gaddafi was committing the crimes he was accused of. He was guilty of not fitting into their plan.

Hillary had described the TNC as Libya's governing body in July 2011, "as steadfast in its commitment to human rights and fundamental freedoms".

But Gaddafi's government had compiled evidence in a report that a US intelligence asset delivered to members of Congress. This report stated "There is a close link between Al Qaeda Jihadi organizations and the opposition in Libya."

Hillary had suggested that Al-Qaeda allies had no role in the opposition. When she was asked about NATO Commander's reference to "flickers in the intelligence of potential" Al-Qaeda involvement Hillary stated, "We do not have any specific information about specific individuals from any organization who are part of this".

But in an email from Sidney Blumenthal he had told Hillary that the incoming TNC would most likely not represent a democracy. And that the government would be based on Sharia or Islamic law.

This is an email from Jake Sullivan to Cheryl Mills and Victoria Nuland on August 21st, 2011

subject: tick tock on Libya

(T)his is basically of(f) the top of my head with a few consultations of my notes. But it shows S' leadership/ownership/ stewardship of this country's Libya policy from start to finish. let me know what you think. toria, who else might be able to add to this?

Secretary Clinton's leadership on Libya HRC has been a critical voice in Libya and administration deliberations at NATO and in contact with meetings as well as the public face of the US effort in Libya. She was instrumental in securing the authorization, building the coalition, and tightening the noose around Qadhafi and his regime.

February 25th HRC announces the suspension of operations of the Libyan embassy in Washington.

February 26th HRC direct efforts to evacuate all US Embassy Personnel from Tripoli and orders the closing of the embassy.

February 26th HRC made a series of calls to her counterparts to help secure passage of UNSC 1970 which imposes sanctions on Gaddafi and his family and refers Qadhafi and his cronies to the ICC

February 28th HRC travels to Geneva Switzerland for consultations with European Partners on Libya. She gives a major address in which she says: "Colonel Qaddhafi and those around him must be held accountable for these acts which violates International legal obligations and common decency. Through their actions they have lost the legitimacy to govern. And the people of Libya have made themselves clear: It is time for Qadhafi to go- now without further violence or delay." She also works to secure the suspension of Libya from membership in the Human Rights Council.

Early March HRC appoints special envoy Chris Stevens to be the US representative to Benghazi.

March 14th RC travels to Paris for the G8 foreign ministers meeting. She meets with TNC representatives Jabril and consulted with her colleagues on further Security Council action. She knows that a no fly zone will not be adequate.

March 14-16 HRC participates in a series of high-level video and teleconferences which she is a leading voice for strong UNSC actions and a NATO civilian protection mission.

March 17- HRC secures Russian abstension and Portuguese and African support for UNSC 1973 ensuring that it passes. 1973 authorizes a no-fly zone over Libya and "all necessary measures"- code for military action- to protect civilians against Gaddafi's Army.

March 24th HRC engages with allies and secures the transition of command and control of the civilian protection mission to NATO. She announces the transition in a statement.

March 18-30 HRC engages with UAE Qatar and Jordan to seek their participation in coalition operations. Over the course of several days all three devote aircraft to the mission.

March 19th HRC travels to Paris to meet with European and Arab leaders to prepare for military action to protect civilians. That night the first US airstrikes halt the advance of Gaddafi's forces on Benghazi and target Libya's air defenses.

March 29th HRC travels to London for a conference on Libya where she is a driving force behind the creation of a contact group comprising 20-plus countries to coordinate efforts to protect civilians and plan for a post Qadhafi Libya. She's instrumental in setting up a rotating chair system to ensure regional buy in.

April 14 HRC travels to Berlin for NATO meetings. She is the driving force behind NATO adopting a communiqué that calls for Qadhafi's departure as a political objective and lays Out 3 clear military objectives end of attacks and threat of attacks on civilians, the removal of Qadhafi forces from cities they forcibly entered, and the unfettered provision of humanitarian access.

May 5 HRC travels to Rome for a contact group meeting. The contact group establishes a coordination system and a temporary financial mechanism to funnel money to the TNC.

June 8th HRC travels to Abu Dhabi for another contact group meeting and holds a series of intense discussions with Rebel leaders.

June 12 HRC travels to Addis for consultations and a speech before the African Union pressing the case for a democratic transition in Libya.

July 15th HRC travels to Istanbul and announces that the US recognizes the TNC as the legitimate government of Libya. She also secures recognition from the other members of the contact group.

Late June HRC meets with house Democrats and Senate Republicans to persuade them not to de-fund the Libya operation.

July 16th HRC sends Feltman, Cretz, and Chollet to Tunis to meet with Qadhafi envoy "to deliver a clear and firm message that the only way to move forward is for Qadhafi to step down".

Early August HRC Works to construct a $1.5 billion assets package to be approved by the security Council and sent to the TNC. That package is working through its last hurdles.

Early August after military Chief Abdel Fattah Younes is killed S (Secretary or Hillary) sends a personal message to TNC head Jalil to press for a responsible investigation and careful and inclusive approach to creating a new executive council.

Early August HRC secures written pledges from the TNC to an inclusive pluralistic, democratic transition. She continues to consult with European and Arab colleagues on the evolving situation.

Hillary travelled all these miles to all these countries and met with all of these individuals and groups to gain support and aid for the overthrow of Gaddafi. But when her people in Benghazi needed her help she was completely silent.

One of the items mentioned in the e-mail that refers to Hillary being instrumental in setting up a rotating chair system to ensure regional buy-in;

This most likely refers to the different country's companies receiving contracts in Libya. Emails from Hillary and Sidney Blumenthal seems to confirm that when they spoke of the oil.

And why did they pay the TNC $1.5 billion? If these were people of Libya that wanted to overthrow Gaddafi for a democracy why would they have to be paid such an excessive amount to do so?

*****

Internal State Department documents show that slain U.S. Ambassador to Libya, Chris Stevens, and the security officers assigned to protect him repeatedly sounded alarms to their superiors in Washington about the intensifying lawlessness and violence in Eastern Libya.

On the day that Ambassador Stevens and three other Americans were killed, September 11th 2012, the ambassador sent a cable labeled 'sensitive'. In the cable he noted "growing problems" with security in Benghazi and "growing frustration" with the Libyan police and security forces, on the part of local residents. Ambassador Stevens said that these forces were "too weak to keep the country secure".

Steven's also noted a meeting he had held two days earlier with local militia Commanders. They boasted to Stevens of exercising control over the Libyan Armed Forces and threatened that if the U.S.-backed candidate for prime minister were to prevail in Libya's internal political jockeying, "they would not continue to guarantee security in Benghazi".

Approximately a month earlier Stevens had signed a two-page cable that was labeled "sensitive", and was sent with the SIPDIS caption, that he titled, The Guns of August: Security in Eastern Libya. With the SIPDIS caption, this ensured that it would be sent through the Pentagon's Secret Internet Protocol Router Network (SIPRnet). This is a government clearinghouse which covers and reaches all U.S. security agencies. According to Ken Timmerman, author of DARK FORCES; "Sending a SIPDIS cable was the diplomatic equivalent of a cry of desperation. Clearly, he was hoping that someone would understand how dire the situation had become, perhaps the CIA or General Carter Ham at AFRICOM, and weigh in with the White House or the secretary of state personally. This cable was also stamped "Routine" by the State Department routing officer. Help was not on the way." (General Carter Ham, along with Andy Wood wanted to keep the group of Army Green Berets and Delta Force operators at the Benghazi compound.) "At the next country team meeting at the embassy, the spiraling violence in Benghazi and the rise of the al Qaeda–affiliated Ansar al-Sharia prompted Ambassador Stevens to launch a formal review of their security posture. By this point, they had lost two of the State Department's three specialized Mobile Security Detachments and were relying for point protection on the Delta Force operators and Army Green Berets under Andy Wood's command. Everyone knew that the State Department had refused to extend the SST beyond August 5, and that the last MSD was also on its way out. Stevens asked the outgoing RSO, Eric Nordstrom, to draft an action request cable for the secretary of state. "According to one participant, this 'fell like a dead fish on the table,' because everyone, including Ambassador Stevens, knew that the Embassy lacked support from Washington, D.C., and could do little about it. Stevens sent out his action request cable, stamped SENSITIVE, on July 9. It painted a dire picture of a wilderness outpost that Washington completely disregarded. From the current quota of thirty-four U.S. security personnel spread between Tripoli and Benghazi, the State Department was cutting back to twenty seven by July 13, and down to seven on August 13, when Wood and the SST were scheduled to leave. Rather than treat Tripoli's request with the urgency it required, the State Department filed the cable along with routine traffic coming in from the 270-odd U.S. diplomatic posts around the world." On August 8, the Ambassador noted that in just a few months time Benghazi has moved from trepidation to euphoria and back as a series of violent incidents has dominated the political landscape... The individual incidents have been organized" which was a product of the security vacuum that a diverse group of independent actors are exploiting for their own purposes".

"Islamist extremists are able to, what we have seen are not random crimes of opportunity but rather targeted and discriminate attacks." In a two-page document, the ambassador's final comment was, "Attackers are unlikely to be deterred until authorities are at least as capable." "[E]ven in the assessment of its own commander, Fawzi Younis, SSC Benghazi has not coalesced into an effective, stable security force." Stevens had reported to his superiors that the US Consulate in Benghazi had been damaged by an improvised explosive device and that an Islamist group had claimed credit for the attack and had "described the attack as targeting the Christians supervising the management of the consulate".

The damage to the consulate was a hole approximately 30 ft. wide.

Stevens aids were reporting back to Washington, by September 4th on the "strong Revolutionary and Islamist sentiment" in the city.

Approximately two months before, Ambassador Stevens had notified the Department of Homeland Security, the Department of Justice, and other agencies about a "recent increase in violent incidents" that included attacks against Western interests". And on June 25th, Stevens wrote, "Until the government of Libya is able to effectively deal with these key issues, the violence is likely to continue and worsen".

Stevens wrote, "Islamic extremism appears to be on the rise in eastern Libya. The al Qaeda flag has been spotted several times flying over government buildings and training facilities..."

The documents also contain evidence that the ability of the attackers to plan their assault on the consulate and annex grounds without being detected was most likely due to the State Department's denials of requests for enhanced security in Benghazi in the months leading up to 9/11.

In a February 1st memorandum to top DS officials, Eric Nordstrom, warned that "Al-Qaeda affiliated groups, including al-Qaeda in the Islamic Maghreb (AQIM) and other violent extremist groups are likely to take advantage of the ongoing political turmoil in Libya. The US government remains concerned that such individuals and groups...may use Libya as a platform from which to conduct attacks in the region.

On February 11th, a colleague of Karen Keshap's, Shawn P Crowley, apologized to her and other officials in an email for "being a broken record" on the subject of inadequate security in Benghazi. Crowley added, "Tomorrow Benghazi will be down to two DS agents... This will leave us unable to do any outreach to Libyan nationals... and we will be extremely limited in the ability to obtain any useful information for reporting".

Karen Keshap, a State Department manager wrote to main State in Washington, "DS is hesitant to devote resources and as I indicated previously this has severely hampered operations in Benghazi. That often means that DS agents are there guarding a compound with two other DOS (Department of State) personnel present. That often also means that outreach and reporting is nonexistent."

Eric Nordstrom, regional security officer who testified before a house hearing in a February 12 email to a colleague wrote, "I've been placed in a very difficult spot, when the ambassador (Gene Cretz at that time) that I need to support Benghazi but can't direct MSD (a mobile security detachment) there and been advised that DS (Diplomatic Security) isn't going to provide more than 3 agents over the long-term."

By February 20th Eric Nordstrom noted the easy access that neighborhood militias had "military grade weapons such as RPGs and vehicle mounted, crew-served machine guns or AA weapons (23 mm) as well as "AK-47s, heavy weapons, and vehicle mounted weapons."

Representative Darrell Issa, the Chairman of the House Oversight and Government Reform Committee, and representative Jason Chaffetz released these documents.

In a letter to President Obama on October 19th and accompanied by the documents, the lawmakers faulted the administration both for providing inadequate security before 9/11, and for allegedly obfuscating the nature of the events on 9/11;

"Multiple warnings about security threats were contained in Ambassador Stevens own words in multiple cables sent to Washington DC., and were manifested by two prior bombings of the Benghazi compound and an assassination attempt on the British ambassador. For this Administration to assume that terrorists were not involved in the 911 anniversary attack would have required a willing suspension of disbelief."

Spokesman Victoria Nuland declined to comment on published reports stating that an official working for the CIA had informed the Obama Administration on September 12th that the Benghazi murders were an act of terrorism.

When questioned by representative Mike Pompeo, Hillary Clinton denied receiving any requests for additional security for Benghazi. Mike Pompeo stated, That's over 600 requests. He asked if none of these had reached her. She said, "That's correct."

Regarding Libyan's guarding Ambassador Stevens, a diplomat in Libya said, "I would never depend on the brigades. The mistakes of the Americans was not following the trail of Islamic radicals".

One diplomat said that the United States was the only one out of approximately 10 foreign missions in Libya who would allow the local militia to be their quick reaction force. Everyone else depended on their own military forces from their own country to provide their own security.

An European diplomat said, "A few months ago there was a small attack here and the Libyans fled. After that I decided to only use special forces."

"We never considered using the brigades," speaking of the 17 February Martyrs Brigade.

"We used to take training from the Americans on diplomatic security," said a diplomat. He was surprised that Steven's had not been evacuated at the very first when the threat began.

During a ceremony honoring Stevens, Hillary said that a joint State and Defense Department task force would "review high-threat posts to determine whether there are other improvements we need in light of the evolving security challenges we now face."

But the diplomats said they believed one such improvement had become obvious in the months after a NATO air campaign helped topple the Gaddafi government: Don't expect local forces to protect you when they can't even protect themselves against local extremists and terrorists groups in a city not defined by reprisal attacks.

And even the leaders of the 17 February Brigade said that they never considered themselves responsible for consulate security.

Naji Muftah, co-founder of the brigades VIP unit, said that his group was not in charge. "How could four people secure a consulate?" He said.

Security for the Special Mission Compound that was attacked in Benghazi in 2012, was previously handled by a Libyan militia who was carefully vetted by the United States. But most of the militia members were fired when Hillary's State Department hired the Blue Mountain Group based in Wales, who was new to the security business. They received a $9.2 million annual contract with the U.S. hired by Hillary's State Department. Instead of providing real security the Blue Mountain Group hired 20 local militia men. They were hired by running ads in Libyan newspapers.

The Blue Mountain group was hired by Hillary "over internal objections". The security specialist who trained the Libyan militia who were carefully vetted by the United States, before the Blue Mountain group was hired, stated that the guards who were hired by BMG were members of Ansar al-sharia and Al-Qaeda groups. They were the terrorist groups who attacked the compound and killed four Americans. The brother of the local Al-Qaeda leader was one of the guards hired by the BMG who was involved in the attack.

A security specialist stated, "Whoever approved contracts at the state department hired the Blue Mountain Group and then allowed the Blue Mountain Group to hire local Libyans who were not vetted. He also said that the Special Mission Compound had made a request of a .50 caliber truck mounted machine gun. But that request had been denied due to the fact that it might have "upset the locals". Was this done on purpose? To fire the original security who was trained and then carefully vetted by the United States? And then hire a new security business that would hire locals to protect the Ambassador and all of the other Americans? It would have been a way to get rid of any witnesses to the U.S. involvement in the gun-running to Syria.

John "Tig" Tiegen, who was a CIA contractor and who fought the attackers in Benghazi, said that "many of the Libyans who attacked the consulate" were "the actual guards (Blue Mountain Group) the State Department under Hillary Clinton" had hired.

"Many of the local Libyans who attacked the consulate on the night of Sept. 11, 2012, were the actual guards that the State Department under Hillary Clinton hired to protect the Consulate in Benghazi. The guards were unvetted and were locals with basically no background at all in providing security. Most of them never had held a job in security in the past. Blue Mountain Libya, at the time of being awarded the contract by our State Department, had no employees so they quickly had to find people to work, regardless of their backgrounds," he said.

In an email sent to the Citizens Commission on Benghazi, Weeam Mohamed, a former guard who witnessed the Benghazi attack sent an email to the Citizens Commission on Benghazi, stated that at least four of the guards hired by the Blue Mountain Group took part in the attack after opening doors to allow their fellow terrorist's in.

"In the U.S. Mission, there were four people [who] belonged to the battalion February 17.

"Always armed. And they are free to move anywhere inside a building mission.

"And therefore, they had a chance to do an attack on the mission's headquarters. They have all the details about the place. At the same time they have given the United States a painful blow," Mohamed wrote in his email.

In an email written by a State Department Contracting officer was stated that there was "a tremendous rush to get the original contract awarded". Why was that? Again possibly to get rid of evidence. They did not want to 'upset the locals', they were in a hurry to award the contract, they spent $9.2 million on the Blue Mountain Group, but they did not send anyone to help the Americans. Was one of the jobs of the Blue Mountain Group to attack the compound instead of protecting it?

Sharyn Atkinson lists 8 major warning signs before the Benghazi attack;

2011: Ambassador premonition: "…Things could go wrong."

In 2011, al-Qaeda was known to be in Tripoli to exploit Libya's unsettled status and to try to obtain some of the thousands of missing MANPADS (man portable air-defense systems): shoulder-fired missiles seized by rebel forces that stormed Qaddafi government bases. U.S. Ambassador Cretz realized there were seriously dangerous tensions among anti-Qaddafi factions: Islamists and secularists. "I think there is a genuine cause to be concerned that things could go wrong," he told reporters.

Dec. 2011: "Islamic terrorist elements…gaining operational capability."

In December 2011, A major terrorist plot targeting foreign diplomatic missions in Libya, Operation Papa Noel, was circumvented…Later, the written emergency-evacuation plan for the U.S. mission in Benghazi warned,… "Islamic terrorist elements do exist in this area of the country, and have been reported by open sources to be gaining operational capability."

In 2012, Al-Qaeda on-line that they would attack the Red Cross, the British, and then the Americans in Benghazi.

On April 10, 2012, The United Nations convoy traveling in Benghazi carrying United Nations envoy Ian Martin had an I.E.D. thrown at it.

On May 22, 2012, The Benghazi offices of the International Red Cross was hit with a RPG (rocket-propelled grenade). The Red Cross decided to leave Benghazi.

On June 6, 2012, a hole was blown on the outside wall of the Special Mission Compound in Benghazi by an I.E.D. (improvised explosive device).

On June 11, 2012, The British ambassador's convoy in Benghazi was hit with a rocket-propelled grenade. The U.K. then left Benghazi.

In 2012 an al-Qaeda demonstration took place in the middle of Benghazi.

"They had a parade down the streets. They raised their flag on one of the county buildings," says one observer.

But State Department officials stated;

"We had no actionable intelligence . . . about this threat in Benghazi. . ."

The acting Deputy Assistant for Operations in the State Department's Counterterrorism Bureau, Mark I.Thompson, testied that then-Secretary of State Hillary Clinton willfully blocked his department's involvement on the night of the September 11 Benghazi attacks. He has been threatened and intimidated by unnamed State Department officials about stating this in public. He testified that al-Qaeda was involved all along.

While the Benghazi facilities were under attack on September 11th, Hillary phoned Libyan President Magariaf at 6:49 p.m. Washington time. Hillary asked the president to "to provide additional security to the compound immediately as there is a gun battle going on which Ansar al-Sharia is claiming responsibility for."

How did Hillary know Ansar al-Sharia was claiming responsibility for the attack? An investigation had proven the terrorist group did not post it on-line as Hillary had stated. Even if they had, that was only 2 hours and 20 minutes after the attacks began when Hillary stated it was Ansar al-Sharia. Why would no help be sent since it was a terrorist attack? It has been shown many times that help could have been deployed and at least likely prevented the deaths at the CIA annex.

Hillary's statement 3 hours later blamed the attack on an internet video.

Then at 11:12 p.m., Hillary emailed her daughter: "Two of our officers were killed in Benghazi by an al-Qaeda like group." Ansari al-Sharia is the arm of al-Qeada on the Arabian peninsula.

Hillary received a confidential email after midnight from Blumenthal, "Magariaf and the attacks on Libya." "Senior advisers including members of the Libyan Muslim Brotherhood." Magariaf was told the Benghazi and Tripoli attacks were inspired by "a sacrilegious internet video on the prophet Mohammed." (There were no attacks in Tripoli).

"...trying to link him directly to foreign intelligence services. According to a separate sensitive source Magariaf noted that his opponents had often tried to connect him to the US Intelligence Central Agency (CIA) through the National Front for the Salvation of Libya (NFSL) a group Magariaf led in the 1980's."

"The attack on the US missions were as much a result of the atmosphere created by this campaign (to connect Magariaf to the CIA) as the controversial internet video." (That was also a lie).

Magariaf spent 30 years in exile. He spent most of it in the United States. He headed the NFSL, the main opposition group to Gaddafi.

The day after the Benghazi attack and murders, the Clinton Foundation received a request. Amitabh Desai, the foundation's director on foreign policy received an email from senior Magariaf aide Fathi Nuah; "Magariaf will be in New York for the UN General Assembly and wishes to "meet President Clinton and participate at the Clinton Global Initiative."

Dr. Fathi Nuah was exiled in the United States for decades. He worked in opposition to the Gaddafi regime. Fathi Nuah is "engaged in developing major business" in Libya in "education, oil, construction and commerce sectors."

Hillary's emails show that on the day that four Americans were killed intelligence from Libyan President Muhammed Yussef el Magariaf show that the attack was carried out by Ansar al-sharia which is led by the former LIFG General Abdelhakim Belhadj.

Ambassador Chris Stevens was the designated chief US liason to Belhadj. Stevens had met with Belhadj to coordinate military action against Gaddafi. Belhadj had also met with leaders of the anti-Assad "Free Syrian Army" in 2011 under CIA supervision. And Ambassador Stevens was brokering arms deals taken from Gaddafi's cache and shipping the Libyan arms to Syria and the Syrian jihadists who were trying to overthrow Bashar al-Assad. Assad had given military assistance to Gaddafi to help in the fight against the Jihadi terrorists. Hillary's State Department put Abdelhakim Belhadj in power. He is the organizational commander of the ISIS in Libya. Belhadj coordinates and supports the ISIS training centers in Derna, Libya. Derna has been long known for jihadi militancy. On October 18, 2011, Hillary travelled to Libya to celebrate her overthrow of Mummer Gaddafi. Hillary was in the company of a man known as, Detainee M, who headed up the government security service who protected her while she was there. He had been known to British authorities as so dangerous that his movements were legally restricted.

It was revealed, accidentally, by the Benghazi committee in October, 2015, that Hillary knew that the U.S. government was using a Libyan intelligence source who has been accused of involvement in a major terrorist attack against Americans, Moussa Kassa. Moussa Kassa is presently living as a free citizen, provided by the U.S. and British governments.

Hillary's email shows that her private server was used for her own Black Operations for coordination purposes and gaining support for arms to Syria from other U.S. government agencies. More so, it shows that she was in league with the terrorists. It is possible that Ansar al-Sharia was acting on her orders to attack the compound in Benghazi to cover her and Obama's illegal weapons supply to Syria.

Documents released by government watchdog group, Judicial Watch, show that top administration officials were given intelligence reports within hours of the Benghazi attacks that stated the Islamic terrorists's had planned up to 10 days before the attack. Their goal; to assassinate as many Americans as possible.

Judicial Watch documents prove that the US government officials knew of the illegal weapons being shipped from Benghazi to Syria. They knew these weapons were to be used against the Syrian Assad regime by radical Islamic terrorists. Very importantly, the documents show an intel analysis in August 2012, that show that the rise of al-Qaida in Iraq terrorists grew into the Islamic State of Iraq and Syria (ISIS) and that Obama's foreign policy of regime change in Syria would fail.

The day after the Benghazi attacks, in a redacted, memorandum the Defense Intelligence Agency (DIA) reported to then-Secretary of Defense Leon Panetta, the U.S. military's Joint Chiefs of Staff, the White House National Security Council, and Hillary that the Islamic terrorists planned their mission approximately 10 or more days prior to the the attacks.

"The redacted DIA memo also states that the majority of the terrorists that attacked the compound are "under the age of 28 with a large number between the ages of 17-21 years of age."

This sounds eerily familiar to the refugees who are swarming into the U.S. and are doing so due to Obama's disregard of the threat.

Tom Fitting of Judicial Watch stated;

"These documents… point to [the] connection between the collapse in Libya and the ISIS war – and confirm that the U.S. knew remarkable details about the transfer of arms from Benghazi to Syrian jihadists.

"These documents are jaw-dropping. No wonder we had to file more FOIA lawsuits and wait over two years for them. If the American people had known the truth – that Barack Obama, Hillary Clinton and other top administration officials knew that the Benghazi attack was an al-Qaida terrorist attack from the get-go – and yet lied and covered this fact up – Mitt Romney might very well be president. And why would the Obama administration continue to support the Muslim Brotherhood even after it knew it was tied to the Benghazi terrorist attack and to al Qaeda?

"These documents also point to connection between the collapse in Libya and the ISIS war – and confirm that the U.S. knew remarkable details about the transfer of arms from Benghazi to Syrian jihadists."

"These documents show that the Benghazi cover-up has continued for years and is only unraveling through our independent lawsuits. The Benghazi scandal just got a whole lot worse for Barack Obama and Hillary Clinton."

A Defense Intelligence Agency report in 2012 states; "The West, Gulf countries [the Islamic regimes ruling Saudi Arabia, Qatar, United Arab Emirates, etc.], and Turkey support the Syrian opposition," it explains, adding that, as The New American reported at the time, al-Qaeda supported the Syrian uprising from the beginning as well. "There is the possibility of establishing a declared or undeclared Salafist [fundamentalist

Islam] principality in Eastern Syria (Hasaka and Der Zor), and in order to isolate the Syrian regime."

"The Salafist, the Muslim Brotherhood, and AQI [Al Qaeda in Iraq] are the major forces driving the insurgency in Syria."

The Defense Department's intelligence analysts reported; "This creates the ideal atmosphere for AQI [al-Qaeda Iraq] to return to its old pockets in Mosul and Ramadi, and will provide a renewed momentum under the presumption of unifying the jihad among Sunni Iraq and Syria, and the rest of the Sunnis in the Arab world against what it considers one enemy, the dissenters.

"ISI [Islamic State in Iraq] could also declare an Islamic state through its union with other terrorist organizations in Iraq and Syria, which will create grave danger in regards to unifying Iraq and the protection of its territory."

It does not reflect a "broader failure of policy" as some would state, they were helping create an Islamic State.

*****

Another reason Hillary wants Citizens United overturned is that they had obtained documents that show that in 2013 the State Department was interested in purchasing land for a new consulate in Eko Atlantic a development on the coast of Lagos. Eko Atlantic is funded by a company owned by the brothers Ronald and Gilbert Chagoury. The Clinton Foundation has ties to Gilbert Chagoury and Eko Atlantic. The Clinton Foundation received over $1 million from Gilbert Chagoury and the Chagoury Group pledged to commit $1 billion through Eko Atlantic to fight coastal erosion as part of the Clinton Foundation's Initiative on Climate Change. Hillary's State Department delayed a Foreign Terrorist Organization (FTO) on Nigerian Islamist Group Boko Haram which would have hurt the Chagoury's business in Nigeria. Boko Haram was the terrorist organization who had captured over 200 school girls.

Bill Clinton appeared in Eko Atlantic's promotional video. In 2013 he also attended the project dedication ceremony. A document released by Judicial Watch shows a top Clinton Foundation official had asked 2 of Hillary's aides at State to put Gilbert Chagoury in contact with the State Department's "substance person" on Lebanon. Chagoury is the owner of the wealthy Lebanese Construction conglomerate and long-time friend of Bill Clinton. In 2000, Chagoury was convicted of laundering millions. Switzerland convicted Chagoury of money laundering and aiding a criminal organization in connection with billions stolen from Nigeria. Chagoury confessed in a British Court to bribery in 2001. Chagoury donated $1-5 million to the Clinton Foundation. And in 2009, the Chagoury Group pledged $1 billion to the Clinton Global initiative.

CHAPTER 19

Retired State Department whistleblower Raymond Maxwell told investigators that he had caught Hillary's Chief of Staff and deputy Chief of Staff shredding documents in the state department basement. According to Maxwell he was told by the first two that they had been instructed to remove any documents that could be politically damaging. An office director who worked for Maxwell told him they were instructed to go through the stacks and pull out the items that could catch anybody in the front office, the seventh floor, where the secretary's office is in a bad light. He left a short time later because he said he 'didn't feel good about it'. Raymond Maxwell was one of the four State Department officials disciplined in the wake of the 2012 Benghazi attack. He was put on administrative leave and has spoken out about how he felt he was used as a scapegoat. He was eventually cleared and then retired.

In an interview with Raymond Maxwell, representative Jason Chaffetz said Maxwell told him those scrubbing the documents were looking for information that would catch Hillary and senior leaders in a bad light.

Early in May 2016 the State Department revealed that it could not find the emails of Bryan Pagliano for the four years that he was employed there. Pagliano was the information technology expert employed by the state department to troubleshoot Hillary's email issues. He was also employed by Hillary to move her regular State Department email account and her secret State Department email account from their secure location.

According to Wikipedia, Special access programs (SAPs) in the federal government of the United States of America are security protocols that provide highly classified information with safeguards and access restrictions that exceed those for regular (collateral) classified information. SAPs can range from black projects to routine but especially-sensitive operations, such as COMSEC maintenance or Presidential transportation support. In addition to collateral controls, a SAP may impose more stringent investigative or adjudicative requirements, specialized nondisclosure agreements, special terminology or markings, exclusion from standard contract investigations (carve-outs), and centralized billet systems.

According to an unidentified FBI insider Hillary sold SAP programs and although she would not have had access to them someone in the government leaked them to her and she sold them to her donors for her own personal gain.

Examining 81 of Hillary's email chains, the FBI determined that they included classified information which related to the CIA, the FBI, NSA, the Pentagon, and the National Geospatial Intelligence Agency (NGA). Hillary compromised classified materials which covered the full range of American espionage: human intelligence or HUMINT from CIA, signals intelligence or SIGINT from NSA, and imagery intelligence or IMINT from NGA.

Seven email chains included Special Access Program (SAP) information, which is highly protected by the Intelligence Community. SAP information is shared only on a restricted, need-to-know basis.

Hillary also compromised Gamma material which is the most sensitive material at NSA.

GAMMA compartment is NSA handling that is applied to extraordinarily sensitive information such as decrypted conversations between top foreign leadership.

According to Wikipedia; United States government classification system is established under Executive Order 13526, the latest in a long series of executive orders on the topic.[1] Issued by PresidentBarack Obama in 2009, Executive Order 13526 replaced earlier executive orders on the topic and modified the regulations codified to 32 C.F.R. 2001. It lays out the system of classification, declassification, and handling of national security information generated by the U.S. government and its employees and contractors, as well as information received from other governments.[2]

Why should we be surprised Obama penned another Executive order concerning the system of classification.

Not long after FBI Director, James Comey announced that he recommended that no charges be brought against Hillary, an FBI insider revealed the truth why no formal charges were brought against her.

Among many other things uncovered by the investigation, the insider said that the FBI uncovered that every department and agency within our government is intertwined in some way with the Clinton Foundation. This involvement with the Clinton Foundation includes leaders at every level within those departments and agencies. It also includes numerous world leaders. The insider said that the Clinton Foundation and members of government both had knowledge of ongoing human trafficking, and were doing nothing about it. If the FBI took down Hillary they would be taking down the whole system with her. So the FBI including the Justice Department did nothing, nothing even though she could have become President of the United States. Maybe they were those responsible for Hillary's loss in the election.

On Aaron Klein Investigative Radio;

A former highly placed NSA official, William Binney, an architect of the NSA's surveillance program, said that the NSA has all of Hillary's deleted emails. He said that the FBI could access them if they decided to do so.

Binney referred to former FBI Director Robert S. Mueller's testimony in March 2011, before the Senate Judiciary Committee. Mueller then stated that the FBI has the ability to access various secretive databases "to track down known and suspected terrorists.".

"Now what he (Mueller) is talking about is going into the NSA database, which is shown of course in the (Edward) Snowden material released, which shows a direct access into the NSA database by the FBI and the CIA. Which there is no oversight of by the way. So that means that NSA and a number of agencies in the U.S. government also have those emails.

"So if the FBI really wanted them they can go into that database and get them right now," he stated of Clinton's emails as well as DNC emails," Binney said.

When asked if NSA has all of Hillary's emails including those that were deleted, Binney's answer was, "Yes. That would be my point. They have them all and the FBI can get them right there."

*****

Everything Hillary touches is tainted with corruption. The New York Times editorial, on the Orlando shooting by Omar Mateen, did not mention the fact that he was a Muslim and that he had pledged his allegiance to ISIS. It is a fact that ISIS executes those who are of the LGBT community, as well as Christians, even children. In the editorial, instead of faulting radical extremism this was stated: "The precise motivation for the rampage remains unclear..."

Progressive organizations in the media also avoided blaming ISIS or radical Islam for the mass shooting. They have idiotically laid the blame on guns and supposed bias against the LGBT community by Republicans and Christians.

Writing for Salon, Amanda Marcotte stepped over the proverbial edge and criticized conservatives for citing radical Islam as the cause for the mass shooting and said that there is no difference between Christianity and Islam regarding violence. Who in their politically correct or politically incorrect mind would make a statement like Marcotte's? So Marcotte is saying that the Pope's view regarding violence is the same as Omar Mateen's who had pledged his allegiance to ISIS? So the Pope's view and ISIS' view is the same?

Also avoiding linking the Orlando shooting to ISIS, ACLU attorneys blamed (in tweets) the "Christian Right" for the terrorist attack due to the 200 LGBT bills that were introduced this year. What will they do next, lay the blame on the LGBT community?

Think Progress, said that Christian's views for the LGBT community are as violent as radical Islam. Do they even know what the tenets of radical Islam are? In no way are Christians views the same as radical Islam toward the LGBT community. The Christian Community embraces the LGBT community as individuals while radical Islam executes them.

This definitively looks like a campaign of disinformation placing blame for a particular incident on something or someone other than the true threat. Are reporters and journalist not held to a standard of reporting the truth? The actual truth not just their opinions or lies? They are not representing the truth to the LGBT community. They have a right to know that there is a real threat to their security by radical Islam. When one knows where a threat is coming from they are better armed to protect themselves. This is where the danger lies in not referring to the terrorists as radical Islamists.

*****

Since President Obama has been in office a terrorist attack averaging one a year has taken place on American soil.

June 2016: Omar Mateen shot and killed 49 people and wounded 53 at the Pulse gay nightclub in Orlando, Florida. The local police shot and killed him.

December 20015: Syed Rizwan Farook and Tashfeen Malik shot and killedt 14 people and wounded 21 others which occurred at the Inland Regional Center in San Bernardino, California.

July 2015: Mohammad Abdulazeez killed four Marines and a Sailor at a military recruiting center and US Navy Reserve center in Chattanooga, Tennessee. President Obama would not call the killings terrorism.

May 2015: Muslims Nadir Soofi and Elton Simpson, directed by ISIS, shot a security guard at the Curtis Culwell Center in Garland, Texas, before police took them down.

April 2013: Brothers Dzhokhar and Tamerlan Tsarnaev, from Chechnya, and Muslim, exploded a pair of pressure-cooker bombs at the Boston Marathon which killed three and wounded more than 260. At least 17 people lost limbs.

September 2012: Terrorists attacked the Special Mission Compound in Benghazi, Libya, killing the US Ambassador Chris Stevens, Sean Smith, Glen Doherty, and Tyrone Woods. Obama and Hillary lied to the American people, and blamed the attack on an anti-Muslim video.

November 2009: Army Maj. Nidal Hasan opened fire on fellow soldiers at Fort Hood, Texas, killing 13 and wounding 32. President Obama ruled it "workplace violence," even though Hasan was in contact with an al Qaeda leader before the shootings and praised Allah as he opened fire. This is where Major General John G Rossi was stationed at that time. Rossi supposedly committed "suicide" on July 31, 2016, two days before taking his new command.

June 2009: Abdulhakim Muhammad, trained by al-Qaeda, fired on an Army recruiting office in Little Rock, Ark., killing Pvt. William Long and wounding Pvt. Quinton Ezeagwula.

In 2012 Hillary's state department and the DHS shut down the case against the mosque that the Orlando terrorist, Omar Mateen attended. The case against the mosque came to the attention of the state Department's and DHS' Civil Rights and Civil Liberties office due to the Obama Administrations belief that it unfairly singled out Muslims.

Retired Homeland Security agent, Philip Haney, reported that the mosque that, Omar Mateen, the Orlando Florida terrorist attended several times each week was protected by Hillary's State Department even after the Islamic attack in San Bernardino California.

Haney's report of the intelligence collected on the worldwide Islamic movement, Tablighi Jamaat, connected the movement to several terrorist organizations and also financing at the very highest levels for Hamas and al-Qaeda. And the Fort Pierce mosque, the one that Omar Mateen attended, is closely linked with the Institute of Islamic Education which was a major part of Haney's case on Tablighi Jamaat. But Haney's report was heavily edited by the State Department. The Obama administration had ordered the deletion of 67 records related to the report on The Institute of Islamic Education.

"This case struck me as very similar to the San Bernardino shooting case. I suspected that they were both part of a national and international network of organizations," Haney said.

"It's exactly how I would have approached a case if I was still active duty," he said.

"The FBI had opened cases twice on him, and yet they found no evidence to charge him. It means they didn't go through the same basic, analytical process that I went through over a three- or four-hour period in which I was able to link the mosque to my previous cases."

So if Obama's Administration, Hillary's State Department, and DHS had followed through on Haney's report, the Orlando shooting very possibly would not have happened.

Why did the FBI ask law enforcement agencies who responded to the Pulse Nightclub shootings to withhold records from the public?

The written request from the FBI told agencies to "immediately notify the FBI of any requests your agency receive" so "the FBI can seek to prevent disclosure through appropriate channels, as necessary."

*****

In 1998, Congressman Dana Rohrabacher, disclosed detailed information that U.S. aerospace companies had helped China improve its strategic nuclear missiles as part of a major ICBM modernization effort. The companies listed were Loral Space and Communications Ltd., (big Clinton foundation donor), Hughes Electronics and Motorola as supplying the Chinese with space launch technology which China used to improve its nuclear missiles.

At a fundraising dinner in New York City in 1996 President Bill Clinton said, "There are no more nuclear missiles pointed at any children in the United States. I'm proud of that."

In 1998 the CIA's National Intelligence Daily stated that "13 of China's 18 long-range intercontinental ballistic missiles are targeted on the United States". The CIA said that China's targeting was made more accurate by Loral's unauthorized help. So how did that happen?

Congressman Rohrabacher continued, "There is ample evidence that American Technology was transferred to this hostile potential enemy of the United States... Providing the Communist Chinese the guidance needed to upgrade and perfect highly sophisticated Weapons Systems increasing the reliability and capability of Communist Chinese rockets... This has given what anyone has to admit is at least a potential enemy of the United States a better ability to deliver nuclear warheads to our country, to American cities, to incinerate millions of our people."

Bernard Schwartz, chairman of Loral Space & Communications between 1992 and 1998 donated over $1.1 million to Clinton and the Democrat Party. President Clinton allowed Schwartz to travel to China with U.S. Commerce Secretary Ron Brown to show his appreciation. President Clinton loosened export controls which enabled Schwartz to purchase Chinese booster rockets for use in launching Loral's satellites.

An internal White House memo originating from the National Security Council dated December 8ᵗʰ 1993, detailed how, Michael Armstrong, the CEO of Hughes electronics pressured the administration into easing the trade restrictions with China. He had threatened to launch a major publicity campaign against the administration's sanctions if they did not relax controls. The launch of a Chinese rocket in 1996, carrying a $200 million Loral satellite, failed when it exploded on the launch pad. The Laurel and Hughes companies put together a team of scientists to investigate. The investigation identified the problems and that information was given to the Chinese Consortium Great Wall Industry, a subsidiary of China Aerospace Corporation. With the information supplied by Hughes and Loral, the Chinese were able to upgrade their nuclear ICBM.

The reason President Clinton allowed this was that the Chinese were secretly giving large donations to the Clinton campaign. China Aerospace Corporation had given $300,000 to Democratic fundraiser Johnny Chung for Clinton's election, Federal investigators have found. Chung kept $200,000 for himself. It was discovered in 1993 that China was selling missile technology to Pakistan. Under tremendous pressure from Congress, Clinton banned the U.S. space industry from using Chinese rockets to launch their satellites. US satellites were put on the "munitions" list which is the list of our most sensitive military and intelligence gathering technology. The reason these commercial satellites are important because they carry technological secrets essential to "significant military and intelligence interests".

But in 1994, President Clinton lifted the ban. Even though reports indicated that China had continued to sell nuclear technology to Pakistan and missiles to Iran, President Clinton signed waivers for four US satellites to be launched by Chinese Rockets. He did this over strong objections from the state and defense departments. And then of course Schwartz and Johnny Chung donated over $100,000 each to Clinton. On that same day, Wang Jun, the Chinese arms dealer, attended one of Clinton's infamous campaign coffees in the White House. Wang Jun owned a very large stake in a Chinese Enterprise that benefited from Clinton's waivers, China International Trade and Investment Corporation. While Clinton personally allowed shipments of US technology that greatly improved the accuracy and reliability of communist China missiles by issuing the waivers, that was grounds for impeachment. It did not matter whether there was any money transactions between Clinton and the satellite companies. President Clinton did a great deal of damage to US National Security.

It was a pay to play.

In 2013, designs for many of the US most sensitive Advanced Weapons Systems had been compromised by Chinese hackers according to a report prepared for the Pentagon and to officials from government and the defense industry.

The Pentagon's highest weapons buyer stated the military's most expensive program the stealthy F-35 Joint Strike reflect Strike Fighter had been hacked and the stolen data used by America's adversaries. Undersecretary, Frank Kendall, did not say who stole the data but China is a strong possibility.

Undersecretary for acquisition technology and Logistics, Frank Kendall said, "I'm confident the classified material is well protected but I'm not at all confident that our unclassified information is as well protected. It's a major problem for us... What it does is reduce the costs and lead time of our adversaries to doing their own designs so it gives away a substantial advantage."

The stolen information made it easier to design countermeasures to US weapons. This improves the possibility that the other countries can hack, jam, and shoot down American aircraft. The data that had been stolen was on how the US and Allied arms manufacturers make Advanced Weapons Systems.

As defense budgets were cut the industry had merged many competing companies into just a few. And the Pentagon responded by consolidating or just canceling competing programs. With just a few companies in the industry an enemy who hacks into a single weapons program will have dangerous information into the majority of the US future fighter fleet.

The designs that were stolen include the advanced Patriot missile system known as Pac-3, an army system for shooting down ballistics missiles known as the terminal high altitude area defense or THAAD, the Navy Aegis ballistic missile defense system, vital combat aircraft and ships including the FA-18 fighter jet the V-22 Osprey, the Black Hawk helicopter and the Navy's Littoral Combat Ship which was designed to patrol waters close to shore. And the most expensive weapons system ever built, the F-35 Joint Strike Fighter, which costs almost $1.4 trillion in 2007.

Independent defense experts said that they were shocked at the extent of the cyberespionage and the potential for compromising US defenses.

Mark Stokes, executive director of the Project 2049 Institute, a think tank that focuses on Asia security issues said, "That's staggering. These are all very critical Weapons Systems, critical to our national security. When I hear this in totality, it's breathtaking."

The first hacking of the F-35 subcontractor BAE Systems was reported in 2007. It happened again in 2013.

Officials said that an AVIC subsidiary, The Chengu Aircraft Industry Group, used the stolen information in building the J-20.

Director of National Intelligence had details of AVIC's past involvement in illicit arms transfers and its role in attaining sensitive F-35 technology through cyber espionage.

In 2011, Pentagon Technologies Security officials opposed a joint venture between General Electric and AVIC due to concerns that US fighter jet technology would be diverted to AVIC's military aircraft programs.

Even though the office of Director of National Intelligence knew of past illegal involvement of AVIC, the Obama Administration ignored those concerns and instead had promoted the systematic loosening of technology controls on transfers to China.

AVIC is Aviation Industry Corporation of China.

The US allies that took part in the F-35 program includes; Australia, Canada, Denmark, Israel, Italy, the Netherlands, Turkey, and the United Kingdom. But why would Obama promote the loosening of technology controls on transfers to China? Could it be related to James Comey's job at Lockheed Martin or HSBC before Obama appointed him Director of the FBI? And the accusation of Marine Field McConnell that Comey leaked the plans to China? Could it have something to do with Obama's focus on Asia?

In 2014, the latest version of China's J-20 stealth fighter jet is the incorporation of the sensitive technology and aircraft secrets that were stolen, according to US officials and private defense analysts.

CHAPTER 20

President Obama has been criticized for not saying "radical Islamic terrorism".

The son of one of the founders of Hamas, Hassan Yousaf stated;

"When the president of the free world stands and says that Islam is a religion of peace, he creates the climate, he provides the climate, the perfect climate to create more terrorism," Yousef stated, who turned against Hamas in 1996.

"There is an Islamic problem, and I think humanity needs to stand against this danger because this danger is not only against the state of Israel, this danger is against the evolvement of mankind. "What is the alternative for Israel and for democracy or for the American Constitution?

"It's the darkness of the sixth century. This is what's the alternative," Yousaf said.

Admiral James 'Ace Lyons has had a 36-year military service as a Surface Warfare Officer including Commander in Chief of the US Pacific Fleet as well as being the senior US military Representative to the United Nations and Deputy Chief of Naval Operations. He was a graduate of the U.S. Naval Academy and has received postgraduate degrees from the U.S. Naval War College and the U.S. National Defense University.

Four star Navy Admiral James Ace Lyons warns America, "Why would an American president embrace the Muslim Brotherhood?"

"The more Islam you have the less Freedom you have.

"The Muslim Brotherhood's Creed is to destroy us from within by our own miserable hands. And replace our constitution with its Draconian Sharia law. The Muslim Brotherhood has been able to penetrate all of our national and intelligence agencies. They have had a tremendous impact on our domestic and foreign policies, a restricted Rules of Engagement that has cost so many American lives that never had to happen. All of the problems we had in carrying out our mission in Iraq and Afghanistan, preventing our people from what we only used to be able to do to win, to be what we used to be in order to win. We have a very serious national security problem. When you have a president not interested in America leading, winning, you can understand our greatest threat to our national security resides at 1600 Pennsylvania Avenue." He stated that never did he believe he'd witnessed this great country being taken down and withdrawn from our world leadership role by our own Administration.

Admiral Lyons had also warned Congress that the Muslim Brotherhood had infiltrated every US National Security Agency under Obama's administration. His warning had come just days before President Obama would invite more than a dozen Muslim Brotherhood leaders to a private meeting in the White House. The press was not allowed to attend. Lyons said "that the 'transformation of America has been in full swing ever since 2008".

"Fundamentally transform America", Obama's stated promise, has been kept.

"No question we've got a hell of a job ahead of us with the Muslim Brotherhood penetration in every one of our national security agencies including all our Intelligence agencies and has been reported by some our lead intelligence agency headed by a Muslim convert (a reference to CIA director John Brennan long rumored to have converted to Islam in the 1990's in Baghdad). This is not going to be an easy task."

Lyons said that Obamas non-presence in Paris was an embarrassment for all Americans. And he said that it was also a signal to the Islamic Jihadists. It has been one of many signals he sent over the years in the White House.

"Political correctness has neutralized all our political leadership. Les Gel called for the entire firing of the entire executive branch of government including Valerie Jarrett but he left one out, the one man who really determines American policy."

"We have had many opportunities over the years to change the course of history starting with Carter. When the Iranians took over our Embassy we could have cut off Islamic fundamentalism at the knees but we did not act. He rejected what could have been a very dramatic action with minimum involvement and it would have been dead."

Lyons said that there is no radical Islam. "Islam is Islam."

About the bombing of the Marine Barracks Admiral Lyons said that,

"The guy that sabotaged the strike was the Secretary of Defense Weinberger, not once but twice. Reagan approved, the French wanted to combine a strike, Reagan approved it but Weinberger would not issue the order. They pleaded with him but he wouldn't do it."

Lyons said that this was stated by Erdogan of Turkey, "Islam is Islam, there are no modifiers. Democracy is the train we ride to our ultimate objective."

Islam is a political movement masquerading as a religion. Admiral Lyons, said, "Obama has a strategy, anti-American, anti-western, pro-islamic, pro-Iranian, and pro-muslim Brotherhood."

"The final year of Obama's presidency should scare the hell out of us," Admiral Lyons stated.

"Hillary Clinton's unsecured email server has likely been hacked by nearly every enemy America has in the world. She has been totally compromised. She is damaged goods. They know everything about her. There is no way that she can be permitted to be in the White House."

Admiral Lyons stated that, "The Muslim Brotherhood has been working on penetrating our government since the 1960's. And now they have carte blanche into the White House and they won't stop in their Crusade until Sharia is the law of the land replacing the US Constitution and America turned into an Islamic Nation. Freedom and Islam cannot possibly go hand in hand."

"In Obama's Marxist background he viewed America as the cause of many of the world's problems and therefore anything that undercuts Americans influence and Power is seen as being objectively Progressive. His strategy is anti-American, anti-western, pro-islam, pro Iranian, and pro-muslim Brotherhood."

"The Muslim Brotherhood has been penetrating our government since the 1960s much like the Communists in the thirties forties and fifties.

"The Muslim Brotherhood's creed is to destroy us from within by our own miserable hands, and replace our Constitution with it's draconian sharia law.

"This was proven by the FBI's Holy Land Foundation 5 file in Dallas Texas in 2008. All these, Islamic Society of North America, and C.A.I.R., they're all Muslim Brotherhood front groups like the Muslim Students Association events sprinkled throughout many of our campuses in the country. There's no such thing as violent extremism or radical Islam. Because that implies that there is some sort of secular Western Islam there is not any and Erdogan when he was Prime Minister of Turkey said it best, Islam is Islam. There are no modifiers. Democracy is the train we ride to our ultimate objective and that's total world domination with Islam as the predominant religion.

It's totalitarian in nature to control every aspect of your daily life. It's no different than what we faced with Communism years ago."

Admiral Lyons is now CEO of Lyon, LLC, a Global consultancy firm specializing in international trade, defense procurement and counter-terrorism.

President Obama has been replacing those in the military with those who will do exactly what he wants. Major Jason Brezler, a Marine, sent a dire warning to fellow soldiers in Afghanistan about a corrupt Afghan police chief who was sexually enslaving young children. It's called, "bacha bazi", or, "boy play". The terrorists are now using boys to attack American soldiers. Because he sent it using his personal email, he was involuntary discharged from the military. But his warning of an attack did come true.

The ACLJ is fighting for Major Jason Brezler. They have helped reinstate Sergeant Charles Martland after he faced expulsion for defending an Afghan boy from sexual abuse. These men are standing up for what is right and they are being expelled from the military. What in the Holy Name of God is happening to this country?

Retired four-star general, Jack Keane has been a longtime critic of President Obama's foreign policy. He has warned Congress that the US is losing the war with the Islamic State.

"Moreover I can say with certainty that the strategy will not defeat ISIS."

Keane said that disagreeing with President Obama can be dangerous for the careers of military leaders.

On a radio interview on Kilmeade and Friends, Keane said that there is a pattern of generals who disagree with the president leaving the military earlier than expected. General Keane also said that when President Obama declared his intention to defeat ISIS he severely restricted the military's options from the very beginning. A normal military campaign procedure, according to Keane, usually includes officials putting together different plans with each one detailing the various levels of risk. The president then makes a judgment call based on the plan. But that military campaign procedure was something that has never happened under Obama's administration. He wanted no boots on the ground and no civilian casualties for the air campaign. These demands hampered efforts to swiftly defeat Isis.

"It's also a fact that a number of our general officers, not all of them but a number of them, were asked to leave before what would normally be accepted as routine tenure for that particular position, and General (James) Mattis is a case in point who had very strong views on Iran," Keane said.

General Keane referencing the Iranian nuclear deal pointed out that, "Iran always cheats and the only reason we know that it's not because of inspection, but because of informants. Iran is attempting to show it is the dominant power in the Middle East and that the U.S. is no longer a strong ally."

"General Flynn you know very well and had on your show with an outspoken proponent for understanding radical Islam how dangerous this particular threat was and was trying to communicate that. He was not able to serve out his full tenure. So yes that's another fact that we can substantiate if there were Generals who did leave earlier than what their tenure would be and the characteristics they all shared together as they did disagree with the administration on various points."

General Flynn had stated, "I mean, there's a lot of frustration within the ranks, and there's a lot of frustration I know in the senior leadership about what we're not able to do."

CHAPTER 21

Hillary stated "I have a better track-record", and that she "is a progressive who gets things done".

Well some of the things she has gotten done and Hillary's major accomplishments were catastrophic. Six countries that were in her path to getting things done were Honduras, Haiti, Afghanistan, Libya, Syria, and Ukraine. The harm she did to each country was not in the interest of their citizens.

During the Benghazi attack, Hillary never gave the order to mobilize the State Department's Foreign Emergency Support Team (FEST) which would secure the compound.

Honduras is ruled by a fascist government, because of what Hillary and Obama did in 2009. Honduras is ruled by a fascist government. All of the lives but the top percentage of the population have experienced hell on earth because of their actions.

The flight of many children to the U.S. was caused by Hillary's support in the coup d'etat in Honduras on June 28th, 2009. As Secretary of State she helped create the seriously disastrous conditions that caused the children to leave. Hillary told CNN's Christiane Amanpour in 2014 that, "It may be safer for the children to remain in the US" but "they should be sent back".

Hillary's State Department played a dark part in the Honduran disaster. It is a human rights and security disaster. The coup deposed democratically elected president Jose Manuel Zelaya.

The U.S. Embassy in Tegucigalpa sent a cable to Washington with the subject: Open and Shut: The Case of the Honduran Coup, declaring that there is no doubt that the events on June 28th constituted an illegal and unconstitutional coup.

The embassy described the removal of President Zelaya from Honduras as an abduction and kidnapping. The cable was sent by the US Embassy to several people which included, Harold Koh, the State Department's legal adviser. The cable was also sent to the White House and to Secretary of State Hillary Clinton. In an interview with the New York daily news, columnist Juan Gonzalez pressed Hillary on her decisions during the coup in Honduras and if she had any concerns about her role in the aftermath of the coup. She stated; "Well let me again try to put this in context. The legislature, the National Legislature in Honduras and the National Judiciary actually followed the law in removing president Zelaya. Now I didn't like the way it looked or the way they did it but they had a very strong argument that they had followed the Constitution and the legal precedence. And as you know they really undercut their argument by spiriting him out of the country in his pajamas where they sent the military to take him out of his bed and get him out of the country. So this began a very mixed and difficult situation.

If United States government declares a coup, you immediately have to shut off all aid, including humanitarian aid, the Agency for International Development aid, the support that we were providing at that time for a lot of very poor people, and that triggers a legal necessity. There's no way to get around it. So our assessment was, we will just make the situation worse by the Honduran people if we declare a coup and we immediately have to stop all aid for the people, but we should slow walk and try to stop anything that the government could take advantage of without calling it a coup."

But she left out the part that Zelaya was a democratically elected president of Honduras. The United Nations along with different governments around the world condemned Zelaya's ouster as a coup and called for his restoration as president.

A professor of history and expert on U.S. relations with Honduras, Dana Frank, said that it was "chilling that a leading presidential candidate would say this was not a coup... She's baldly lying when she says the United States never called it a coup".

President Obama said, "We believe the coup was not legal, and that president Zelaya remains the president of Honduras, the democratically elected leader of the country."

But the United States, in 2009, changed it's position and decided for elections instead of bringing Zelaya back.

When talking about Hillary's role in the 2009 coup Berta Caceras, a fearless environmentalist and one who fought for indigenous land rights, said "We're coming out of a coup that we can't put behind us. We can't reverse it. It just kept going. And after, there was the issue of the elections. The same Hillary Clinton, in her book Hard Choices, practically said what was going to happen in Honduras. This demonstrates the meddling of North Americans in our country."

The paperback edition of Hard Choices, by Hillary, completely left out the discussion of the Honduran coup.

A year after the 2010 Haiti earthquake, Hillary flew down to Port-au-Prince to speak with the Haitian president. Her goal was to persuade him to change the results of the first-round election for his successor. Billions of aid dollars were on the line. Hillary wanted her own puppet in government. Hillary got her way. A few months later, Michel Martelly was inaugurated president of Haiti. Again, putting those in office to do her bidding.

Hillary had set the stage for a coup d'etat in the Ukraine when she made Victoria Nuland the State Department's official spokesperson. When Vice President Dick Cheney was in office, Nuland had been his chief foreign-affairs advisor. Nuland then became the organizer of the February 20, 2014 coup in Ukraine. This coup caused a bloody civil war and replaced Ukraine, Viktor Yanukovych, with an anti-Russian, Arseniy Yatsenyuk, a U.S. puppet. Victoria Nuland is obsessed with hatred of Russia. If she were Hillary's Secretary of State or in any other office, should Hillary be President of the United States significantly if both held high offices, war with Russia may be inevitable.

The Jasmine Revolution, or the Tunisian uprising, caused the overthrow of the country's president, Zine El Abidine Ben Ali.

Radical Islamic extremists began and then further agitated the protesters which turned into a full scale revolution.

The Tunisian protests of 2011 were spurred by political assassinations. And the Democratic Patriot's movement leader, Chokri Belaid on February 6th, 2013, and the People's Movement leader and member of parliament Mohamed Brahmi on July 25th, 2013, murders were blamed on Islamic extremists with Boubacar Hakim. Hakim was under suspicion of smuggling weapons from Libya.

Hussein Ibish warned that there is a historical pattern for islamists helping to topple the government in the name of pluralism and political reform and then seizing power for a theocratic dictatorship.

"The model is Iran. It is possible to go from the frying pan to the fire."

Extremist cleric Sheikh Abu Muhammad al-Maqdisi who was the mentor of slain al Qaeda leader in Iraq, Abu Musab al-Zarqawi had urged supporters to "seize the moment", according to a summary prepared by the Middle East Media Research Institute. He called on extremists to boycott existing parties and work through "reviving mosques, opening libraries, spreading relevant propaganda, and performing "missionary work" among the Tunisian people".

Al-Qaeda in the Islamic Maghreb leader, Abu Mus'ab Abdel Al-Wadoud praised the demonstrators, calling on them to intensify their efforts and spread them to other Arab and Muslim countries. This call was heard on a radio message.

The EnNadha, the Islamic political party, had been banned from Tunisia for decades by Ben Ali. The leaders were jailed or sent into exile.

Some observers of the opposition's rise, stated their concern openly of the Islamic extremists in Tunisia.

The EnNadha movement is said to have been shaped by Qutbism and is highly influenced by the Muslim Brotherhood. Following the overthrow of Ben Ali, the EnNadha party, led by Rasid al-Ghannushi, was legalized. The Muslim Brotherhood's stated goal is to instill the Koran and Sunnah as the sole reference point for... ordering the life of the Muslim family, individual, community... and state.

Their mottos include;

"Islam is the solution",

"Allah is our objective; the Koran is the Constitution; jihad is our way; death for the sake of Allah is our wish."

Hillary was Secretary of State when the 2006-2010 drought was taking place and causing relocation of large numbers of the population of Syria. U.S. State Department cables, of the Assad government urgently requesting aid from foreign governments to help farmers fight off starvation, passed up the chain of command to Hillary. But Hillary's State Department ignored the requests. She used this humanitarian crisis in Syria of children, women, and men as an opportunity to promote the revolution.

In Syria, the Arab Spring was not what the Obama administration and Hillary tried to portray. The demonstrations against Assad were Sunni jihadist fighters who where sent to Syria, by the U.S., Saudi Arabia, Turkey, and Qatar. The U.S. government was assisting jihadists to overthrow the non-sectarian, secular Shiite leader, Assad, and replace him with a fundamentalist Sunni dictator.

President Putin is not the bad guy everyone wants to make him out to be in the case of Syria. Obama and Hillary were backing ISIS to overthrow Assad. Putin is fighting against that. Obama had wanted Turkey to assist but they would not do so. Obama also tried to get Russia to stop fighting ISIS and let them have Aleppo. Well why doesn't Obama quit backing ISIS? And why would Obama want ISIS to control Aleppo? It is a terrible humanitarian crisis. But it is not Putin's fault. It is the fault of Obama and Hillary for giving ISIS the assistance to attempt to overthrow Assad. What would Syria be if Assad and Russia stops fighting and allows ISIS to takeover? Look at Libya. But US Ambassador to the UN, Samantha Powers, refused to accept Syria's rationale of fighting terrorists. And is it any wonder why nothing is being resolved? The ambassadors of Great Britain, France, and the United States contemptuously walked out of the chamber when Syria's UN ambassador spoke at an emergency Sunday meeting on September 25th. Sadly, that shows that the US has no interest in ending these war crimes it is committing against the children, women, and men of Syria. And what Great Britain, France, and the United States have in common is all three countries took part in the overthrow and murder of Gaddafi, and taking the lead, Obama and Hillary.

In a leaked email Sidney Blumenthal told Hillary that just as Gaddafi had died in his home town of Sirte that Assad's family home is in Qardaha, outside of predominantly Alawite Latakia. There is an indication that if Assad fled to Latakia, where his fellow Alawites and a Russian military base could protect him at least temporarily, Qardaha might also serve as Assad's "Sirte". Blumenthal states in the email to Hillary, that if Assad fled to Latakia it would represent a "very short lived endgame," and Assad, unlike Gaddafi, is not willing to fight to the death. But Gaddafi was not willing to fight to the death. Hillary would not allow him to surrender.

This is one of the emails from Sidney Blumenthal to Hillary concerning Syria;

CONFIDENTIAL July 24, 2012 For: Hillary From: Sid Re: Syria, Turkey, Israel, Iran SOURCE: Sources with access to the highest levels of the Governments and institutions discussed below. This includes political parties and regional intelligence and security services.

1. According to an individual with access to the highest levels of major European governments, the intelligence services of these countries are reporting to their principals that the commanders of the Israeli military and intelligence community believe that the civil war in Syria is spreading to neighboring countries, including Lebanon, Jordan, and Turkey. These European officials are concerned that the ongoing conflict in Syria will lead to uprisings in these countries that will bring increasingly conservative Islamic regimes into power, replacing existing secular or moderate regimes. This individual adds that, Israeli security officials believe that Prime Minister Benjamin Netanyahu is convinced that these developments will leave them vulnerable, with only enemies on their borders.

2. In private conversations senior Israeli Intelligence and Military commanders state to their European associates that they have long viewed the regime of Syrian President Bashar al Assad, while hostile, as a known quantity and a buffer between Israel and the more militant Muslim countries, a situation that is threatened by the growing success of the rebel forces of the Free Syria Army (FSA). This source is convinced that these Israeli leaders are now drawing up contingency plans to deal with a regional structure where the new revolutionary regimes that take over the various countries will be controlled by the Muslim Brotherhood and possibly more problematic groups such as al Qaeda, which doesn't bode well for the Israelis.

3. At the same time, looking at the tensions between Israel and Iran as part of the overall situation in the region, these European heads of state are receiving, reporting, indicating that if Israel were to attack the Iranian nuclear facilities at this time it would only exacerbate relations with their neighbors. In addition, such an attack may lead to further deterioration in the world economy, which would in turn be blamed on Israel. These sources believe that such an attack would also unite the Iranian population against the United States and strengthen their ties to the Mullahs, rather than weaken them. These particular individuals fear that this in turn would accelerate Iranian efforts at building a nuclear arsenal, seeking additional support from their contacts in Russia and China.

4. According to a source with direct access, Turkish Army commanders have stated in private discussions with the highest levels of their Government that an Israeli attack on Iran will surely start a regional war "before the first Israel air-strike sortie has returned to base". Turkish intelligence estimates, supported by their liaison contacts in Western European intelligence services, advise that thousands of missiles and rockets would fall on Israel fired from Iran, Lebanon, Syria, and Gaza.

5. (Source Comment: The Turkish Army estimates that Syria and Lebanon Hezbollah forces have access to over 200,000 surface to surface rockets and missiles. Their military analysts also believe that an assault from such a force would overwhelm Israel's defenses.

And Israel has Obama and Hillary to thank for that situation.

The Halifax International Security Forum (HISF) was formed in 2009 as a covert arm of the US states. It is mainly funded by the Department of National Defense (DND). The two leading officials of HISF, president David Van Praagh, and Vice President Joseph Hall, both US citizens and experienced agents whose salary is paid by the Department of National Defense were deployed to Egypt by the US National Democratic Institute of the National Endowment for Democracy (NED) during the Tahrir Square uprising. Hall opened the first NDI office in Cairo in 2005 and was in Cairo in January and February of 2011. Directors of the HISF include three members of the Council of Foreign Relations, (CFR), and the president of Freedom House. They were getting ready for the Arab Spring.

The Arab Spring revolutions have four unique features in common;

1) None of the revolutions were spontaneous. All revolutions had careful and lengthy planning, 5 years and more, supplied by the State Department, CIA pass through foundations, George Soros, and the pro-Israel lobby.

2) All of the revolutions removed or tried to remove the governments of the countries.

3) None of the revolutions made any reference at all to anti-US sentiment over Palestine and Iraq.

4) All of the instigators in the revolutions were middle-class and well-educated youth, who up and vanished after 2011.

Bensaada, in writing Arabesque$, used websites of key CIA pass through foundations, and Wikileaks. He lists every State Department workshop and conference attended by the Arab Spring militias; the amount of money spent on them by the State Department; key "democracy" promoting foundations; and involvement of Facebook, Google, and Twitter. He also sights Obama's 2008 internet campaign which was training the Arab Spring participants in social media and encryption technology. Bensadaa also lists U.S. embassies visits by the Arab Spring militias; and he shows that these militias had direct contact with Hillary, Obama, John McCain, Condoleezza Rice, and the Serbian trainers from CANVAS. CANVAS is the Center for Applied Non Violent Action and Strategies and is the CIA-backed organization that overthrew Slobodan Milosevic in 2000.

Twelve million dollars was given to the militia groups in opposition to the Syrian regime from 2005-2010, by the State Department. Syrian exiles in Britain were also backed by the U.S. to start an anti-government cable TV channel which they transmitted into Syria.

In Arabesque$, he gives 11 key U.S. assets who engineered the overthrow of Gaddafi and his regime. These assets were also being trained along with the Middle Eastern militias which was provided by the State Department. And to coincide with the 2011 uprisings in Tunisia and Egypt, they started nonviolent Facebook and Twitter protests. The CIA, Chad, Mosaad, and Saudi Arabia trained the ones in exile in guerilla warfare. Some of these same people led Islamic militias to try to overthrow Assad in Syria, after the assassination of Gaddafi.

In 2006, Syrian militias received U.S. training by the U.S. in cyber-activism and nonviolent resistance. In a 2011 film, on How to Start a Revolution, Ausama Monajed is featured. Along with others, Monajed worked closely with the US embassy. This was funded by the Middle East Partnership Initiative (MEPI). MEPI is a State Department program that operates in countries such as Libya and Syria. These countries have banned USAID.

They posted on Twitter and Facebook in 2011, in which they called for a Day of Rage. Along with allies, Saudi Arabia, Turkey, Qatar, and Jordan, they used Islamic terrorists when nothing happened with their online call for a day of rage. There were many from the militias from Libya, to declare war on the Assad regime.

Ahmad Bensaada's, Arabesque$, book review is by Dr. Stuart Jeanne Bramhall, a retired psychiatrist and political refugee in New Zealand. Her book, The Most Revolutionary Act: Memoir of an American Refugee, describes the circumstances that led her to leave the US in 2002.

One of the most dangerous men to the criminal element at the highest levels of the U.S. Government is, William Robert "Tosh" Plumlee. Plumlee has an extensive history and knowledge of the criminal part of the U.S. government. He has had first hand experience in their methods and operations. Tosh Plumlee goes way back to the 1950's, back to the Castro days. Their criminal actions have global implications and will very likely lead the U.S. into World War 3. Plumlee was a C110 pilot who flew guns ammunition all over the world under Direct Commercial Sales of the State Department. Plumlee said they received unknown money from unknown sources. But he does differentiate that there are good and bad elements in the government and the CIA.

As stated on Canada Free Press;

For his candor and hours after the interview, he confided to me that he was informed by at least one highly placed government source that his public interview on our show was heard and documented by the Department of Justice. He was informed, as I was, that his disclosures angered the Department of Justice as well as some in the CIA hierarchy and other government offices, and that he had no "right" to discuss such matters. This, despite the inconvenient fact that he would be guilty of a felony by not disclosing illegal government operations to authorities. But when the authorities, or those we have elected to oversee and stop such egregiously illegal actions fail to do anything other than respond by asking for campaign contributions via form letters, he felt he had to go public. And so he did, with a clear conscious and without regard to the peril he now faces.

He said that the bad element wants him dead while the good element wants him to continue. That way he can inform them.

These secret operations, that the CIA did not know existed, has come out in the courts.

These secret operations have access to our arsenal and take them from special operations under the guise of training troops in foreign countries to defend their countries. And then they are used to destabilize these governments. Just as what happened in Tunisia, Egypt, Libya, and Syria. That is the reason the Homeland Security has been buying odd caliber ammunition in huge amounts. They supply the Syrian rebels and then the ammunition will not be traced back to the U.S.

Plumlee said that this shadow government controls the U.S., not our elected officials, not our Constitution. They are using the threat of Al-Qaeda. Although now they openly arm al-Qaeda. But Navy Seal and drone operator, Travis Lively, said that al-Qeada does not exist. The threat is coming from this shadow government. Plumlee said the Syrian rebels were given chemical weapons by Saudi Intelligence.

Plumlee's contact in the Middle East and a high ranking NATO official had reports of complaints from Ambassador Stevens about his dispatches and cables he had sent to the State Department about weapons being delivered into radical arms including Stinger missiles. Ambassador Stevens questions were, "Where are they coming from? What do I have to do? What should I do?" And he was ordered to stand down.

The ambassador's people had written a series of field reports and cable dispatches advising the State Department that rebel factions had been armed with U.S. weapons

A Pentagon source, a week after the attacks, said that the Ambassador said, "No", to giving al-Qaeda heat seeking missiles. They had 3 warehouses full of them.

So they had them ordered all killed, using Benghazi "al-Qaeda" security forces to wipe out witnesses of the weapons and so that they could expunge the cables. That is the real story of Benghazi.

Glen Doherty, Tyrone Woods, Sean Smith, and Ambassador Chris Stevens were murdered because Hillary and her State Department, and the Obama administration did not want any witnesses or any evidence left of their shipment of arms to Syria and wherever else they were sent to. And they did not want known the fact that they were trying to deliver these to Isamic terrorists. This is why it is important to bear in mind the existence of a shadow government in our own government. No conspiracies, these are facts. This shadow government goes back to the 1950's. It includes Castro, the Iran-contra, the Arab Spring which encompasses Tunisia, Egypt, Libya, and Syria. Research documents this. A good place to start is with Rattler's Revenge, by government insider Col. Donn de Grand Pre. It is a 4 volume collaboration of historical information that shows how the U. S. has been sold out to the global elite for no other reason than globalization. The European Union, the Arab Spring, the refugee crisis not only in the U. S. but in every country, the progressive's desire for the control of the world by one central government, one central bank, the United Nations, which Obama wanted to give the control of small arms to, are all part of this.

The U.N.'s definition of Small arms, includes weapons capable of being carried and fired by one person which would include every handgun and rifle one owns.

Sen. James Inhofe (R-Okla.) introduced an amendment that would prevent the United States from entering into the United Nations Arms Trade Treaty in order to uphold the Second Amendment. His amendment passed on a 53-46 vote. Thankfully they voted against the treaty but by a very narrow lead.

was released obligates States to establish "national control systems" to meet the particulars of the treaty. And, where no "law" can be established, the treaty invites new "regulations" on gun ownership.

And, the language makes specific note that the treaty places no limit upon greater gun control efforts within individual nations. That is because the treaty requires each country to enact national legislation sufficient to meet the minimum goals outlined in this treaty. That includes creating gun registries, coordinating background checks, putting controls on imports/exports, and so forth.

There is no protection of the individual's right to bear arms in this treaty. Instead, the State, is given the right to arms ownership in order to maintain internal order. The individual is not.

CHAPTER 22

M any people have lost their lives due to those in the American government who believe in the Yglesias principle. It is basically the U.S government's belief that it is entitled to use violence at will.

And the Yglesias principle also pertains to violence and murder of three Kennedy's in 30 some years.

The assassination of John F Kennedy Jr.

John F Kennedy JR's plane crash in 1999 was blamed on his own recklessness. But Don Jefferies' investigation found that it was in fact another Kennedy assassination. JFK JR was scheduled to meet with Wayne Madeen, who he had hired, the following week, and one of his jobs would be to investigate the assassination of his father, President John F. Kennedy. Steve Sbraccio, reporter for WCVB-TV who had covered the story of JFK JR's death, wrote Don Jeffries in a 2006 email telling him, "I've always felt there was something wrong about that crash... from the way the police swept through that beach forcing everyone off, to the way they kept the wreck site closely guarded until they pulled up every bit of debris..."

A reporter from the Martha's Vineyard Gazette claimed to have seen an explosion in the air and then he seemed to vanish from off the face of the earth. Sbraccia sent Jefferies another email in 2012. "I can swear in court that man was real-and I reported exactly what he told me he saw."

There were also other people who claimed to have seen the explosion. After the accident, trying to track down the Martha Vineyard Gazette reporter researcher, John Dinardo was refused by the paper the name of the reporter who saw the explosion. Jeffries came up against the same resistance from the editor who claimed to have personally covered the story for the paper. She told Jeffries that she had no recollection of all of the reports about a mid-air explosion or of the reporter. The mainstream media at that time continued the lie that Kennedy should not have flown that evening because of bad weather. But the evidence proved that the skies were clear. FAA Flight Specialist Edward Meyer released a public statement, "Nothing of what I have heard on mainstream media makes any sense to me... The weather along his flight was just fine."

Meyers emailed Jeffries in 2012, "That every report I saw, read, or heard said that visibility was too low for JFK JR to make his approach..."

Meyer told Don Jeffries that the NTSB report contradicted that, "EVERYTHING that was said by the media... He was fully licensed to fly that night and there were no weather reports that contradicted the VFR flight conditions that the plane was flying in."

News reports had initially described a call at 9:39 p.m. from Kennedy to the FAA and reported all was well and that he was awaiting landing instructions. Coast Guard petty officer Todd Bergen was interviewed by WCVB about the call from Kennedy to the FAA which would have been taking place at the exact moment officials would later claim Kennedy's plane was crashing. None of Jefferies emails were responded to by the reporter who interviewed Bergen on air. And Jeffries could not locate her again. VFR would later claim that there was never a 9:39 p.m. communication from Kennedy even though there were many local news reports and widely distributed accounts about the call from UPI and ABC News. Jeffries had video tapes of the original WCVB coverage and it included many references to the 9:39 p.m. phone call from Kennedy. When researchers obtained the videotapes they discovered that all references to the 9:39 p.m. call had been edited out. Jeffries said that the fear on the part of those who were associated in some way with events that he had chronicled were still evident even decades later. When he first contacted the nephew of Deputy Seymour Weitzman he kept repeating, I don't know anything. Deputy Weitzman was in the center of what happened on November 22nd 1963, the assassination of JFK. Later on the House Select Committee on Assassinations would find that Weitzman had been committed to a mental institution supposedly due to his preoccupation and fear of the conspirators he felt had been behind the assassination of JFK.

Although most people believe that JFK JR was not going to go into politics, he had stated the same day that he died that he would run for senator of New York, the same seat Hillary was running for. Just think. If JFK Jr would not have been killed, or murdered, he very possibly would be the President of the United States today.

Even though it has been proven that Hillary has lied, and that she has worked to overthrow governments, filling the coffers of the Clinton Foundation, some people still vote for her. Something is definitely going on with the Republican Congressmen and Congresswomen support of Hillary.

Never in history has so many of the Republican officials changed their views and decided to vote for a Democrat. Surprisingly, or maybe not surprisingly, George Bush Senior is voting for Hillary.

None of it makes sense until you look a little deeper, along with the fact that so many in Washington have ties to the Clinton Foundation. Hillary will continue the Permanent War Economy, that began at the end of World War 2, if she is President. And of course the Military Industrial Complex will continue to enrich those who have companies who want to do business with the government.

Dwight Eisenhower had warned the United States of the danger of the Military Industrial Complex. Eisenhower expressed concerns about the growing influence of what he termed the military-industrial complex.

Before and during the Second World War, American industries had successfully converted to defense production as the crisis demanded, but out of the war, what Eisenhower called a permanent armaments industry of vast proportions emerged. This conjunction of an immense military establishment and a large arms industry is new in the American experience Eisenhower warned, [while] we recognize the imperative need for this development. We must not fail to comprehend its grave implications we must guard against the acquisition of unwarranted influence...The potential for the disastrous rise of misplaced power exists and will persist. Eisenhower cautioned that the federal government's collaboration with an alliance of military and industrial leaders, though necessary, was vulnerable to abuse of power. Ike then counseled American citizens to be vigilant in monitoring the military-industrial complex. Only an alert and knowledgeable citizenry can compel the proper meshing of the huge industrial and military machinery of defense with our peaceful methods and goals, so that security and liberty may prosper together.

LATEST INFORMATION UPDATE

Obama care has done so much damage. Not only have health care centers and health insurance companies had to go out of business, but companies that have to lay off employees are fined under Obamacare. One company was fined approximately $3.6 million due to layoffs.

Obamacare has caused millions of full-time jobs to turn into part-time jobs. It has imposed a tax on lower-income workers who cannot afford it, forced millions of people out of insurance they liked. Obamacare restricted access to doctors for millions of others. It created an enormous bureaucracy that discourages our doctors and nurses. And Obamacare suppresses health-care system innovation.

The number of records set by Obama during his presidency has harmed America.

Those records include;

$20 trillion in national debt,

$100 trillion in unfunded liabilities owed due to entitlements,

Made it more difficult for businesses,

81,640 pages of regulations as of November 17th, the most regulations passed in a single year,

The only president to ever surpass the production of the 80,000 mark of regulatory pages and achieved this mark four times,

Also the only presided to produce the most regulatory pages in one day, 572 pages on November 17.

"In other words, each year every person, regardless of age, in the nation is responsible for paying roughly $540 in regulatory costs. These burdens might take the form of higher prices, fewer jobs, or reduced wages," Sam Batkins said, AAF's director of regulatory policy at the watchdog group.

"The Obama Administration surpassed 500 major regulations last summer, imposing $625 billion in cumulative costs. Earlier this year, regulators published the administration's 600th major rule, increasing burdens to $743 billion. Now, thanks to data from the last term of the Bush Administration and another billion-dollar rule from EPA, the regulatory tally has surpassed $1 trillion. These figures are direct estimates from federal regulators, but it will take more than an effort from these regulators to amend hundreds of major regulations."

The Obama Administration's new orders are to release Haitians caught at the border.

And "...is moving to release hundreds of Haitians being held in detection centers in Arizona and California. The result of that release will be a new marketing tool for Mexican cartels and human smuggling organizations," said Hector Garza, National Border Patrol Council Local 2455 President during an exclusive interview with Breitbart Texas.

All the Haitians have to do when arriving in Mexico is claim to be African and they then receive a 20-day permit to pass through the country northward. They arrive in the U.S. and ask for asylum.

"The move continues to overwhelm U.S. authorities as the number of asylum seekers continues to rise, adding more work to the already overwhelmed agents who, according to NBPC officials, [on purpose deprived by Obama] lack manpower, equipment, and help from Washington."

Dr. Jane Orient, executive director of the Association of American Physicians and Surgeons stated that, "Tuberculosis is one of the most lethal infectious diseases in history." But refugees with an outbreak of deadly infectious tuberculosis was allowed to be sent to Indiana by President Obama. Also Obama is allowing Syrian immigrants to enter without proper medical examinations.

Chris Cabrera, Southern Texas Border Patrol agent, said, "...The ongoing invasion at the border with Mexico is exposing Americans to numerous health risks. What's coming over into the U.S. could harm everyone. We are starting to see scabies, chicken pox, methicillin-resistant Staphylococcus aureus infections, and different viruses. Syrian refugees have brought leishmaniasis, a terrifying parasitic flesh-eating disease prevalent in Syria, to Turkey and Lebanon."

"It is important to bear in mind that contrary to what left-wingers say, it is not nutty or racist to be concerned about foreigners importing diseases; population movement is how diseases spread. Aliens and even some citizens may unwittingly bring in pathogens for which Americans have not developed immunity. Sometimes these maladies cause death on an epic scale. For example, centuries ago Europeans brought pathogens like the smallpox virus on their bodies to the new world. Indigenous Indian communities were wiped out because they had never encountered it before."

In his first year in the White House, President Obama had lifted an entry ban on immigrants with HIV. His plan is to lift the entry ban on three more sexually transmitted diseases (STDs). Obama's actions guarantees more infections in the United States, according to the Health and Human Services Department.

The military aerial support program known as Operation Phalanx has been shutdown by DHS officials...The DHS said that illegal crossings have declined along the Texas-Mexico border...But throughout the year Breitbart Texas has reported of the increase in numbers of immigrants crossing the border... Immigrants started flooding across the border at record numbers in the months leading up to the election....Utilized by Operation Phalanx were the National Guard UH-72 Lakota helicopters specially equipped with surveillance equipment which included night vision... The program was launched in 2010 and was fully funded until 2017, but Obama began scaling back the program in January 2016.

The Obama administration is doing everything they can to help as many immigrants cross the border even if it means no vetting whatsoever.

The Conflict Armament Research, (CAR) a London-based independent organization that tracks illicit weapon movements, had given its most extensive report in several years on illegal weapon flows in the Sahel. The CAR report confirms that the arms and weapons which were taken from Gaddafi's weapons store after his overthrow have mobilized Islamist insurgencies since 2012 in North and West Africa.

Also being used by the jihadists in the Sahel are assault rifles which flowed from Syria and Iraq.

The supply of weapons are coming from ISIS. Very concerned by the report, are European counter-terrorism officials and those in the Sahel and West Africa. The study was funded by several EU governments. They fear that the weapons which include shoulder-launched surface-to-air missiles are very likely being smuggled into Europe along immigrant routes. The weapons will then be used for terrorist attacks in European capitals.

The CAR study researchers believe that Islamist groups attacks in the Sahel, which included international hotels, "have a common source of supply or constitute a single cell, and point tentatively to possible links or commonalities of supply sources between Islamist fighters in West Africa and those operating in Iraq and Syria."

The Syrian jihadists obtained massive amounts of weaponry from the Libyan shipments to Syria that were illegally backed by Hillary and Obama.

Putin said that WW III will not start in Iran but in Syria. Syria is his "red line in the sand."

Until 2012, there had not been nuclear exercises conducted since the fall of the Soviet Union.

Under the command of President Vladimir Putin large-scale exercises of Russia's Strategic Nuclear Forces were also conducted.

S-400 missiles had been deployed to areas of Syria by Russia in readying for NATO'S "aircap" over Syria.

A ten-mile "buffer zone " already exists along it's borders as a safe area for the refugee's.

But Syria's Assad knows that at any time a full U.S./NATO force could reign down on him. And the excuse of chemical weapons could be falsely attributed to Assad.

After the overthrow of Qaddafi a flow of over 40 million tons of weaponry was taken from Libya and shipped to Syria. And intelligence knew that included chemical weapons and many surface to air missiles.

According to the Inspector General's report, the State Department cannot account for $6 billion. This was over a six year period covering partial time while Hillary was Secretary of State.

The report states that it is a "significant financial risk and demonstrates a lack of internal control over the Department's contract actions" which "could expose the department to substantial financial losses."

This "creates conditions conducive to fraud, as corrupt individuals may attempt to conceal evidence of illicit behavior by omitting key documents from the contract file."

An OIG audit of the closeout process for the U.S. Mission in Iraq showed that 33 of 115 contract files asked for in accordance with the audit could not be provided by the contract officials. These files were worth $2.1 billion.

There were 82 contract files. And 48 of those 82 were incomplete.

The "incomplete files...did not contain all of the documentation required by regulations." These incomplete files were worth $2.1 billion.

In an audit by the States Bureau of African Affairs;

They "were unable to provide complete contract administration files for any of the eight contracts that were reviewed".

These contracts in the audit were worth $34.8 million.

The OIG's Officer of Investigations uncovered a contract file that did not contain documentation which should show modifications and task orders that were given to the company that was owned by the spouse of a contractor employee. The employee was working as a Contract Specialist for the contract worth $52 million.

"In a number of recent OIG inspections, OIG identified contract file management deficiencies. For example, COR files for a $2.5 million contract lacked status reports and a tally of the funds expended and remaining on the contract," this was stated in the report.

After the Clinton Foundation was given $2.35 million during 2009-2013 by the chairman of Uranium One, Hillary voted to give Russia 20% of the Uranium production capacity of the United States.

Bill Clinton was paid $500,000 for a Moscow speech by a Russian investment bank, which promoted Uranium One stock, after Russia declared that it was taking over Uranium One

IRS filings for 2014 for the Clinton Foundation show $93.1 million were spent with less than $5.2 million going to charitable grants.

So the claim that 90% of the money donated to the Clinton Foundation paid out in charity is false. Only 5.7% of their budget went to charitable grants, "the rest went to salaries and employee benefits, fundraising and 'other expenses.'"

$34.8 million: compensation, employee benefits, and salaries.

$50.4 million: other expenses.

$851 thousand : professional fundraising expenses.

"Watered-down" HIV/AIDs drugs distributed to patients in sub-Saharan Africa by The Clinton Health Access Initiative (CHAI). According to a congressional report, this "likely increased" the risks of morbidity and mortality.

Among the haters of Israel that President Obama keeps in his circle are, Professor Derrick Bell who stated, "Jewish neoconservative racists... are undermining blacks in every way they can", Spokesman for Palestine Liberation Organization Rashid Khalidi, pro-Hamas negotiator Robert Malley, UN Ambassador Samantha Power who had suggested using American troops to guard against Israelis to protect Palestinians, and Zbigniew Brzezinski, former Jimmy Carter National Security Advisor.

In May 2008, President Obama told Benjamin Netanyahu that "settlements have to be stopped in order for us to move forward." So then Netanyahu announces a settlement freeze to comply with Obama. But the Palestinians still refused to negotiate. And Obama's statement against Israel when it should have been against the Palestinians was that, "they still found it very hard to move with any bold gestures."

In Obama's 2009 Cairo speech, he said that Israel was created due alone to the Jewish suffering of the Holocaust. Obama said that Palestinians have also been similarly victimized by the Jews, "They endure the daily humiliations – large and small – that come with occupation. So let there be no doubt: the situation for the Palestinian people is intolerable. America will not turn our backs on the legitimate Palestinian aspiration for dignity, opportunity, and a state of their own."

He must not know anything about the Holocaust if he equates Jewish suffering of the Holocaust to the Palestinians.

President Obama had threatened to put separation or "daylight" between the United States and Israel. In 2009 Obama told Jewish leaders, "Look at the past eight years. During those eight years, there was no space between us and Israel, and what did we get from that?"

What we did get from that, actually what Israel got from that, was for Israel to have to forcibly remove thousands of Jews from the Gaza Strip. Also they got the election of Hamas in the Gaza strip, and a war started by the Palestinians and Hezbollah. Then Obama reprimanded the Jews about their need for Israeli "self-reflection." But he had no complaints about what the Palestinians were doing against Israel.

In 2009, President Obama told the United Nations that "America does not accept the legitimacy of continued Israeli settlements." But what Obama actually was referring to, as his definition of Israeli settlements, were building bathrooms in a home which was already owned by Jews in East Jerusalem. Obama still again had no critical statements against the Palestinians.

Following his criticism about Israeli settlements, Obama sent Vice President Joe Biden to Israel. Biden riled against the Israelis for building bathrooms in their own homes in Jerusalem, the eternal Jewish capital. And Hillary spoke to Benjamin Netanyahu on the phone for an hour in a rant telling him that he had "harmed the bilateral relationship." David Axelrod calls the building plans of bathrooms an "insult" to the United States. Netanyahu's visit to the White House a week and a half later, ended with Obama making him leave through a side door.

The April 2010 Washington summit on nuclear proliferation became an Arab mandate on the evils of Israel's nuclear weapons due to President Obama.

In June 2010, a leak to the Times of London by an anonymous "US defense source" stated that Israel had brokered a deal with the Saudis to use their airspace to strike Iran. After the leak the deal was then withdrawn.

Hillary's State Department said in May 2011, that Jerusalem was not a part of Israel. Then based on pre- 1967 borders, Obama made demands on Israel to make concessions to the Palestinian. The pre-1967 borders era is called "Auschwitz borders" by Israelis due to it making their defenses less capable.

In November, 2011, President Obama and French President Nicolas Sarkozy were heard on an open microphone discussing Netanyahu. President Sarkozy said, "I can't stand him, he's a liar," Sarzoky said.

"You're tired of him? What about me? I have to deal with him every day." This was Obama's answer.

The U.N.'s hypocrisy is shown by them both blaming and honoring Israel while Israel is trying to save lives.

The highest honor had been awarded to Israel by the UN's World Health Organization, type 3 certification. Israel is the only country in the world to attain that high level of recognition.

Then the UN'S WHO also passed a resolution condemning only Israel.

Israel was the only country the U.N. Commission on the Status of Women (CSW) condemned for violating women's rights anywhere, for violating the rights of Palestinian women.

In rebuke of America's closest ally in the Middle East, Vice President Joe Biden had "overwhelming frustration" with Israel's government. He said that Netanyahu's government was leading Israel in the wrong direction.

In December 2011, of course Hillary had to condemn the State of Israel. She said that it was moving in the "opposite direction" of democracy and that that Israel reminded her of Rosa Parks. Rosa Parks stood up or rather sat down for what was right. She also said that Israel reminded her of religious people not listening to women sing. Among some segments of the Orthodox this was a long lived policy. And she also said that Israel reminded her of extremist regimes. Her comparison was that it was "more suited to Iran than Israel."

Information from "senior Obama administration officials" said that Israel had financed and trained the Iranian opposition group Mujahideen-e-Khalq. Also "four senior diplomats and military intelligence officers" revealed the "United States has recently been granted access to Iran's northern border."

Columnist Ron Ben-Yishai of Yidioth Ahronoth wrote that the Obama administration wants to "erode the IDF's capacity to launch such strike with minimal casualties."

Quoted by David Sanger, to gain the Jewish votes in June 2012, Obama, Joe Biden, and then-CIA director Leon Panetta, talked about the President's deep involvement in the Stuxnet plan to take out Iran's nuclear reactors by a computer virus. But before then it had been thought that Stuxnet was an Israeli project. The Obama administration denied leaking the information. But the State Department released emails a year later which proved that Sanger had regularly corresponded with all of Obama's top officials. And it included correspondence concerning Stuxnet.

In Decmber, 2012, Hillary spoke at the Saban Forum on US-Israel Relations where she stated that Israelis have a "lack of empathy" for Palestinian. She also stated that the Israelis needed to "demonstrate that they do understand the pain of an oppressed people in their minds."

That must have something to do with why Hillary would not get out of the car, when her and Bill were going to a party, due to her seeing a Jewish menorah in the window. Bill said that it was because Hillary was really tight with the Palestinians.

President Obama forced Netanyahu to call Turkish Prime Minister Tayyip Erdogan in March 2013. The call was for Netanyahu to apologize for Israel's actions to stop a terrorist-arming flotilla from entering the Gaza Strip to aid Hamas. Obama did not want Israel's Netanyahu to stop aid to Hamas. Erdogan had recently said that Zionism was racism.

In May 2013, members of the Pentagon under Obama, leaked information that Israel had attacked the Damascus airport. The reason stated was to stop a shipment of weapons to terrorist groups. The leaked information endangered American lives. Obama officials had to apologize for this leak in which they blamed "low-level" employees.

The Obama administration leaked specific information regarding Israeli Arrow 3 anti-ballistic missile sites in June 2013. Weeks later, US sources told CNN that Israel attacked a Syrian installation full of Russian-provided missiles. And in the same month, "American intelligence analysts" told the New York Times that Israeli strikes had not been effective. The information that was leaked by the Obama Administration was classified.

In June 2014, three Jewish teenagers were kidnapped, including an American, and were murdered by Hamas. The Obama administration immediately called on Israel, not in a compassionate gesture, but for restraint. The Obama Administration said it would continue to work with a Palestinian unity government which included Hamas. Jen Psaki, the State Department spokeswoman, said that the Obama administration wanted "the Israelis and the Palestinians continue to work with one another on that, and we certainly would continue to urge that... in spite of, obviously, the tragedy and the enormous pain on the ground." And throughout the Gaza War, the Obama administration criticized Israel's prosecution of the war. Even though Hamas fired rockets on Israeli civilians. And tunnels were also uncovered demonstrating Hamas' intent to kidnap Israeli children.

In the middle of a shooting war of August 2014, Obama actually stopped a weapons shipment to Israel. According to the Wall Street Journal, Obama found out that Israel had asked the Defense Department for shipments of Hellfire missiles. Obama himself blocked the shipments to Israel.

The court Jew for the Obama administration, Jeffrey Goldberg, in October 2014, released an article in The Atlantic where he quoted Obama officials calling Prime Minister Benjamin Netanyahu a "chickenshit." But Goldberg, laid the blame on Netanyahu. In 2008, Goldberg also wrote that any Jew who feared Obama on Israel was an "obvious racist".

In January 2015, a group, "One Voice," funded by American donors, paid for the Obama campaign team which was led by Obama's 2012 field director, Jeremy Bird. Obama's team was working to defeat Netanyahu in Israel. The announcement came only days after Speaker of the House John Boehner invited Netanyahu to speak before a joint session of Congress. Obama then announced that he would not meet with Netanyahu. Obama made the excuse that the meeting would come too close to the election.

Netanyahu won the re-election in March 2015 but President Obama refused to call to congratulate him for two days. And when he did call, Obama threatened to remove American support in the international community while also moving to loosen sanctions and weapons embargoes on Iran.

The New York Times Magazine and bestselling author of the book on the Clintons, "Guilty As Sin," Ed Klein, stated that according to his source only days before Hillary lost the election Bill and Hillary had a screaming match that ended with Bill Clinton throwing his phone off the roof of his penthouse apartment in Arkansas.

Also stated in Klein's report, "one of Bill's closest advisers," who said he was with Former President Clinton "in Little Rock when he had this shouting match with Hillary on the phone and she accused (FBI Director) Comey for reviving the investigation into her use of a private email server and reversing her campaign's momentum."

"Bill didn't buy the excuse that Comey would cost Hillary the election. As far as he was concerned, all the blame belonged to (Hillary's campaign manager Robby) Mook, (campaign chairman John) Podesta and Hillary because they displayed a tone-deaf attitude about the feeble economy and its impact on millions and millions of working-class voters." Klein's source said.

"Bill was so red in the face during his conversation with Hillary that I worried he was going to have a heart attack. He got so angry that he threw his phone off the roof of his penthouse apartment and toward the Arkansas River."

His source said that Clinton felt ignored by Hillary and her campaign when he advised on their onslaught of attacks on Trump, in which he felt were not working.

"Bill always campaigned as a guy who felt your pain, but Hillary came across as someone who was pissed off at her enemy [Trump], not someone who was reaching out and trying to make life better for the white working class," Klein's source told him.

In the fiscal year 2016, The Dept. of Health and Human Services' Office of Refugee Resettlement released 52,147 more illegal immigrant "children" into the United States averaging about 149 per day.

The Office of Refugee Settlement had released 5,203 children in September alone.

In 2014 through 2016 the Office of Refugee Resettlement released 133,502 unaccompanied children into the United States. Of those children released in 2015, 68% were male with 68% claiming to be between the ages of 15-17. Less than 1 out of 5 were under 12 years of age. So where are all of the little children who need help? Why do only those "claiming" to be 15-17 year old males need help?

Executive vice president of the Conference of Presidents of Major American Jewish Organizations, Malcolm Hoenlein, said that he had "some concerns about what Obama and others may do" regarding the Israeli-Palestinian peace process before Jan. 20.

"This is based on things I heard from him a year ago about his priorities and the understandable importance of his legacy to him," Hoenlein said. "And I listen to his speeches and I have seen some of the harsh statements that are being issued…about Israeli settlement policies. The language being used is much stronger than we've seen in the past and I'm afraid that this could be indicative of what a forthcoming UN Security Council resolution against settlements, or something that goes even further, might look like."

The F.B.I. had sent two secret letters to the State Department and had shown that the investigation into Hillary's use of private email was due to a "Section 811" referral from the inspector general.

Section 811, Under the Intelligence Authorization Act of 1995, "is the statutory authority that governs the coordination of counterespionage investigations between executive branch departments or agencies and the FBI."

ISIS would not be "almost a nation" if President Obama had not pulled out U.S. troops too early from the Middle East. US tanks and supplies were left for anyone to take. ISIS did take them. It was as if Obama wanted them to take them. The tanks along with everything else that was left there were then used by ISIS to increase in size and power.

"During the investigations, Yousaf al Salafi revealed that he was getting funding – routed through America – to run the organization in Pakistan and recruit young people to fight in Syria," a source said on condition of anonymity.

Yousaf al Salafi also said that he, along with a Pakistani Imam, was recruiting people to go to Syria. They were being paid approximately $600 per person from Syria.

"The US has been condemning the IS activities but unfortunately has not been able to stop funding of these organizations, which is being routed through the US.

"The US had to dispel the impression that it is financing the group for its own interests and that is why it launched offensive against the organization in Iraq but not in Syria."

Those named in a 2012 document that was declassified recently were "Salafist, the Muslim Brotherhood and AQI [Al-Qaeda in Iraq] major forces driving the insurgency in Syria." And that "the West, Gulf countries, and Turkey support the opposition while Russia, China and Iran support the regime."

The declassified document, showed that in 2012 the Obama administration was alerted that these Islamic jihadists would establish a "Salafist principality in eastern Syria". But he continued to support the opposition.

Putin said that WW III will not start in Iran but in Syria. Syria is his "red line in the sand."

Until 2012, there had not been nuclear exercises conducted since the fall of the Soviet Union.

Under the command of President Vladimir Putin large-scale exercises of Russia's Strategic Nuclear Forces were also conducted.

S-400 missiles had been deployed to areas of Syria by Russia in readying for NATO'S "aircap" over Syria. A ten-mile "buffer zone " already exists along it's borders as a safe area for the refugee's. But Syria's Assad knows that at any time a full U.S./NATO force could reign down on him. And the excuse of chemical weapons could be falsely attributed to Assad. After the overthrow of Qaddafi a flow of over 40 million tons of weaponry was taken from Libya and shipped to Syria. And intelligence knew that included chemical weapons and many surface to air missiles.

Former FBI Agent James Kallstrom has stated that Obama's Syrian Refugee program is a cover up.

Kallstrom said that Obama is acting in direct opposition of the American people. He said that the statistics and Obama's support of his Syrian Refugee plan does not make sense.

He is basically saying that Obama is trying to destroy America from the inside out.

The accommodation of Muslims in the United States is absolutely ridiculous. A woman who was flying United Airlines out of Los Angeles had her seat given away because her seat was by two Muslim men. The boarding agent told her, "The two gentlemen seated next to you have cultural beliefs that prevent them from sitting next to, talking to, or communicating with females." So she had to take another seat.

Keith Ellison, the first Muslim elected to Congress, cannot explain away evidence that his association with the anti-Semitic, anti-white Nation of Islam was much closer than he has claimed. Ellison was known to be a supporter and activist for Louis Farrakhan's Nation of Islam. He even spoke on behalf of the controversial group as a "representative." In 2006, during his first campaign for Congress, Ellison had written a letter to the Jewish Community Relations Council of Minnesota & the Dakotas. He wrote that he had never been a member of the Nation of Islam.

But in 2006, after being sworn in to Congress, he posed for photographs with then-House Speaker Nancy Pelosi. They both had their hands on a copy of the Quran.

When Ellison talked with Sean Hannity, he responded to Hannity's montage of President Obama's statements about the upcoming automatic budget cuts by exclaiming, "Quite frankly, you are the worst excuse for a journalist I've ever seen." The interview went downhill from there. In the letter to the Jewish group, Ellison further claimed that his association with the Nation of Islam was limited to an 18-month period in which he was helping to organize the Minnesota contingent at the 1995 Million Man March. You can watch the video; https://shariaunveiled.wordpress.com/tag/keith-ellison-black-panther-member-nation-of-islam-member-cair-hamas-member/

A U.S. service member fighting along side with the Kurdish-leg Syrian Democratic Forces in northern Syria died from injuries from a blast by an improvised explosive device, military officials said.

The death is believed to be the first American military casualty since the start of the operation against Islamic State fighters. Since the Obama administration backs ISIS in Syria the soldier was killed with the help of his own government.

Throughout Obama's time in government he has been against voter ID legislation. He even described it as being designed to "systematically put up barriers and make it as hard as possible for our citizens to vote."

In August 2015, Obama criticized the 30 U.S. states that require some form of ID in order to vote.

Ellen DeGeneres was at the White House to accept a Presidential Medal of Freedom Award. Obama was the one to present it to her.

DeGeneres had trouble getting into the White House because she forgot to bring a photo ID and could not talk her way through security.

And then Ted Cruz posted on twitter;

"I thought Obama didn't believe in photo I.D?" Good one Ted!

Secretary of State John Kerry has secretly negotiated to take illegal immigrants from terrorist countries from Australia which does not want them.

The chairmen of the House and Senate judiciary committees are demanding the Obama administration provide details of a secret resettlement deal in which the U.S. has agreed to take up to 1,800 mostly Muslim immigrants who have been rejected by Australia as illegal aliens.

In a letter, sent by two lawmakers, on November 22, to Kerry and DHS Secretary Jeh Johnson, they wrote that it amounts to an international treaty that Secretary of State John Kerry negotiated without consulting or notifying Congress according to Article II, Section II of the U.S. Constitution. Australia effectively said "no" to the United Nations' plan to open up Western democracies for millions of refugees fleeing not only the Syrian war but conflicts in Afghanistan, Somalia, Sudan and even countries like Pakistan that are not at war. Germany alone has accepted 1.5 million Muslim refugees and subjected itself to thousands of sexual assaults on its women and girls.

"This situation is concerning for many reasons; your departments negotiated an international agreement regarding refugees without consulting or notifying Congress… The individuals who will be resettled are coming from countries of national security concern. In fact, two of the countries are officially designated by the State Department to be State Sponsors of Terrorism. [This] deal is not only a matter of grave national security concern, but it could also be illegal."

"This is a backroom deal, wheeling and dealing with another country's refugee problem," he said.

"I don't believe for a moment it's a one-time deal. That's for public consumption. Traditionally, the details of all refugee resettlement deals are completely transparent… If [these refugees] have been vetted and deemed inadmissible [in Australia], [under American laws] the U.S. can't say, 'You don't want them, so we'll take them.'"

Immigrants who tried to get to Australia were not welcomed. So the United Nations is looking for countries that will take the immigrants.

The U.N. worked with the Obama administration and Kerry confirmed he had reached a deal to take an undetermined number of the 2,465 immigrants for permanent resettlement in the United States...But information about the immigrants on how many will end up in which American cities has not been released.

"...It begs the question why Australia and other countries refuse to admit these individuals, what other countries are doing to help alleviate the situation, what kind of precedent this sets for future refugees interdicted at sea by Australian forces and prevented from entering Australia, and how a similar situation will be prevented in the future."

Denver Sheriff Department To Pay $10,000 Fine For Requiring Job Applicants To Be Citizens

"This is insane!"

The Denver Sheriff Department has agreed to pay a fine... from the Obama administration for making citizenship a requirement for hire from 2015 to early 2016.

...The department will also be required to go through old applications and search for those who were disqualified for not having citizenship. The Sheriff Department will have to reconsider those applicants for future job position.

Under the Immigration and Nationality Act, the Sheriff's department should have considered all applications regardless of citizenship as long as applicant was a work-authorized immigrant.

"The Justice Department's investigation found that from approximately Jan. 1, 2015, until approximately March 23, 2016, the Denver Sheriff Department discriminated based on citizenship status by requiring applicants for deputy sheriff positions to be U.S. citizens and publishing job postings with U.S. citizenship requirements, in violation of the INA," the DOJ statement said.

"The INA's anti-discrimination provision prohibits employers from limiting jobs to U.S. citizens except where the employer is required to do so by law, regulation, executive order or government contract. The Denver Sheriff Department was not subject to one of the INA's exceptions."

"The Denver Sheriff Department maintains its commitment to treat all people with dignity and respect, and is proud to have one of the most diverse workplaces in Colorado," Simon Crittle, spokesman for the DSD, wrote.

It is illegal to hire illegal immigrants! Oh that's right. Obama siigned an Executive Order for that. Who wants an illegal immigrant as a deputy Sheriff? I wonder if any illegal immigrants are on Obama's security detail?

The Obama administration is working to pass countless last-minute regulations.

But the Republican-led U.S. House of Representatives voted 240-to-179 to allow Congress to stop and un-do any last minute rules and regulations approved by Obama.

Rep. Darrell Issa, the bill's sponsor explained, this bill stops Obama's last-minute, shameful regulations forever:

"This bipartisan bill is about reviving the separation of powers to ensure our laws are written by the Representatives we actually vote for – not unelected and unaccountable bureaucrats who are on their way out the door. Presidents of both parties have made a habit of enacting scores of last-minute regulations, with little oversight, to sneak in as much of their agenda as possible before the clock runs out on their time in office. The bill helps ensure this President, and any future president, will be held in check and that their policies have the proper level of scrutiny by both Congress and the American people. I'm pleased to see the House pass this important measure and look forward to its quick passage by our colleagues in the Senate."

The day after the election Geert Wilders stated;

Yesterday, in the biggest democracy on earth, we witnessed a political revolution. The American people sent a powerful message to the world:

Enough is enough, we want to be free again, we want to be great again! Against the media, against the establishment, against the elites, against all the odds, Donald Trump won the American elections. And what a victory! A stunning and truly historic achievement, with the White House, the House and the Senate in Republican hands for the first time since 1928. —Geert Wilders "The Second American Revolution Has Come"

The leader of the Party for Freedom, Wilders has been the source of great controversy in the Netherlands and abroad for his criticism of Islam and what he describes as the Islamization of the Netherlands. At his trial, he faced five counts of criminal offenses. The first charge was of criminally insulting Muslims because of their religion. The remaining four charges pertained to incitement of hatred and discrimination of Muslims, Moroccans, and other non-Western immigrants because of their race or ethnicity. These charges stemmed from articles Wilders had written between 2006 and 2008, as well as his short film Fitna. These statements included a call for a ban on the Quran, warnings against an "Islamic invasion," and a "tsunami of Islamization." He also labeled Islam a fascist religion, described Dutch-Moroccan youths as violent, and compared the Quran with Hitler's Mein Kampf. He has also referred to Mohammed as "the devil." And all of it is the truth.

On 23 June 2011, Wilders was acquitted of all charges, with Judge Marcel van Oosten noting that his statements, although "gross and denigrating," had not given rise to hatred against Muslims, and as such were "acceptable within the context of public debate."

Part of Geert Wilders' statement at his "hate speech" trial;

I stand here before you. Alone. But I am not alone. My voice is the voice of many. ...A worldwide movement is emerging that puts an end to the politically correct doctrines of the elites and the media that are subordinate to them. And I tell you, the battle of the elite against the people will be won by the people. Here, too, you will not be able to stop this, but rather accelerate it. We will win... and it will be remembered well who was on the right side of history. Common sense will prevail over politically correct arrogance.

The voice of freedom cannot be imprisoned; it rings like a bell. Everywhere, ever more people are saying what they think. They do not want to lose their land, they do not want to lose their freedom.

REFERENCES

http://www.politifact.com/truth-o-meter/statements/2015/jan/23/andy-puzder/ceo-carls-jr-says-obamacare-has-caused-millions-fu/

https://edwardsnowden.com/surveillance-programs/

http://usscompton705.com/remember.html

http://canadafreepress.com/article/dnc-intimidation-of-tom-bauerle-loved-ones-exposed-by-wikileaks1

http://www.thepoliticalinsider.com/top-official-set-testify-hillary-found-dead-breaking-news/

http://www.newsbbc.net/2016/08/official-who-served-dnc-election-fraud.html?m=1

http://www.spacepolicyonline.com/news/molly-macauley-renowned-space-economist-killed-while-walking-her-dogs

http://www.businessinsider.com/dnc-seth-rich-wikileaks-politicize-2016-8
Family of slain DNC staffer: Those attempting to politicize death are 'causing more harm than good'

http://m.washingtontimes.com/multimedia/image/screen-shot-2016-10-28-at-100618-ampng/Maj. Gen. John Rossi committed suicide: U.S. Army investigation

http://mobile.wnd.com/2014/01/on-bad-behavior-nidal-hasan-whining-about-jail/

http://wallstreetonparade.com/2016/10/banker-deaths-and-wikileaks-deaths-have-a-common-thread/

http://www.citadel.edu/root/pow-mia/i-am-old-gloryhttps://www.smartmatic.com/

https://www.theguardian.com/technology/2016/jun/30/apple-iphone-camera-disable-remote-sensors-patent Apple gets patent for remotely disabling iPhone cameras, raising censorship fears http://www.gilat.net/

Aaron Klein http://www.breitbart.com/jerusalem/2016/09/09/leaked-memo-george-soros-foundation-seeking-expand-u-s-online-voting/ NEW YORK – George Soros's Open Society Foundations is seeking to expand the use of electronic and online voting systems nationwide, according to a leaked Foundations document reviewed by Breitbart News http://www.karebearaaa.bravepages.com/patrioticpoems.html

Amy Moreno http://truthfeed.com/corrupt-hsbc-global-bank-exec-arressted-links-to-hillary-james-comey-and-loretta-lynch/12683/Corrupt HSBC Global Bank Exec Arrested, Links to Hillary, James Comey and Loretta Lynch

Patrick Howley http://www.breitbart.com/2016-presidential-race/2016/09/10/exposed-fbi-director-james-comeys-clinton-foundation-connection/ Exposed: FBI Director James Comey's Clinton Foundation Connection

https://en.m.wikipedia.org/wiki/HSBC

http://21stcenturywire.com/2016/07/13/fbi-director-comey-board-member-of-clinton-foundation-connected-bank-hsbc/FBI Director Comey was board member of HSBC – Clinton Foundation & Drug Cartel 'bank of choice'

Lauren Italiano http://nypost.com/2016/07/31/report-raises-questions-about-clinton-cash-from-russians-during-reset/

http://m.washingtontimes.com/news/2009/jan/23/clinton-foundation-mum-on-stock-buyer/Clinton Cash by Peter Schweizer,

http://dailycaller.com/2016/09/16/just-5-7-percent-of-clinton-foundation-budget-actually-went-to-charity/

content://com.sec.android.app.sbrowser/readinglist/1122031404.mhtml

http://www.naturalnews.com/055898_Hillary_Clinton_email_server_pedophilia.html

Medea Benjamin http://m.huffpost.com/us/entry/11779826 Hillary Clinton, The Podesta Group And The Saudi Regime: A Fatal Menage A Trois

http://www.breitbart.com/radio/2016/11/04/erik-prince-nypd-ready-make-arrests-weiner-case/Erik Prince: NYPD Ready to Make Arrests in Anthony Weiner Case

http://conservativetribune.com/ex-cia-chilling-hillary-revelation/

http://www.judicialwatch.org/press-room/weekly-updates/clinton-scandal-update/

http://www.judicialwatch.org/press-room/weekly-updates/clinton-scandal-update/content://com.sec.android.app.sbrowser/readinglist/1122031404.mhtml

http://lucianne.com/thread/?artnum=888447

https://www.globalmbwatch.com/2016/07/24/featured-hillary-clintons-vp-pick-the-us-muslim-brotherhood-we-warned-you-in-2007-about-tim-kaine2/

http://www.thedailybeast.com/articles/2016/10/03/tim-kaine-s-time-with-a-marxist-priest.html

13 HOURS THE INSIDE ACCOUNT OF WHAT REALLY HAPPENED IN BENGHAZI, MITCHELL ZUCKOFF with the Annex Security Team 2014

http://abc7news.com/news/former-cia-contractor-speaks-out-about-benghazi-attack/1351333/

https://sofrep.com/46262/13-hours-director-refutes-cia-claim-about-stand-down-order-controversy/

https://conservativedailypost.com/if-you-thought-obama-didnt-know-you-should-probably-read-this-for-your-own-eyes/

Dark Forces by Kenneth Timmerman, 2014

content://com.sec.android.app.sbrowser/readinglist/1230190742.mhtml

http://beforeitsnews.com/alternative/2016/10/judge-napolitano-says-the-nsa-hacked-clintons-emails-3427010.html

content://com.sec.android.app.sbrowser/readinglist/1230185612.mhtml

https://theconservativetreehouse.com/2013/04/30/benghazi-lies-the-truth-begins-to-crack-through-a-little/

http://www.naturalnews.com/051324_House_Speaker_John_Boehner_Obama_Administration.html

https://johnib.wordpress.com/tag/brig-gen-robert-lovell/

http://www.americanthinker.com/blog/2014/05/the_appalling_obama_foreign_policy_team_the_case_of_tommy_vietor.html

http://ijr.com/opinion/2016/10/260611-survived-benghazi-attacks-heres-suggest-start-fighting-islamic-terrorism/?utm_source=twitter&utm_medium=social

https://sofrep.com/49885/exclusive-sofrep-interview-kris-tanto-paranto-secret-soldier-benghazi/

http://www.usatwentyfour.com/col-andrew-wood-u-s-rescue-team-way-benghazi-ordered-turn-back/

http://www.fury.news/2016/09/bombshell-rescue-team-way-benghazi-got-order-last-minute/

http://www.judicialwatch.org/press-room/press-releases/judicial-watch-new-benghazi-email-shows-dod-offered-state-department-forces-that-could-move-to-benghazi-immediately-specifics-blacked-out-in-new-document/

http://www.theblaze.com/news/2015/12/08/judicial-watch-releases-compelling-benghazi-email-it-says-worsens-the-scandal-of-benghazi/

https://en.m.wikipedia.org/wiki/Lockheed_AC-130

http://www.foxnews.com/opinion/2011/05/11/dont-hear-george-soros-ties-30-major-news-organizations.html

http://www.foxnews.com/politics/2016/05/25/state-department-audit-faults-clinton-on-email-use.html

http://www.globalresearch.ca/who-pocketed-gaddafis-billions/5310459?print=1

https://en.m.wikipedia.org/wik/Title_18_of_the_United_States_Code

http://m.washingtontimes.com/news/2015/sep/16/nobel-panel-saw-obama-peace-prize-mistake-new-book/

http://dailycaller.com/2016/11/04/hillary-emails-so-bad-clinton-campaign-wanted-public-to-focus-on-benghazi-instead/

http://www.ibtimes.co.uk/isis-funding-routed-through-us-claims-islamic-state-commander-pakistan-1485622

http://thehill.com/homenews/administration/304343-obama-commutes-sentences-for-72-inmates

http://bearingarms.com/jenn-j/2016/11/07/obama-grants-commutations-federal-inmates-gun-offenses/

http://www.nbcwashington.com/news/local/Immigrants-Responsible-for-Gang-Violence-Spike-in-Frederick-County-Sheriff-Says-on-Capitol-Hill-376285141.html

http://m.washingtontimes.com/news/2016/sep/7/abid-riaz-qureshi-nominated-us-district-court-coul/

http://www.breitbart.com/2016-presidential-race/2016/11/04/final-warning-america-immigration-officers-clintons-plan-open-borders-will-unleash-violence-american-communities-2/

http://www.breitbart.com/big-government/2014/10/27/u-s-civil-rights-commissioner-warns-of-executive-amnesty-s-negative-impact-on-african-americans/

http://clashdaily.com/2014/12/death-cult-10-assaults-beheadings-happened-american-soil/

http://milosevic.co/572/christopher-black-terrorism-a-matrix-of-lies-and-deceit/

http://conservativetribune.com/ex-cia-chilling-hillary-revelation/

http://dailycaller.com/2016/11/04/hillary-emails-so-bad-clinton-campaign-wanted-public-to-focus-on-benghazi-instead/

http://www.thepoliticalinsider.com/former-fbi-official-risking-his-life-just-exposed-obama-in-a-huge-way/

http://americannews.com/former-fbi-official-james-kallstrom-risks-everything-to-expose-this-about-obama/

https://patriotpost.us/pages/134

http://www.thegatewaypundit.com/2016/09/german-officials-encourage-women-wear-sneakers-outrun-migrant-rapists/

http://www.dailywire.com/news/1152/six-reasons-why-west-should-stop-taking-muslim-aaron-bandler

http://mobile.wnd.com/2016/09/feds-spend-another-10-million-to-register-immigrant-voters/

http://thefreethoughtproject.com/anti-war-dissenters-military-detention/

http://www.washingtonsblog.com/2011/08/libyan-war-gaddafi-falls-but-why-did-we.html

https://www.theguardian.com/commentisfree/cifamerica/2011/apr/21/libya-muammar-gaddafi

http://www.marketoracle.co.uk/Article27208.html

http://www.cnbc.com/id/42308613

http://www.thenewamerican.com/economy/markets/item/4630-gadhafi-s-gold-money-plan-would-have-devastated-dollar

http://www.americanthinker.com/articles/2015/12/america_has_jumped_from_the_middle_east_frying_pan_into_the_fire.html

http://canadafreepress.com/article/hillary-fights-to-keep-wall-street-speeches-secret http:// thefreethoughtproject.com/anti-war-dissenters-military-detention/ Matthew Vadumhttp://aclj.org/executive-power/obama-administration-pledges-to-turn-over-documents-on-iran-lie-on-election-day-as-new-collusion-revelations-surface

Hard Choices, Hillary Clinton 2014

https://ronabbass.wordpress.com/2016/06/20/a-matrix-of-lies-and-deceit-us-war-on-terror/

https://patriotpost.us/pages/134

"The Case Against Hillary Clinton" by Peggy Noonan, p. 55

"Unlimited Access", by Clinton FBI Agent in Charge, Gary Aldrige

"I've Always Been A Yankee Fan" by Thomas D. Kuiper, pg.68

"Inside The White House" by Ronald Kessler

"The First Family Detail," by Ronald Kessler

http://www.teaparty.org/list-hillarys-filthy-fking-potty-mouth-puts-trump-shame-190963

http://www.thepoliticalinsider.com/confirmed-obamas-intelligence-chief-admits-hes-lying-about-isis-heres-the-truth/

http://www.washingtonsblog.com/2011/08/libyan-war-gaddafi-falls-but-why-did-we.html

http://m.washingtontimes.com/news/2015/jan/29/hillary-clinton-libya-war-genocide-narrative-rejec/

http://www.foxnews.com/world/2016/11/07/benghazi-guards-turned-on-us-diplomats-in-2012-attack-sources-say.html

http://nypost.com/2016/06/16/america-has-suffered-a-terror-attack-every-year-under-obama/

https://sharylattkisson.com/8-major-warnings-before-benghazi-terrorist-attacks/

https://thelastgreatstand.com/2016/07/31/shocking-nsa-whistleblower-says-nsa-hillarys-deleted-emails-video/

http://www.investors.com/politics/editorials/why-does-obama-keep-missing-red-flags-before-islamic-terror-attacks/https://conservativedailypost.com/breaking-julian-assange-just-delivered-the-next-batch-of-emails-shes-toast/http://

nypost.com/2016/06/16/america-has-suffered-a-terror-attack-every-year-under-obama/

http://www.breitbart.com/texas/2016/11/17/obama-releases-detained-haitian-migrants-trump-win/

http://www.breitbart.com/texas/2016/11/20/report-outgoing-president-shuts-border-aerial-surveillance-program/

https://patriotpost.us/pages/134

http://www.thegatewaypundit.com/2016/09/german-officials-encourage-women-wear-sneakers-outrun-migrant-rapists/

content://com.sec.android.app.sbrowser/readinglist/0731152727.mhtml. FEATURED: Hillary Clinton's VP Pick & The US Muslim Brotherhood- We Warned You In 2007 About Tim Kaine

Meghan Bartlett http://m.washingtontimes.com/news/2015/sep/16/nobel-panel-saw-obama-peace-prize-mistake-new-book/

Allen Cone http://www.upi.com/Top_News/US/2016/09/07/Obama-nominates-first-Muslim-American-federal-judge/3431473253719/

http://conservativetribune.com/ex-cia-chilling-hillary-revelation/

http://www.inspiretochangeworld.com/2016/06/us-war-terror-matrix-lies-deceit/

Jim Hoft http://www.thegatewaypundit.com/2016/09/german-officials-encourage-women-wear-sneakers-outrun-migrant-rapists/

http://www.judicialwatch.org/blog/2016/04/obama-allots-19-mil-to-register-immigrant-voters/

http://thefreethoughtproject.com/anti-war-dissenters-military-detention/ Matthew Vadum

http://canadafreepress.com/article/hillary-fights-to-keep-wall-street-speeches-secret

http://aclj.org/executive-power/obama-administration-pledges-to-turn-over-documents-on-iran-lie-on-election-day-as-new-collusion-revelations-surface

http://mobile.wnd.com/2016/10/judge-wont-release-drafts-of-whitewater-indictment/

http://m.washingtontimes.com/news/2016/oct/5/marc-turis-charges-dropped-in-libya-weapons-scheme/

Hard Choices, Hillary Clinton 2014

http://www.westernjournalism.com/retired-general-reveals-demoralizing-experience-of-serving-under-obama/http://dailycaller.com/2016/07/13/new-ties-emerge-between-clinton-and-mysterious-islamic-cleric/

http://www.judicialwatch.org/blog/2010/02/napolitano-hosts-terrorist-groups-d-c/

http://www.collective-evolution.com/2014/11/28/10-things-about-gaddafi-they-dont-want-you-to-know/

http://www.counterpunch.org/2015/10/20/libya-from-africas-wealthiest-democracy-under-gaddafi-to-terrorist-haven-after-us-intervention/

http://thepoliticsforums.com/threads/69258-Muslim-Plan-to-Infiltrate-Every-Element-of-Society-amp-Church

Phil Butler http://www.globalresearch.ca/arab-spring-the-fall-of-all-freedom/5544453

http://aclj.org/israel/aclj-takes-on-the-most-significant-us-federal-court-case-in-defense-of-the-israels-legitimacy-as-a-jewish-state

http://www.thepoliticalinsider.com/confirmed-obamas-intelligence-chief-admits-hes-lying-about-isis-heres-the-truth/

http://usherald.com/breaking-wikileaks-founder-just-exposed-even-documents-just-devastated-hillary-campaing/

http://freedomoutpost.com/u-s-spy-exposed-by-unsecured-emails-now-executed-by-iran-hillarys-server-now-has-its-first-dead-body/

https://sharylattkisson.com/8-major-warnings-before-benghazi-terrorist-attacks/

http://www.judicialwatch.org/bulletins/clinton-inc-benghazi/

http://www.foxnews.com/politics/2014/09/15/damage-control-ex-official-claims-clinton-allies-scrubbed-benghazi-documents-in.html

http://dailysignal.com/2014/09/15/benghazi-bombshell-clinton-state-department-official-reveals-alleged-details-document-review/

https://www.lewrockwell.com/2016/07/roger-stone/clinton-corruption/

http://breakingdefense.com/2013/06/top-official-admits-f-35-stealth-fighter-secrets-stolen/2/

http://usherald.com/breaking-admiral-ace-lions-warns-america-why-would-an-american-president-embrace-the-muslim-brotherhood-video/

http://www.westernjournalism.com/retired-general-warns-what-happens-when-you-disagree-with-obama/

http://www.cnn.com/2015/06/08/politics/hillary-clinton-libya-election-2016/http://haitiantimes.com/7-articles-to-read-uncovering-hillary-clintons-haiti-record-14284/

https://www.ff.org/hillarys-many-libya-problems/LISTS7 Articles To Read Uncovering Hillary Clinton's Haiti Record

https://tonyseed.wordpress.com/2016/04/14/the-arab-spring-us-black-ops-and-subversion/The Arab Spring: US black ops and subvers

http://canadafreepress.com/article/cia-whistleblower-faces-the-ire-of-an-angry-justice-department-over-benghaz

http://henrymakow.com/2015/07/JFK-Jr-Death-Was-No-Accident%20.htmlkJFK Jr.'s Death Was No Accident

http://www.globalresearch.ca/arab-spring-the-fall-of-all-freedom/5544453 Arab Spring: The Fall of All Freedom

http://www.shoebat.com/wp-content/uploads/2012/08/Abedin_Affairs_with_Al_Saud_0813123.pdf

http://northwestlibertynews.com/julian-assange-wikileaks-release-proof-hillary-rigging-elections/

http://washingtonbabylon.com/the-accoona-scam-who-bought-bill-clintons-worthless-stock-shares-for-700000/

http://www.homelandsecurityus.com/archives/10636

http://www.cnn.com/2015/06/08/politics/hillary-clinton-libya-election-2016/http://haitiantimes.com/7-articles-to-read-uncovering-hillary-clintons-haiti-record-14284/

https://www.ff.org/hillarys-many-libya-problems/LISTS7 Articles To Read Uncovering Hillary Clinton's Haiti Record

http://www.breitbart.com/texas/2016/11/18/mexican-cartels-coaching-illegal-immigrants-request-asylum-border-patrol-union-says/

http://www.thepoliticalinsider.com/obama-regulations-record-that-will-make-you-sick/

http://www.thepoliticalinsider.com/obama-regulations-record-that-will-make-you-sick/?utm_source=SailThru%26utm_newsletter&utm_medium=email&utm_campaign=TPI%20Newsletter%2012-5-16%20Curated/Horizon%20Tier%201&utm_term=Tier%201%20Real

http://www.thepoliticalinsider.com/breaking-u-s-house-just-voted-to-stop-obama-this-prevents-obama-from-creating-last-minute-regulations/

https://www.americanactionforum.org/insight/passing-1-trillion/

http://www.breitbart.com/texas/2016/11/17/obama-releases-detained-haitian-migrants-trump-win/

http://www.breitbart.com/texas/2016/11/20/report-outgoing-president-shuts-border-aerial-surveillance-program/

http://www.globalsecurity.org/military/library/news/2016/11/mil-161120-voa01.htm?_m=3n%2e002a%2e1873%2erh0ao09cc5%2e1q0g

http://canadafreepress.com/article/the-hidden-real-truth-about-benghazi

http://m.washingtontimes.com/news/2014/apr/4/state-dept-misplaced-6b-under-hillary-clinton-ig-r/ http://www.foxnews.com/opinion/2016/03/29/can-t-make-it-up-un-names-democratic-israel-as-world-s-top-human-rights-violator.html

http://www.jerusalemonline.com/blogs/lou-brifman/op-ed-is-america-a-true-ally-of-israel-24863?utm_source=ActiveCampaign&utm_medium=email&utm_content=Netanyahu+s+lawyer+takes+polygraph+test+about+submarine+deal++and+more+news+from+Jerusalem Online&utm_campaign=Evening Newsletter+-+Recurring

Ben Shapiro http://www.breitbart.com/national-security/2015/03/20/a-complete-timeline-of-obamas-anti-israel-hatred/A Complete Timeline of Obama's Anti-Israel Hatred

http://www.globalsecurity.org/military/library/news/2016/11/mil-161120-voa01.htm?_m=3n%2e002a%2e1873%2erh0ao09cc5%2e1q0g

http://canadafreepress.com/article/obama-ends-air-watch-on-drugs-illegals?utm_source=CFP+Mailout&utm_campaign=475483c4fe-CFP+Daily+Mailout&utm_medium=email&utm_term=0_d8f503f036-475483c4fe-297732117&mc_cid=475483c4fe&mc_eid=c9d72098f8

http://conservativetribune.com/obama-admin-risk/

Read more at http://mobile.wnd.com/2016/11/report-hillary-physically-violent-after-losing/#vCvbWEfgCkWKSgQD.99

http://www.cnsnews.com/news/article/penny-starr/feds-number-unaccompanied-alien-children-resettled-us-87-percent-27840

http://nypost.com/2016/04/19/biden-slams-netanyahu-moving-israel-in-the-wrong-direction/

http://www.ibtimes.com/hillary-clintons-exasperated-anti-israel-commentary-sparks-outrage-380338

https://www.algemeiner.com/2016/10/10/report-obama-administration-manufacturing-crisis-with-israel-to-apply-pressure-on-jewish-state-ahead-of-lame-duck-period-push-for-palestinian-state/

http://www.ibtimes.co.uk/isis-funding-routed-through-us-claims-islamic-state-commander-pakistan-1485622

http://reagancoalition.com/articles/2015/former-fbi-official-james-kallstrom-risks-everything-to-expose-this-about-obama.html

Ben Shapiro http://www.breitbart.com/national-security/2015/03/20/a-complete-timeline-of-obamas-anti-israel-hatred/A Complete Timeline of Obama's Anti-Israel Hatred

https://unitedwithisrael.org/watch-the-u-n-blames-israel-for-saving-the-world/?utm_source=MadMimi&utm_medium=email&utm_content=UN+Blames+Israel+for+Saving+the+World%21+Protest+France%27s+Labeling+of+Israeli+Products&utm_campaign=20161201_m135880060_UN+Blames+Israel+for+Saving+the+World%21+Protest+France%27s+Labeling+of+Israeli+Products&utm_term=_0D_0A_09_09_09_09_09_09_09_09_09_0D_0A_09_09_09_09_09_09_09_09_0D_0A_09_09_09_09_09_09_09_09_09Whttp://www.globalsecurity.org/military/library/news/2016/11/mil-161120-voa01.htm?_m=3n%2e002a%2e1873%2erh0ao09cc5%2e1q0g

http://canadafreepress.com/article/obama-ends-air-watch-on-drugs-illegals?utm_source=CFP+Mailout&utm_campaign=475483c4fe-CFP+Daily+Mailout&utm_medium=email&utm_term=0_d8f503f036-475483c4fe-297732117&mc_cid=475483c4fe&mc_eid=c9d72098f8

tp://www.wsj.com/articles/secret-recordings-fueled-fbi-feud-in-clinton-probe-1478135518

content://com.sec.android.app.sbrowser/readinglist/1125174717.mhtml

content://com.sec.android.app.sbrowser/readinglist/1125123601.mhtml

content://com.sec.android.app.sbrowser/readinglist/1125174623. mhtmlhttps://m.youtube.com/watch?v=SwrprHZKN4I.

http://mobile.wnd.com/2013/02/muslim-congressman-was-farrakhan-spokesman/

http://www.foxnews.com/world/2016/11/24/us-service-member-killed-by-explosive-device-in-syria.html

http://www.westernjournalism.com/ted-cruz-roasts-obama-after-ellen-degeneres-denied-entry-into-white-house/

http://mobile.wnd.com/2016/1/obama-fast-tracks-plan-to-take-muslim-migrants-rejected-by-australia/http://www.conservativezone.com/articles/president-obamas-last-stand/

content://com.sec.android.app.sbrowser/readinglist/1124201436.mhtml

content://com.sec.android.app.sbrowser/readinglist/1125193112.mhtml

http://canadafreepress.com/article/trump-voters-support-geert-wilders?utm_source=CFP+Mailout&utm_campaign=fded74a3af-CFP+Daily+Mailout&utm_medium=email&utm_term=0_d8f503f036-fded74a3af-297732117&mc_cid=fded74a3af&mc_eid=c9d72098f8

https://en.m.wikipedia.org/wiki/Trial_of_Geert_

Printed in the United States
By Bookmasters